CONFLICT OVER THE BAY

CONFLICT OVER THE BAY

NORMAN L.R. FRANKS

GRUB STREET · LONDON

Published by
Grub Street
The Basement
10 Chivalry Road
London SW11 1HT

First published by Wm. Kimber 1986
Updated and revised 1999
Copyright © 1999 Grub Street, London
Text Copyright © 1999 Norman Franks

British Library Cataloguing in Publication Data
Franks, Norman L.R. (Norman Leslie Robert), 1940-
Conflict over the bay
  1. World War, 1939-1945 – Biscay, Bay of (France and Spain)
  – Aerial operations, British 2. World War, 1939-1945
  – Biscay, Bay of (France and Spain) – Aerial operations, American
  I. Title
  940.5'44'941

ISBN 1-902304-09-8

Typeset by Pearl Graphics, Hemel Hempstead
Printed and bound in Great Britain by

Biddles Ltd, Guildford and King's Lynn

CONTENTS

ACKNOWLEDGEMENTS

As with my previous books I have been more than pleased with the response received from former members of the Royal Air Force (and in this instance the Royal Australian Air Force too), without whose help the true stories cannot be told.

To all those I have met or with whom I have corresponded I give my sincere thanks:

Wing Commander W.E. Oulton CB CBE DSO DFC	58 Squadron
Flight Lieutenant R.H. Collishaw	58 Squadron
Wing Commander G.C.C. Bartlett AFC	58 Squadron
The late Group Captain P.G. Stembridge DFC AFC	172 Squadron
Flight Lieutenant D.H. Hobden	172 Squadron
Flight Lieutenant E.C.C. Goodman	172 Squadron
Flight Sergeant D.A. Radburn	172 Squadron
Wing Commander D.M. Gall DFC	201 Squadron
Wing Commander P.J. Cundy DSO DFC AFC TD	224 Squadron
Squadron Leader T.M. Bulloch DSO DFC	224 Squadron
Flight Lieutenant E.S. Cheek AFC DFM	224 Squadron
Flight Lieutenant J.H. Brooks	224 Squadron
Flight Lieutenant J.S. Powell CGM	224 Squadron
Flight Sergeant A. G. Dyer	224 Squadron
Flight Sergeant J. McMahon	224 Squadron
Flight Sergeant F.T. Holland	224 Squadron
Flight Lieutenant G.D. Williames	228 Squadron
Flight Sergeant G. Kneale	228 Squadron
Flight Sergeant J.H. Wright	423 Squadron
Flight Lieutenant D. Marrows DSO DFC	461 Squadron
Flight Lieutenant P.T.Jensen	461 Squadron
Flight Lieutenant G.M. Watson	461 Squadron
Flight Lieutenant G. L. Donnelly DFM	461 Squadron
Flight Lieutenant H.E.R. Barrett	502 Squadron
Flight Sergeant W. Owens	547 Squadron

Flight Sergeant F G Duff	547 Squadron
Flight Lieutenant F.P.G. Hall DFC	10 OTU
Wing Commander J. Singleton DSO DFC AFC	25 Squadron
Flight Lieutenant W. G. Haslam DFC	25 Squadron
Flight Lieutenant M.C. Bateman DFC	236 Squadron

I should also like to thank my good friend Chaz Bowyer, Mrs Evelyn Boyd one time with Air Historical Branch, MoD, The Keeper of the Public Record Office, Kew, and to my two pals Geoff Thomas and Martyn Ford-Jones for continued help with photographs and maps.

Thanks are also due to Juan Carlos Salgado and Franz Selinger. Also to author Chris Goss, and Graham Day at AHB.

Also to my friend Eric Zimmerman, who helped considerably to update this second edition, and to C V T Campbell who pointed out errors I had made in the first edition. And all at Grub Street Publishers, and of course to my darling wife Heather who gives meaning to my life.

CHAPTER ONE

THE BATTLE OF THE BAY

Following the fall of France in 1940, Germany was able to take over and develop the important naval bases along the French west coast that overlooked the mighty Bay of Biscay. Beyond the Bay lies the Atlantic and routes to Africa and South America. From the Brest Peninsula in the north the Biscay coast line stretches some 500 miles south-east and then south to Bayonne where it joins the northern coast of Spain. This Spanish coast runs westwards for 400 miles to Cape Ortegal, Coruna and Cape Finisterre.

With the ports of Brest, Lorient, St Nazaire, La Pallice and Bordeaux under their command, the German Navy quickly established their submarine bases at these French harbours. If war with Britain continued beyond the summer of 1940, they would be well situated to attack Atlantic shipping from France, rather than the long haul from Germany's only sea exit around Kiel in the north. As the war did continue after 1940, the U-boats from the French ports began increasingly to sail out into the Atlantic to harass ships and convoys bringing supplies to a now beleaguered Britain – dependent on food and war materials from overseas.

Thus began a great struggle between the U-boats and the men of the Royal Navy and the Merchant Navy, who fought the Battle of the Atlantic. The Royal Air Force too were participants in this all important battle but its aircraft at first were few, and their range of operation limited. Like all RAF commands, they had prepared for a war limited between Germany and Britain in the North Sea, with France as an ally. RAF Coastal Command expected to have to face German sea power in the North Sea and in the North Atlantic, but with the fall of Norway and then France, the men of Coastal Command were suddenly faced with an impossible task. The Germans could strike almost anywhere from the Biscay bases, or from Northern Germany, while the RAF were handicapped in numbers and capabilities.

Over the next two years the battle continued. Submarine numbers increased while Coastal Command too expanded. Its equipment improved too. In the beginning Coastal's aircraft were Hudsons, Whitleys, and

Hampdens, plus Sunderland and Catalina flying boats. By 1943, four-engined Halifax aircraft had joined the ranks as well as two four-engined American aircraft – the Consolidated B24 Liberator and Boeing B17 Flying Fortress. With these three aeroplanes, an improved Sunderland plus the Catalina, the range of Coastal Command's war arm was extended far out into the Atlantic. Wellingtons too were still on strength, but used mainly at night, equipped with Leigh Light searchlights.

Nevertheless, the U-boats continued to sink Allied shipping at an alarming rate. Their Atlantic wolf-pack tactics could decimate convoys despite gallant defensive actions by destroyers, sloops and corvettes.

There were two other ways of trying to combat the U-boats. One was to bomb and destroy their bases, but secure in their re-inforced concrete U-boat pens, even the heaviest bombs bounced off these seemingly attack-proof shelters. The second option was far easier. Hit the U-boats as they left or were returning to their bases. Heading into or back to France from the Atlantic, the U-boats had no choice but to cross the Bay of Biscay. This area came under the jurisdiction of No.19 Group of Coastal Command, commanded, at the beginning of 1943, by Air Vice-Marshal Sir Geoffrey Bromet CBE DSO. Operating almost exclusively in and around the Bay area, the group had believed it had destroyed one U-boat in 1941 (now known to be incorrect) and just five in 1942, (three in the Bay and two further west by convoy escort aircraft, but including the first Leigh Light kill [July]).

The Germans knew very well that they were vulnerable while traversing the Bay, so generally they crossed it at night when they were fairly safe from attack, submerging during the daylight hours. Recharging their batteries during the hours of darkness, they could safely remain under water in daylight.

Locating a surfaced U-boat was not difficult. Air-to-Surface Vessel (ASV) radar had been available to Coastal Command since 1940. The early Mark I ASV sets were far from 100% reliable and barely effective against U-boats, but they did help aircraft contact Allied convoys. They also helped navigation as coast lines could be detected over twenty miles away. Mark II ASV was developed in1940, but as the development team (Pye Radio Ltd and E.K. Cole Ltd) also produced AI (Airborne Interception) radar sets for nightfighters, this had priority over pure ASV radar production. Nevertheless, ASV Mark II came along slowly and together with a new aircraft aerial system designed by the Telecommunications Research Establishment, improved its range considerably. It also incorporated sideways-looking coverage. Although with the Mark II the operator could only select forward or sideways coverage – not both at the same time – its potential was far better. Sideways coverage extended ten miles to either side, forward radar five miles. These ranges were gradually improved upon over the following months.

One of the vagaries of the ASV radar was that a contact went off the screen at about one mile when it disappeared in the ground (sea) clutter on the radar screen, as the aircraft reduced height for an attack. However, at one mile the radar was no longer being used for by then any surfaced U-boat would have been held visually for sometime by the approaching aircraft's crew. Yet it was this problem that gave the U-boat immunity at night. It was little use finding a U-boat on radar in a black night over the Bay, if one couldn't know when one was over her to drop bombs or depth charges.

This problem was solved by Squadron Leader Humphrey de Verd Leigh DFC, an administrative officer at HQ, Coastal Command. A pilot during World War One, who had flown anti-submarine patrols in that war, he overheard a conversation in 1940 about the problem of attacking U-boats at night. Pondering this problem, his solution was to fit a powerful searchlight to a Wellington aeroplane. Once an ASV operator guided the pilot on an attacking course for a U-boat it only needed the light to be switched on when less than a mile from her!

There were a number of associated problems to be overcome but finally trials were carried out in the spring of 1941. Yet it was to be a year before 172 Squadron had five combat-ready Wellingtons equipped with Leigh Lights and with crews trained in their use. Their first success came on 4th June by a Wellington attacking the Italian submarine *Luigi Torelli*, which was damaged. The first definite night sinking by Leigh Light came on 6th July.

* * *

Another development in the war against the U-boat came at the end of 1942 when the ASV Mark III entered service. Technically it was similar to the new H2S ground-mapping radar developed for Bomber Command. Both used the new centimetric wavelength radar. When used in aircraft of Coastal Command it would prove a definite leap forward in the Bay war.

One of the new Halifax squadrons was No 58, commanded by Wing Commander Wilfred Oulton:

> 'After the shocking and unsustainable shipping losses during 1942/43, Churchill over-ruled Bomber Command and agreed to the transfer of 50 aircraft to Coastal with the then new H2S III. This turned out to be Halifaxes for two squadrons, 58 and 502, to operate in the Bay of Biscay. 58 kept their mid-upper turrets and were to operate inside the Bay. 502 swopped their mid-uppers for extra fuel and worked the outer part of the Bay and convoys further out.
>
> 'The plan for the employment of these aircraft, as also for the night searching Wellingtons equipped with the Leigh Light, was based on the premise that a U-boat transiting the Bay would have to surface for several hours at least once every 24 hours, every 200 miles or so.

'I took over 58 in April, at a time when the squadron was rather fed up and discouraged, having flown thousands of hours on Whitleys, then latterly re-equipping with the Halifaxes.'

Wing Commander W.E. Oulton, OC 58 Squadron.

The Germans, of course, knew all about ASV, having fitted a captured set into a four-engined Focke Wulf 200 Kondor in 1941 for tests. The Germans were quickly able to design a simple receiver to detect ASV transmissions from RAF aircraft. Surfaced U-boats picking up such transmissions were able to dive to safety before any attack could be delivered. The device was called Metox, named after the French Metox Company near Paris, one of two French-owned firms to build the receivers. Equipped with Metox German U-boats had been free of any fierce retribution by Coastal Command, but all that was about to change.

The new ASV radar used frequencies outside the scope of the Metox search receiver and once the Germans discovered the RAF were using centimetric radar (from a shot down bomber carrying H2S) the race was on to produce a receiver to pick-up the new wave-lengths.

Meanwhile, armed with Leigh Light equipped aircraft and the new Mark III ASV, all out efforts were being made by 19 Group to combat U-boats crossing the Bay. Air Vice-Marshal Bromet mounted operation 'Enclose' between 20th and 28th March 1943. Under his command he now had 32 Leigh Light Wellingtons of 172 and 407 (RCAF) Squadrons which were also equipped with ASV Mark III, while his other squadrons still had ASV Mark II. This operation brought 26 U-boat sightings and 15 attacks, but only netted one U-boat, which was thought to have been sunk by 172 Squadron who also claimed damage to another.[1]

The successful crew of 172 Squadron was commanded by Pilot Officer P.H. Stembridge. In his crew was Eddie Goodman, senior wireless and radar operator and Dennis Hobden (wireless operator/radar operator/air gunner):

Flight Sergeant E.E.C Goodman, 172 Squadron:
'The way one got into the Leigh Light business came about when forming an experimental flight (No 1417) at Chivenor in 1942. Our first training with it was in May. I was crewed with a Flight Lieutenant A.W. Southall (DSO DFC) who had been a full time WEM (wireless electrical mechanic) from Cranwell. So apart from his flying abilities he was a very clever man. The flight was commanded by Squadron Leader J.H. Gresswell (who then went to Commanding Officer of 179 Squadron) and all our flying throughout April and May 1942 was all training. Some were against our own submarines or on buoys and light ships in the Bristol Channel.

---

[1] It has now been discovered that this attack had been upon U-448 which suffered no damage. During the 'Enclose' operation a Whitley from 10 OTU sank U-665 on the 22nd.

'Although we were the leading crew in doing the experiments with the Leigh Light we weren't the first crew of 172 Squadron to fly operationally, because Flight Lieutenant Southall was such a perfectionist that he wanted to wait until he was convinced we were absolutely ready. Unlike some of the other crews, we spent every minute of the day living in the aircraft practising getting out in a hurry and things like that. It was round about the beginning of June 1942 when we as a crew went operational for the first time.

'Because of the success 172 Squadron were having it was decided to extend the squadron and a lot of new crews came in who had been trained in Canada and I left Flight Lieutenant Southall's crew and went, supposedly, as a fairly experienced person, with a new crew under Pilot Officer Peter Stembridge. Throughout August 1942 we were training with our new crew. We became operational in September and began to fly frequently every other night on 8-9 hour patrols.'

Flight Sergeant D.H. Hobden, 172 Squadron:
'I flew with Flight Lieutenant Peter Stembridge, the second pilot was a Flying Officer Boyd, and the navigator Flying Officer Peter Dene. They were known as Big Peter and Little Peter for Stembridge was small in stature whilst Dene, an ex- Hendon police graduate was very tall.

'I was wireless operator, radar operator and air gunner. Generally we carried three wireless operators/air gunners/radar and the three of us did an hour on each position in continuous rotation.

'I hated night flying and you may be aware of our expression only birds and fools fly and birds don't fly at night. Day time was training, air testing and if on operations on any evening, pilots forbade drinking alcohol 24 hours beforehand and insisted we rested in the afternoon prior to take off.

'We would look anxiously at the weather hoping for a cancellation or, at least, decent flying weather with a chance to get back to base in the morning without being diverted elsewhere.

'There was always an advantage to operations and that was beforehand we would go to the operations canteen for eggs and chips – highly thought of at that time – and then briefing. The operations room controller was a Brighton man whose family kept a string of highly thought of pubs and restaurants in the town. His name was Eric Edlin. He looked like Charles Laughton. He knew he looked like Charles Laughton and aped his best Captain Bligh attitudes!

'Briefing meant information as to where we would search down in the Bay, the likely position of U-boats and weather. The trips were quite long and tedious but looking at the radar screen meant trying to pick out something interesting that might prove to be U-boats. The original ASV radar was a different visual principle to centimetric radar. Training for this had been at Prestwick. We had the screens showing a vertical base line and blips on either side indicating a contact which then had to be lined up and distance relayed to the captain. It had about three ranges on it and often could be used as a radar beacon which was useful for navigation particularly on the way home if the navigator was uncertain of his whereabouts.

'The blips would give an indication of surface vessels but I nearly got our crew killed one night. We had set off for Chivenor and were proceeding along the coast of north Devon. There were plenty of clear blips on the screen but I kept silent as there was always lots of shipping proceeding along at that spot. All of a sudden the second pilot Jimmy Boyd screamed, "Bloody Barrage Balloons!" We were flying over shipping equipped with balloons. Had never seen anything like it before. Stembridge was a brilliant skipper and we managed to avoid a crash but my name was unmentionable for a few days afterwards!

'Came the time when we received word that we were to change to a new type of radar which gave us a visual plan of the sea and land. At first, believe it or not, I hated it. We had got used to ASV whilst on the new type it was difficult to pick out blips at close range. Really it was just a case of getting used to it and, of course, it was immensely superior to the old ASV. It meant a lot of training but we soon got used to it.'

Pilot Officer P.E. Stembridge, 172 Squadron:
'I had carried out, with my crew, many night anti-submarine sweeps/patrols over the Bay of Biscay before we sighted and attacked our first U-boat during the night of 22/23rd December 1942. At that time we were still flying the Leigh Light Wellingtons Mark VIII (Pegasus engines and ASV Mark II). Until that night our crew had had no tangible success against the U-boats although we hoped that at least, by our presence, we might be "keeping them down", causing them to "crash-dive" (lowering their crews' morale) when they detected our aircraft on our ASV transmissions – before we had even got them on our ASV – and forcing them to surface more often in daylight (in transit through the Bay) thus presenting more targets for our daytime colleagues.

'On many sorties we had investigated, with the Leigh Light, a considerable number of ASV contacts but virtually all had proved to be French or Spanish fishing boats. Many of those boats carried lights but obviously we had to illuminate and investigate all ASV contacts because one might just turn out to be a U-boat; a U-boat, with no lights, might be hiding alongside a lighted fishing boat or be in the midst of a group of such boats; furthermore, one suspected that a U-boat commander, with some experience of Leigh Light operations in the Bay, might be persuaded to show lights in the hope that we would be deceived thereby and would not bother to illuminate that contact. Carrying out the homing and investigating procedures every time (sometimes twenty, thirty or more during a sortie) was very frustrating and one wondered at times if the searchlight and/or its batteries would "pack up"; also one reckoned that any U-boats in the vicinity would probably dive if they saw a Leigh Light being operated anywhere near them. I used the words "virtually all" above because I recall, that, on the night of 18/19th November 1942, we homed on to a rather unusual ASV "blip", switched on the Leigh Light at one mile, height 500 feet, and, because nothing was seen on the surface, descended rather leisurely (as opposed to an attack run to 100 or 50 feet) whilst continuing our approach. On reaching the "contact" we had the slightly un-nerving experience of passing just under and to the side of a barrage balloon, decoy or otherwise, some 200 miles from land, and just seen in the "side-effect" of our Leigh Light beam. Fortunately, we had missed the cable which was trailing into the sea and, as it was obviously a hazard to other aircraft, particularly at night, we shot it down in flames; this took a little time as we had to circle it in darkness, from slightly above, and use our rear-turret guns on it; we could not of course illuminate it with the Leigh Light whilst circling.

'Our luck changed on the night of 22/23rd December 1942 – an early Christmas present! At this stage let me emphasise that I had a very competent crew who flew some 500 operational hours on Wellingtons with me and, in particular, Sergeant (later commissioned on our crew) Eddie Goodman was an "ace" on both ASV II and III and this could make all the difference between picking up, particularly on a cluttered screen, an ASV contact on a U-boat or not, especially if the U-boat was not fully surfaced. Anyway, at just after 0315 hours we got an ASV II contact at six miles; we switched on the Leigh Light at one mile and, at the end of the beam, there was a fully surfaced U-boat heading west at good speed. It is, and was, difficult to describe one's immediate feelings on seeing an enemy submarine for the first time, especially after many long sorties without a sighting, and particularly at night – a very sinister sight, I recall. In brief, I felt a combination of surprise, excitement, elation, intense satisfaction, etc. but all subordinated to carrying out immediately the correct attack procedure in the ensuing seconds – we might never sight another U-boat. The U-boat started to dive as soon as it was illuminated but its conning tower was still visible when I dropped a

"stick" of four depth charges (D/Cs) at an angle of about 60°
(because of the "stick" spacing and because the lethal range of our
D/Cs was only six yards) just ahead of the U-boat. The rear-gunner
reported that the D/Cs had exploded across the centre of the conning
tower swirl. Flame floats had been dropped with the D/Cs and we
homed back over the position but saw nothing of the U-boat. We
backed-up the flame floats with a marine marker. Shortly afterwards,
when the marker was to port of us, we came under fire from the
starboard side – it appeared to be cannon and/or machine-gun fire
from about two miles or less away. As we had already used our one
and only stick of D/Cs, I made a diving turn to port from 500 to 100
feet, during which the firing followed us round, and then, after a brief
deliberation on tactics, returned to the estimated position of the
source of the firing. However, though we searched the area for 50
minutes, nothing further was seen, either visually or on ASV. It was
assumed at the time that two U-boats had been in company about two
miles apart. We understood later that the initial Intelligence
assessment of our attack was "serious or lethal damage inflicted".
Anyway, it proved to us conclusively that there really were such
things as U-boats in the Bay!'

Flight Sergeant E.E.C. Goodman, 172 Squadron:
'In November, still flying every second night we were very busy.
Very strange sort of job really, flying for hours and hours every night
and more often than not, just not seeing anything. And yet the losses
in aircraft were fairly high relative to other sections of the airforce,
simply through people flying into the sea. We were flying with a
normal altimeter, set on barometric pressure – which was guesswork
from the Met. people on what it might be when we were out six or
seven hours from home. It was only when we received the radio
altimeter that we felt a little more secure in patrolling at 500 feet
or less.
'At the end of December we attacked a U-boat without seeing any
results (22nd December). I remember flying on Christmas Eve and as
Christmas Day arrived people were breaking all the rules, breaking
radio silence to send silly messages and things. Throughout January
1943 we had no sightings and still a tremendous amount of training.
There was no question of being "trained" and being sent out, we were
often up, trying to perfect our techniques and strategies, doing
homings with our ASV. We then began to get the centimetric radar.'

Pilot Officer P.E. Stembridge, 172 Squadron:
'Our re-equipment in February 1943 was most welcome in more
ways than one. Not only had our new Wellingtons Mark XIV got the

new ten centimetre ASV III, obviating the need for the Mark II's numerous "fishing rod" aerials sticking out in all directions (one heard that some local civilians in the Barnstaple area reckoned we were spraying poison gas over Germany from those prominent "rods"), and a stick of six D/Cs instead of four, but also had Hercules engines, significantly more powerful than the Pegasus, and, furthermore, one could "feather" the propellers in case of engine failure. Thus, if one had an engine failure over the Bay of Biscay, one reckoned one had a reasonable chance of getting back to the UK. With the old Mark VIII Wellingtons one was worse off, regarding engine failure (two at risk instead of one), than in a single-engined aircraft. An engine failure (either one) several hundred miles away over the Bay, at a patrol height of 800 – 1,500 feet, was the precursor of a "ditching" at night, probably in rough or very rough seas; it was estimated it would take $2^1/_2$ hours, armed with the hand-axe, to jettison the searchlight/turret and the numerous batteries in the nose.

'I personally knew of only one Mark VIII that successfully got back after a complete engine failure and that was indeed an extraordinary affair. Thus, whilst on an operational sortie, the port engine (I believe it was the port) began to vibrate badly, the pilot shone a torch on it just in time to see the propeller fly away into the night, the vibration naturally increased umpteen-fold and then the engine itself fell off leaving just a few limp fuel, oil and hydraulic pipes, etc. dangling from the face of the engine nacelle. Apparently the pilot was able to maintain height – just – because of the loss of the engine's weight.

'One night in October 1942, my crew was fortunate when, in a Mark VIII heading for the Bay and just past the Scilly Islands, our starboard engine started cutting badly, with loud bangs and jerking the whole aircraft longitudinally; we started losing height (we were at about 1,500 feet) and prepared to ditch in the relatively calm water in the middle of the Scilly Islands. However,the "cutting" became less frequent and we gingerly made our way back at low level to the mainland where we force-landed at RAF Portreath, and the engine stopped completely and required rectification. We were amused to hear that some civilians in the area had reported some low-level AA gunfire that evening – it was apparently our starboard engine "banging-of"! The Pegasus engines did seem to suffer quite a bit from sticky valves; they were probably never meant to cope with continual flying at low level over the salty oceans.

'The Mark XII's were of course faster, particularly in the homing and attack phase and, as their flight endurance was less, our sorties were somewhat shorter and less fatiguing. Soon after midnight on 22nd March 1943, height 1,000 feet and visibility one mile, we had an ASV III contact at seven miles. We homed and at one mile, height 350 feet, turned on the Leigh Light; at $^1/_2$ mile we sighted a U-boat in the act of crash-diving, conning tower and stern still visible. I dropped six D/Cs, from a height of 70 feet, ahead of the conning tower swirl, the stern being still visible. Due to the angle of attack, the D/Cs had more of a cluster effect than a spaced "stick" and the rear-gunner reported what appeared to be one large explosion with the full length of the U-boat visible in the trough caused thereby; as he could not see the conning tower or hydroplanes, he thought the U-boat was keel uppermost. He fired a burst of about 50 rounds from his guns for good measure. I made a wide circle and came back at 250 feet over the flame floats, three minutes later, with the Leigh Light on; we saw two separate patches of very large bubbles but no sign of any part of the U-boat.'

Flight Sergeant E.E.C. Goodman, 172 Squadron:
'On 21st March 1943 we attacked a U-boat which appeared to us to turn over in the sea. As far as I can recall I was on the radio or the radar. I specialised on the radar and later did a radar leader's course.

'On the original ASV was an oblong tube with a time base down the middle and all the ground returns came up at the bottom. Then we'd pick up the blips, either to the left or right of the screen. One eventually got skilled seeing something sometimes right in these sea returns. We'd go off on quite a lot of "wild-goose" chases but as we got more experienced we could attribute some of these to anything from flocks of seagulls to something floating on the water. One which puzzled us one night, we just couldn't make out why he couldn't find this thing, was a barrage balloon, that had got free and was floating down the middle of the Bay of Biscay! We spent ages finding it, then shot it down.

'The advantage of going on to what we called the PPI (Planned Position Indicator) with the circular screen which covered virtually all the aircraft except an area immediately behind, was tremendous. We had a rotating time base and that gave you a blip out from the centre. We had a measuring device round the outside of the screen so that we could call a course from that. Then we had other markings on the screen that gave distances. As time went on we got even more advanced and found that we could push the centre of the screen – which was us – further out. In other words, as we got nearer to the object we were able to expand this base so that the object was really quite large and we could read off more or less exactly where it was to a degree or two. So in theory, instead of the old ASV method of giving your pilot "right, right, left, left" corrections, resulting in one banking to go over the U-boat and dropping all the D/Cs in a salvo instead of a straddle, which was highly inaccurate and was sheer luck if we did any damage, we were now able to, in theory anyway, plot the position of the object we were homing on and track right over it really accurately. That was the theory but often you'd be afraid, having picked something up, say at 25 miles, it took a lot of confidence by the pilot to say, "All right, we'll turn round and approach it from a bit farther so that we can do a more carefully thought out approach"; in case they had picked us up! More often than not, however, we'd say, "OK, we'll head towards it."

'We would put the Leigh Light on at less than a mile, as late as possible obviously. In the days of the normal ASV the crews on the night patrols could see the crew on the conning tower who'd obviously come up for a smoke etc. and those in the front of the Wellington would say they could see the terror on their faces suddenly having this two million candle power light switched on them, fast approaching out of the blackness. We, of course, would be homing on something – we didn't know what it was. It could have been anything, a fishing boat or a merchant vessel etc. We were briefed about our own merchant vessels and sometimes about enemy merchant vessels and told either to ignore them or whatever. But we didn't know what the radar had picked up until it suddenly appeared in the searchlight. As soon as we'd identified it, the light went off and if it was a U-boat we also switched it off, because we then had to circle. We did this as quickly as possible to come in again for another attack – then switch the light back on. Once we'd flown over it and dropped our D/Cs, we'd come round for another look with the light back on to see what had happened.'

On the night of 27/28th March, one of 172's flight commanders, Squadron Leader R.B.Thomson, picked up an S/E contact at eight miles, and switched on their Leigh Light at one mile. They saw nothing but even at this early stage, the Germans were starting to shoot first and dive later. Without the slightest sign of a visual contact, Thomson and his crew encountered gunfire from the blackness, but this same gunfire gave away the U-boat's position. If they had not opened fire they would not have been seen and might have dived unhindered.

The flak gained in intensity as Thomson turned, this time heading for the source of the flak, then switched on the light again, this time picking up a fully surfaced submarine. Only then did the boat begin to dive, but Thomson came in and dropped his depth charges at 100 feet while the conning tower and stern was still visible. They straddled the U-boat, one exploding amidships close to the hull. Even now the guns were still firing, suggesting that the Germans had left at least one man on the bridge as the boat dived. Thomson flew off, returning three minutes later but only a flickering yellow light could be seen about one mile from the flame floats that were automatically dropped when the D/Cs went down. Whether this light came from the life vest of the German gunner was not known for sure.

* * *

Grossadmiral Karl Dönitz, who prior to January 1943 had commanded the U-boat service, and who was now in command of the entire German Navy, noted the increased activity and attacks in the Bay. Although only one U-boat had been lost, several commanders returned to their bases with stories of sudden attacks and narrow escapes. It was becoming increasingly dangerous to cross the Bay, and between 6th and 13th April, Bromet put on a repeat 'Enclose' operation. Eleven sightings and four attacks cost the Germans one more U-boat, again to 172 Squadron, while 210 Squadron damaged a second.[2]

Following this operation, Geoffrey Bromet mounted operation 'Derange', this time covering another area of the Bay. His aircraft now equipped with centimetric radar totalled about 70, not just Wellingtons, but some Liberators and Halifax aircraft too. The Germans, not unaware of this growing problem, had finally to warn their U-boat commanders of the danger. Warn them that their Metox was of no help in alerting them to an approaching centimetric radar-equipped aircraft, homing in on them. In the last week of April two more U-boats received unwelcome night attacks and were damaged.

Pilot Officer P.E. Stembridge, 172 Squadron:
'Just past midnight on 29th April 1943 we detected an ASV III contact at eight miles; at 1½ miles I sighted a wake and, at ¾ mile, we illuminated a fully surfaced U-boat. I dropped six D/Cs from a height of 100 feet, pulling out of a comparatively steep diving turn, so again the D/Cs had more of a cluster effect than a spaced stick. During our attack the U-boat opened fire with cannons and/or machine-guns. This time the rear-gunner, although he reported a single large explosion due to the near-cluster effect, saw no sign of the U-boat, after that attack-run. We made a wide circle and flew back towards the flame floats; we encountered heavy cannon and/or machine-gun fire from the position of attack but could not positively sight the U-boat. We remained in the vicinity for over an hour, having dropped a marine marker to replace the flame floats. During this time the ASV III contact (presumed to be still a U-boat – it showed no

---

[2] As with the previous 'Enclose' operation, more recent research has disclosed that 172 Squadron probably attacked and damaged U-465. Squire of 210 Squadron, previously credited with causing this damage, definitely attacked U-527 which suffered no damage. There is now no known attack which can account for the loss of U-376, listed at the moment as to unknown causes.

lights) remained almost stationary and three lighted fishing boats, observed within seven miles of the presumed U-boat, also remained stationary all the time we were in the vicinity. We had of course sent the appropriate W/T messages to our "Control" (Plymouth). In passing we were pretty sure that, by this stage of the "Battle of the Bay" the U-boats were well aware that our Leigh Light Wellingtons carried only one stick of D/Cs. The ASV contact (U-boat almost certainly) then disappeared and we resumed patrol. The immediate Intelligence assessment of our attack was "damaged, perhaps sunk", but I heard long afterwards that the U-boat was the U-437; we had damaged it and so it was attacked again by the daytime aircraft.

'Regarding night anti-submarine (AS) operations over the Bay, if the U-boat was fully surfaced then even their commendable efforts to reduce the time taken to fully submerge (in their newer boats) to a mere 30 seconds were not good enough when a Leigh Light Wellington suddenly illuminated a U-boat from a range of only one mile and then homed straight on to it, at full power and in a dive (at least a shallow one) at about 180 knots. It was not therefore surprising that, for a period, some U-boats elected to stay on the surface and fight it out rather than crash-dive when detected by Leigh Light Wellingtons. During that period, I recall that when homing on to an ASV contact, we sometimes delayed switching on (referred to as "striking") the Leigh Light until three miles from the contact to lessen the time the U-boat AA gunners could fire up the searchlight beam (wearing very dark glasses!)'

Flight Sergeant E.E.C. Goodman, 172 Squadron:
'The next bit of excitement was on 29th April, (U-437) the night we attacked a U-boat and had confirmation as late as February 1945. As far as I recall, I was on the radar and remained there, for as soon as the aircraft was turning we were wanting to see if we'd still had a contact on the screen. So the radar job was absolutely vital then to find where it was. By this time we were getting rather clever with the radar. We could spot a submerging U-boat as the blip began to disappear – getting weaker and weaker.

The U-boat casualties forced Dönitz to signal his commanders, ordering them to stay submerged during the night, and surface to re-charge batteries during the day. He also made it clear that the RAF had now a radar device against which the submarines were, for the present, totally powerless to detect. German scientists were endeavouring to produce a receiver able to locate emissions from the centimetric radar – to be known as 'Naxos-U' – but until its arrival, the U-boats would remain vulnerable.

Some Germans thought that the RAF was able to receive radiations from the Metox up to thirty miles away, Metox being a super heterodyne receiver, its radiations coming from the local oscillator stage.

In fact in the early days when one had to license a domestic radio, the British General Post Office used a similar method to detect licence dodgers.

Others simply did not believe that this could be done, thinking that the Metox radiations were too feeble. They were correct, the U-boats were being located by the new centimetric radar, and the Leigh Light was proving itself a tremendous asset at night.

For the first time in months of wearying Bay patrols, 19 Group had the opportunity of being at a distinct advantage over its U-boat enemy. As the German U-boat command had now changed its Bay tactics, surfacing by day instead of at night, it was suddenly presenting Coastal Command crews with better numerical chances of sighting them.

In staying on the surface, the U-boat crews had to defend themselves. Gun crews would now be part of the 'bridge party', keeping at least two 20 mm guns at the ready, and supported by more men acting as ammunition hoisters. As the Battle of the Bay progressed, U-boats leaving French bases were equipped with heavier defensive armament. Some gun-armoured shields were also fitted. It was claimed to offer complete protection against .303 and safety against .5 guns although, on later interrogation, some German prisoners were not totally convinced of this.

The responsibility for choosing between diving and fighting lay with the officer of the watch. It was recommended that the U-boat should still dive if it sighted an aircraft in time to avoid a surprise attack. A surprise attack was defined as one in which an aircraft got to within 2,000 to 3,000 metres before being sighted. In these circumstances U-boat commanders were encouraged to fight it out on the surface. One man from each watch now had to be a trained anti-aircraft gunner, able efficiently to operate the 20 mm guns and to this end the Naval flak school at Mimizan in Southern France had been running a five-day short AA course for U-boat gunners, each week since January 1943.

In some respects, Dönitz's tactics seemed logical. A huge lumbering Sunderland, Liberator or Halifax etc. coming down to around 50 feet in a straight approach was a big target. With a U-boat surfaced, its gunners blazing away with single, double or quadruple-mounted 20mm cannon, the aircraft would be shot out of the sky. In reality, however, it wasn't always that simple or easy. Yet as far as Coastal Command Headquarters was concerned, the opportunity was too good to miss. For an aircraft to find and attack a fully surfaced U-boat, get in close enough to drop its bombs or D/Cs to claim a kill, was a definite step forward. And even if the aeroplane was shot down, it was good arithmetic. The cost of a U-boat, with perhaps 40 to 60 men aboard, far outweighed the cost of one aeroplane with perhaps six to ten crewmen. The aeroplane crew had possibly a better chance of surviving. They could crash-land and be in dinghies, having already radioed base of their attack position. If they failed to get home, search and rescue was very possible; certainly their comrades would soon be out looking for them. For the U-boat crew, it was usual only for the few men on the bridge or in the conning tower who might survive a submarine's plummet beneath the waves with hatches open and perhaps a ruptured hull, and sea water in the batteries filling the boat rapidly with chlorine gas.

Coastal Command was suddenly offered a chance to get to grips with the U-boats in the Bay of Biscay. It was too good to miss. For the next three months the battle raged. Tactics were changed, the fight escalating on the sea and in the air. The Battle of the Bay was about to reach a climax.

Of course, operations in the Bay were not only anti-U-boat patrols. There could be a variety of tasks set for the Coastal flyers. There were always fishing boats, trawlers, blockade runners,torpedo boats and destroyers in the Bay. For instance, Dudley Marrows, an Australian with 461 Squadron RAAF had an unusual operation on 10th April 1943:

> *Flight Lieutenant D. Marrows, 461 Squadron:*
> 'While on a normal anti-submarine patrol, we were diverted to locate an enemy merchant vessel in towards the French coast. We located it, but it was being escorted by destroyers and some Ju88s.
>
> 'It was a fine day with some 6/10th shallow cloud. We had to close up through the cloud patches to identify, and periodically came under heavy gun fire from all vessels. Their combined fire however was very accurate indeed with no-one else to share it with. In between we had to seek out cloud cover to avoid the Ju88s (numbers unknown).
>
> 'Thinking I had safely made cloud cover, there was an urgent cry from John (Jock) Rolland our navigator that the Sunderland's tail was sticking out of the cloud top! "Get down, get down! Your tail's out!" Quite like a game of hide and seek, both from the heavy gun fire and from the Ju88s. On the way back, somewhat relaxed we were intercepted by a flight of what we believe to have been FW190s – again we did not wait to make sure, again being lucky enough to have some cloud cover available before they closed.'

Larry Donnelly DFM was a member of Marrows' crew at this time.

> *Flight Sergeant G.L. Donnelly, 461 Squadron:*
> 'We had taken off from PD (Pembroke Dock) at 11.50 hours in Sunderland JM675 'O',[3] and some hours later we entered "Tiger" country and commenced a normal anti-sub patrol. I was doing my stint on the watch tower when I received a message from Group

---

[3] JM675 was lost on operations on 28th May – see Chapter Three.

diverting us to the southern area of the Bay, to shadow a German blockade runner, and "home" onto it, a strike force of Hampdens of 455 Squadron RAAF. As soon as we had worked out an intercept, we set course. The Germans at this time were using fast merchant ships to take precision instruments etc. to the Japanese. The ship would then return loaded with raw materials,e.g. rubber, which the Germans urgently required. Our Intelligence was alerted to this and had obtained information this particular ship was within striking range, hence our diversion and the projected strike.

'The Germans in the meantime had despatched four Narvik class destroyers and a force of Ju88s to escort and protect their ship. When we sighted the target, the destroyers were already there and they opened up on us with their heavy flak, but we circled out of range. At this time there was no sign of the Ju88s.

'I sent a message to Group updating the ship's position and I was instructed to "home in" the Hampden strike force which was on its way. We continued circling and transmitting and the force got nearer, but when it was about five minutes flying time away,the German air cover arrived in the shape of five Ju88s. Our gunners reported they were heading our way, so after informing Group and the strike force, we beat a hasty retreat for the nearest cloud cover. Actually we couldn't have stayed much longer as we were at our PLE (Prudent Limit of Endurance).

'As we left the area, unscathed I'm glad to say, the Hampdens arrived. They, unfortunately, weren't so lucky and took a hammering, but I think they obtained some results.

'We landed back at PD after being airborne for 12 hours and 35 minutes – a fair old flog, but at least we got back which was more than some of the poor Hampden boys!'

Sergeant J.H. Brooks, 224 Squadron:
'As far as our crew was concerned we felt quite excited about the prospect. We were well briefed about the operational objects of the campaign and we felt very much part of it. Prior to this we had been a Very Long Range (VLR) Squadron doing trips of up to 18 hours out to 30°W over the Atlantic. Up to this time we had, as a crew, done 230 hours operations on Liberators, and had one U-boat sighting which we attacked and were later credited with, and one successful attack on a 6,000 ton merchant vessel. Hits on it were confirmed by Beaufighters doing a follow up attack. We discussed it and I remember that we decided that we could well find more U-boats and although there may be a bit more of a chance to get shot down but with the number of sorties going on here was a great deal more hope of being picked up if we were. I was with a very experienced crew

and we planned our course of action for any foreseeable consequence, e.g. Norman Foster, the senior WOP/AG had the basics of navigation and could use GEE and LORAN. We trained the second pilot to use the bomb sight. I could fly a course and was a qualified AG. Every member of the crew could operate the radar and the navigator could do the fuel transfers and calculate fuel consumption. We reckoned we could lose half the crew and still get home.

'We didn't suffer from the tedium of long hours. The WOP/AGs changed stations at intervals of about an hour, turrets to beam guns, radar, to radio. The navigator was busy doing three course winds and looking out. I changed round, flight deck, top turret, 2nd pilot. The 2nd pilot to lookout or top turret.

'Our main concern was that in the event of an attack the damn bomb doors would not open fully and that the depth charges would not drop off. I always stood by on a sighting to prop the doors and drop the charges by hand. I did this on a shipping strike in 1942.'

Sergeant G.D. Williames, 228 Squadron:

'We were all a little apprehensive but very excited when we were switched from the North Atlantic to the Bay. The only enemy aircraft we had seen to date was the occasional sighting of a FW200 Kondor. Now we had Ju88s to contend with. Some of us had seen periscopes but never a fully surfaced U-boat. We had seen the aftermath of wolf-pack attacks on convoys, the lifeboats, wreckage with dead or near dead people on board drifting alone hundreds of miles from the coast, no hope of rescue and the sea too rough for us to land. Now at PD we were going to even things up a bit, on their own doorstep.

'The Sunderland, the best aircraft ever built, thoroughly reliable, easy to live with in the air or on the water. Some years ago I started work for British Aerospace at Hatfield. In conversation with one of our chaps in the factory, he told me he built Sunderlands during the war and was a little apologetic for being in a reserved occupation. He was a little overcome when I shook his hand warmly and thanked him on behalf of all Sunderland crews for a job so well done so many years previously.'

CHAPTER TWO

STAY UP AND FIGHT

At seven minutes into Saturday, 1st May, Flight Sergeant P.W.Phillips in Wellington 'N' of 172 Squadron saw the surfaced U-boat in the beam of his aircraft's Leigh Light. The contact had been made 62 miles away; Peter Phillips made a gentle turn to starboard as he reduced height to the black sea below. Ahead of him, the crew of U-613 and her Commander Helmut Köppe, were unaware of the approaching danger. Below, the operator of the Metox receiver was unconcerned, his apparatus giving no indication of the presence of any ASV radar emissions. The Wellington, equipped with the new centimetric radar, had the contact dead ahead now. At three-quarters of a mile, the light was switched on, and with bomb doors open, Phillips roared in for the kill.

The men on the bridge of the U-boat felt naked and vulnerable as the light exposed them. Yet they were quick to react. The 20 mm cannon blazed out at the fast approaching beam, whose glare blotted out the aeroplane carrying it. The RAF navigator noted their position – 4445° north, 1157° west – approximately 550 miles due west of the coast of France, 250 miles north-west of Cape Ortegal and some 500 miles south-west of Land's End.

As Phillips came over U-613 he released six depth charges and almost simultaneously the crew felt their Wellington shudder. They estimated a perfect straddle with the D/Cs, two going into the water on the near side, four on the other. With the light off, Phillips hauled the Wellington hard round to the left, the light being switched on again as they returned to the area of the attack once more. The illuminated sea foamed and bubbled for four minutes where their D/Cs had gone in, but they saw nothing to confirm a kill. Like so many crews before, they could only claim an attack and hope they had sent their enemies to Hades. If nothing else they had shaken them up, and forced them under, slowing down their forward speed. Having made a sighting position, other aircraft would be able to search the general area. If the U-boat had survived, perhaps another Coastal Command crew would trace them later.

An hour after the attack, the crew of 'N' realised what the shudder had been over the submarine. They had seen no sign of gunfire, but their Wellington had been hit and the hydraulics damaged. As they also discovered when they landed, their port tyre had been punctured. They crash-landed at Predannack, but fortunately nobody was hurt. At this moment honours were one damaging blow to the U-boat side. But the 1st of May was to see further action.

At 11.36 am U-415, commanded by Kurt Neide, was spotted by a Sunderland of 461(RAAF) Squadron (DV968 'M'), piloted by Flight Lieutenant E.C. Smith. This time, in daylight, the German lookouts saw the approaching danger. The Australians made the sighting at between five to six miles and altered course slightly to the left. This time the U-boat dived immediately and was under the surface when the D/Cs went down. As the explosions subsided, nothing was seen, but U-415 had received some damage. She limped on, heading further south-east in order to get closer to the northern Spanish coast.

Then at 5.25 pm she was picked up again, this time by a Whitley VII of 612 Squadron. Flight Sergeant N. Earnshaw had taken off shortly after 1 pm, following a heavy hail shower. Over the Bay, however, the weather was fair with visibility ranging from ten to twenty miles. They were in the 'Derange' area, flying at 3,000 feet on a course of 280° as the U-boat was seen five miles to port, on a course of 100°.

Norman Earnshaw turned towards the submarine which began to turn to starboard. As the range closed and the Whitley lost height, the U-boat gunners began to fire at the approaching aircraft. Then the U-boat, still turning, began to submerge. With her decks awash, the gunners on the conning tower continued to fire but the Whitley was not hit. Six depth charges splashed down, but fell 200 yards off to the right. Earnshaw pulled round to the left into a circle to come over the estimated path of the U-boat. Two more D/Cs were dropped and having circled for a few minutes, the crew spotted some oil, but nothing conclusive.

Neide's U-415 received more damage in this attack, but they had been extremely lucky. They had survived a fairly good attempt to sink them but finally managed to limp into Brest on 5th May. Three other sightings were made on this first day of May. Another Leigh Light Wellington of 172 Squadron located one U-boat at 2.55 am. This too fired at the British aircraft, then crash-dived before Pilot Officer Whiteley could make his attack. At 8.22 Flying Officer Houston of 502 Squadron attacked another surfaced U-boat, while a third was depth charged by Flying Officer Davey of 502 Squadron at 12.38 pm; this latter attack being upon U-185, commanded by August Maus, but she successfully reached Bordeaux two days later.

* * *

Flying in the Derange area shortly after 8 am the next morning Flight

Lieutenant Griffiths of 10 Australian Squadron, put his Sunderland over a surfaced submarine which submerged after the first attack. This was outbound U-664 (OL Adolf Graef) which while undamaged, did have two of her crew injured. 612 Squadron's U-boat searches were rewarded by two attacks. At 10.18 am Sergeant J.L. Richards (Whitley BD682 'W') dived on a surfaced U-boat, his gunners exchanging fire with the Germans. His depth charges under-shot the stern of the boat as she went down. This had been the inbound U-188 (KL Lüdden). Again no damage was inflicted but as with U-664, two men had been injured, including Siegfried Lüdden.

In mid-afternoon Flight Sergeant D. Gunn (BD676 'G') put a stick of D/Cs ahead of the swirl of water where U-257 (KL Heinz Rahe) disappeared just eight seconds earlier. Oil and bubbles were seen but nothing else. It was nothing unusual for a submarine to jettison oil and air, making it look like the vessel had been hit, in the hope the RAF crew would fly off satisfied. In this instance U-257 did suffer some slight damage.

The real success of the day, however, came at 7.15 that evening, again involving Flight Lieutenant E.C. Smith of 461 Squadron, that had helped damage U-415 the day before. Again flying Sunderland 'M' (DV968), they had been airborne just over an hour from Pembroke Dock, when they spotted a Type VIIC submarine, on her way from La Pallice to the North Atlantic on her seventh war patrol. 'Bertie' Smith flew the Sunderland into some broken cloud, flying through them towards the boat ten miles distant. At one mile Smith dropped the Sunderland down to the attack height, the German gunners opening fire from that range. The front gunner in the Sunderland replied with the single Vickers GO gun – then they were over the submarine, four D/Cs dropping across her. Some of the German gunners were blown into the sea, then the U-boat began to circle to the left. Smith came in again to drop another four D/Cs which straddled the crippled U-boat. Completing one and a half circles, the boat slowed, then stopped. Oil had been flowing freely from the submarine which had also started to list badly to port. Once stopped, some of the crew were seen jumping into the sea, then the U-boat began to sink stern first, leaving at least fifteen men in the water.

It had been thought earlier that this attack had been upon U-332, but in fact it was U-465, commanded by Kapitänleutnant Heinz Wolf. She had sailed on 29 April and all 48 of the crew were lost. U-332 was sunk on 29 April, three days after sailing, by a Liberator of 224 Squadron, captained by Flight Lieutenant A R Laughland.

* * *

The two Australian flying boat squadrons with 19 Group were to the fore on the 3rd. At 9.31 am, a Sunderland of 10 Squadron saw and attacked a U-boat, while one minute later 461 Squadron attacked another, over 100 miles to the north-east. This latter Sunderland was piloted by Flying Officer

R.D.J. Baird in 'S' (EJ142).

In Russell Baird's crew was one non-Australian, the Flight Engineer, Sergeant G.M. Watson, an Irishman.

> 'I joined 461 Squadron early in 1943 after OTU at Invergordon, where I was crewed with Ken Field (WOP/AG) and Flying Officer Russell Baird RAAF, and as such was the only Irishman in 461. All the pilots and navigators were Aussies but quite a few engineers and wireless operators were RAF, especially in 461 Squadron which was formed on Anzac Day 1942, out of 10 Squadron.
>
> 'The navigator is the most hard worked man on a flying boat – he has no one to share the very exacting calculations, far away from land and often unable to even see the stars or sun, to use his sextant. Russell Baird, captain of "S", had a first class navigator in Douglas Hughes, as was shown by the account I shall now narrate. We were well south in the Bay of Biscay on 3rd May 1943, flying just below cloud at 2,000 feet, when there, dead ahead, we sighted a U-boat cruising west, fully surfaced. Klaxons screamed and we went down in a steep dive for the attack, but she crash-dived at an incredible rate and there was nothing more than a swirl in the sea to mark her diving position. Useless to drop depth charges. The captain and navigator had to decide a plan of action, after reporting the sighting to HQ. We flew east for half an hour and Doug Hughes gave the captain his reciprocal course. Flying in the cloud, west again, we carried on until Doug gave the order to dive – there, just below us was a U-boat. This time we were closer, before he spotted us, and we screamed down, flat out, dropping a stick of six depth charges just as she went below the waves. There was a tremendous explosion. We searched the area and noticed and photographed an oil slick. HQ Coastal Command would only credit us with a "possible" sinking – but what a fantastic piece of navigation!'
>
> *Sergeant G.M. Watson, 461 Squadron.*

These two attacks were timed at 9.32 and 10.42 am which caused some damage to U-257, but an hour later Sunderland 'S' received an unwanted visitor. They were at 1,000 feet, still in the general area of their U-boat sighting when a single Junkers 88 approached, 500 feet lower. It passed under the Sunderland's nose then came round to the port quarter and attacked with its cannon, but from long range. Twelve shells exploded short of the flying boat, but by then Baird had flown the aircraft into the cover of nearby cloud, and contact was lost.

More sightings were made by Coastal aircraft over the next two days, resulting in another U-boat being damaged. Flying Officer J.M. Hartley in a Halifax of 58 Squadron (HR745 'S') made the first sighting of the day at

7.40 am, 350 miles out of La Pallice. The sea was rough and the U-boat was on the surface, her crew showing some fight. John Hartley made an immediate attack, only to come under fire from a heavy gun on the deck, a 20 mm cannon on the bridge and an estimated five machine-guns aft of the bridge. Taking evasive action during his run-in, Hartley was down to 200 feet on the U-boat's port quarter, and estimated his D/Cs straddled just aft of the conning tower. One sailor was seen to be hit by the aircraft's return fire as Hartley flew over and fall into the sea. Seconds later the U-boat submerged without sign of damage.

However, the target, outbound U-190, commanded by Kapitänleutnant Max Wintermeyer, had suffered some slight damage but it did not prevent her from carrying on with the patrol. Despite the observation of a crewman falling into the sea, the U-boat had no casualties.

Four other sightings were made during the day but no kills were achieved. On the 5th a Whitley of 612 Squadron flown by Flying Officer C.H. Norton, returning after a 12-hour Bay patrol, was diverted from Davidstow Moor to Chivenor, owing to bad weather. The aircraft crashed two miles from Wadebridge, the sole survivor being Sergeant J.E. Edge, the second pilot, who baled out at 1,200 feet.

In mid-afternoon, Sergeant Webb of No 10 OTU spotted a U-boat on the surface four to five miles away. Diving his Whitley from out of the sun, he attacked with six D/Cs, only to discover that four of them hung-up. When he pulled round again, the submarine had gone. The boat had been U-405 (KK Rolf-Heinrich Hopmann) which escaped damage.

No. 10 OTU (Operational Training Unit), a Bomber Command OTU, loaned to Coastal Command, took a large share of Bay patrols during the early phase of the current Bay Operations. Each crew was nearing the moment when they would be posted to an operational bomber squadron, so flying a number of anti-submarine patrols was useful pre-squadron training. And a number of them saw action. Fred Hall, who with his crew was on detachment to 10 OTU at St Eval in mid May recalls:

'We were accommodated in a very nice hotel – The Treyarnon Bay – although we didn't have separate bedrooms. The hotel was situated alongside a most pleasant bay north of Newquay. Transport was provided to get us to and from the aerodrome. Routine was expected to be Air Testing one day, fly operational sweep the next day, then rest on the third day. This consisted mostly of swimming, surfing and sunbathing.'

Sergeant F.P.G. Hall, 10 OTU.

At 3.27 on the afternoon of the 6th a 10 OTU Whitley – Pilot Officer Poore – saw a U-boat four miles away and in the attack dropped six 250lb Torpex D/Cs as she began to submerge. They achieved a good straddle but they failed to explode. Two and a half hours later, Sergeant Barnett of 10 OTU found another U-boat on a Derange patrol. They were at 3,000 feet, Barnett diving the Whitley the three miles towards the submarine.

Half a mile from the target another aircraft was seen astern of the U-boat at zero feet. At the same instant the U-boat opened fire with cannon, the Whitley's front gunner returning fire until his gun had a stoppage. Barnett released six D/Cs set to explode at a depth of 25 feet, from 300 feet up. As the Whitley cleared the U-boat, the rear gunner opened up, seeing hits on the conning tower, then saw three D/Cs explode across her bows. Barnett pulled up into cloud because of the unidentified aircraft. Whether this was a Ju88 or a Sunderland of 228 Squadron that witnessed the attack is unclear, but when Barnett came out of cloud and circled the area there was no sign of the U-boat. The boat has not been identified.

This success was followed by a major victory the next day (the 7th), and brought Coastal Command its next two U-boat kills. Shortly after 4.30 am, two aircraft took off from very different bases. Flight Lieutenant G.G. Rossiter lifted his 10 Australian Squadron Sunderland off from the waters of its base at Mount Batten, while Wing Commander W.E. Oulton took off his Halifax from St Eval.

At five minutes to seven, Wilfred Oulton spotted a U-boat three to four miles away and attacked but saw no results. Half an hour later a S/E contact turned out to be two Spanish trawlers. Returning at 10.15 to the same area where the U-boat had been seen the U-boat was spotted again having resurfaced. She was eight miles away. Oulton flew his Halifax into cloud, coming out at four miles. As he reduced height, the U-boat gunners began to open fire, hitting the aeroplane in one wing and fuel tank. The submarine had been on a course of 260° but changed her heading to the left. Fire from the Halifax hit the conning tower, one man on the bridge being hit. As he roared over the boat, Oulton let go three depth charges. Plumes from the explosions obscured the vessel which finally went below the waves some 30 to 40 seconds later. As the Halifax flew back, the D/C swirl was clearly visible as well as one body. A patch of greenish-blue scum coloured the sea for two or three minutes before this was finally dispersed in the rough sea.

> 'At the beginning of May we ran into this slogging match, beginning on 7th May when I had two separate sightings, both converted to attacks, one just before dawn as we started our routine rectangular creeping line ahead patrol, and another one two hours later. We eventually learned after the war that the second attack had sunk U-663.' [4]
>
> *Wing Commander W.E. Oulton, Commanding Officer, 58 Squadron.*

---

[4] It is now understood that Oulton's attack had been upon U-214 (KL Günther Reeder) and not U-663 which was sunk by 10 Squadron RAAF. U-214 suffered a number of casualties from machine-gun fire including her captain. The boat returned to Brest on the 10th.

Meanwhile, Geoffrey Rossiter, 50 miles to the north-east, at about this same time, saw a submarine wake ten miles to starboard but it disappeared. A few minutes later another wake at six miles and above it a Liberator which dropped a smoke float. Remaining in the general area, his patience was rewarded at 12.20 pm when the crew spotted a fully surfaced U-boat from their height of 2,000 feet. Like Oulton, Rossiter used cloud to approach, breaking cover at four miles. The Sunderland closed in at speed, the front gunner opening fire at two men that could be seen on the U-boat's bridge.

'We saw two men on the U-boat's deck,' Rossiter said afterwards, 'wearing sou'westers and oilskin coats. They seemed to be staring up at us and looked very frightened. We didn't see them again after making a first attack and they may have been killed by our machine-gun fire.' Four D/Cs went into the sea from 50 feet, straddling just forward of the conning tower. Pulling round in a tight turn as plumes completely covered the submarine, Rossiter delivered a second attack placing four more D/Cs across the boat. After this attack the submarine began to travel in tight circles to starboard, at about four or five knots, trailing oil. She gradually slowed to a stop, her stern and rear section of conning tower awash. At 1 pm she went down.

'It disappeared stern first,' reported Rossiter, 'with its bows tilted high in the air. It was a goner all right.' Rossiter circled the spot for over an hour, seeing a number of circular oil patches appear, one drifting away in the sea for some 250 yards.

Below, U-663 went down, 240 miles north-west of Cape Ortegal. U-663, under her commander, Heinrich Schmid. She had sailed on the 5th for operations in the Atlantic, her fifth war patrol. Severely damaged she surfaced on the 8th and gave a report to base but that was the last that was heard of her and her crew of 49. A Halifax of 58 Squadron failed to return from patrol on 7th May, having left St Eval at 5.10 am. At 6.14 the crew, piloted by Sergeant N.F. Robertson RAAF, acknowledged a routine call, then nothing. The crew had run into U-228, commanded by Kapitänleutnant Erwin Christopherson, and was shot down by her gunners. With (what at the time was thought) two Bay killings in one day, three in a week, this gave Coastal Command HQ hope for the future. Already the number of U-boat sightings had increased. Certainly something new was happening in the Bay of Biscay. However, for the next three days bad weather severely restricted operations. The change in the weather began on the night of the 7th, inflicting a severe blow to 59 Squadron as recalled by the unit's Commanding Officer, Geoffrey Bartlett AFC:

'In March 1943, No 59 was taken out of line to return to Thorney Island and re-arm with VLR Liberator Vs. On 11th May we moved to Northern Ireland (RAF Aldergrove), and operations had started with detachments to St Eval. A streak of bad luck – unpredicted deterioration of the weather – when four of our aircraft were airborne on 7th May. B/59 and M/59 were successfully diverted to Thorney Island and Ballyhalbert respectively, but J/59 (one of the Flight Commanders, Squadron Leader W. Cave DFC) was lost, and Flying Officer T.D. Wright and his crew of K/59 eventually had to bale out when they ran out of fuel over Blackburn, Lancashire.

'T.D. Wright, called Peter in the squadron, was RAAF. A very steady going, sensible, reliable fellow – not at all the stereotype "wild" Aussie. We had a high percentage of RAAF aircrew in No. 59 at the time I was in command; and few of them were the wild type. Some pretty high-spirited – but so were a good many of the RAF. Peter and his crew were well up to their job. People who have experienced the stresses of flying in a storm in "radio silence" where one is supposed to pass messages in *Syko* for security reasons will know he faced a real bad situation. Flying Officer Ernie Allen was fortunate to get back into RAF Thorney Island that night, just in the nick of time before a terrific rain storm blotted it out for the rest of the night. And poor old Cave and his crew were never seen again.

'I was particularly saddened by the loss of "Frank" Cave and his crew. He had joined 59 and taken over as a flight commander early in April 1943 to start his second tour. He had the DFC from his first tour (which squadron I do not recall [502, Ed.] and I quickly got to like and trust him. For what proved to be his last flight, he "borrowed" two of my own wireless operators, Tim Summers and Sainthouse, no doubt two of his own crew were off sick or something. I still have a sad little photo of myself with the remaining four of my crew, taken just before I handed over to Peter Gilchrist.'

Wing Commander G.C.C. Bartlett, OC, 59 Squadron.

Nothing of note was logged on the 8th and 10th, although some flying was done on the 9th. Just before dawn, Flight Sergeant James A. Hoather, who had only just been awarded the DFM, took off in a 58 Squadron Halifax at 6.11 am but failed to return, hope fading as his ETA of 3.40 pm came and went. No signals were received or acknowledged, indicating a loss early in his flight. From German records we know that he came upon U-666 (OL Herbert Engel) and was shot down. The sub's crew noted the crash, 500 metres from the boat, at 1028 hours as the aircraft came in for a second run, the first being abortive.

A 10 OTU Whitley had the only reported excitement. Sergeant A J Savage saw a wake, then the surfaced U-boat at 12.28 pm on which he dropped D/Cs (although one hung-up). Twelve minutes later, a little to the north-west he spotted a second U-boat, his front gunner exchanging fire with eight men seen on the conning tower. The Whitley received a hit in the tailplane, but then the submarine dived. This was U-666 again, her gunners scoring hits on a second aircraft this day but this time their fire was not so accurate.

The weather wasn't all that good on the 11th, but success came again. Pilot Officer J.B. Stark of 58 Squadron was airborne at 3.05 am, to fly out on a convoy escort mission, to convoy OS47, ships on their way to West Africa.

Submarine U-528, on her first war patrol, commanded by von Rabenau, had sailed to the North Atlantic from Kiel on 15th April. She was now in the outer part of the Bay making her way to one of the French bases.

About 9 am, two hours after making contact with one of the convoy's escort ships, the Halifax crew sighted a surfaced U-boat but she crash-dived before an attack could be made. Jim Stark flew back towards the Naval escort, reported by signal Aldis, then returned to the U-boat's position which he reached half an hour after the first sighting. There again was the U-boat, fully surfaced on a course of 90°. Stark, at three miles, was coming in out of the early sun, but he was seen and U-528 began to submerge. Stark came in head-on, dropping a stick of D/Cs right in front of her. As Stark pulled round to the left, the exploding D/Cs lifted the stern of the U-boat, which rolled before disappearing. The crew of the Halifax also saw a large piece of debris thrown into the air by what seemed to be a secondary explosion which caused the U-boat's bows to break surface. An oil patch began to appear which spread 100 yards across. The Halifax reached its PLE (Prudent Limit of Endurance) at 10.20, landing back at St Eval at 12.53 pm. Naval escort ships arrived to drop more D/Cs, and later fifteen survivors were picked out of the water by HMSs *Mignonette* and *Fleetwood*. Stark later received the DFC.

Bad weather again restricted operations in the Bay for the next day and a half, but on the afternoon of 13th May, Pilot Officer G.B. Willerton of 224 Squadron took off at 1 o'clock to go into the Bay. On the Brest peninsula was the Luftwaffe unit, V Gruppe of KG40 (Staffels 1 and 3) equipped with twin-engined Ju88 C-6 heavy fighters. They were based at Kerlin Bastard near Lorient, as well as using Bordeaux Merignac aerodrome. The III Gruppe of KG40 (Staffels 7 and 9) equipped with long range four-engine Focke Wulf 200s was at Bordeaux. There were also FW190s at Brest which often flew short range sorties out from the Brest peninsula.

Just as U-boats had to cross the Bay to reach their French bases, so too did Coastal aircraft have to skirt round the Brest Peninsula to reach England. Obviously it was best to give this spot a wide berth, but the occasional navigational error, or shortage of fuel put aircraft closer inshore than was prudent. On a number of occasions FW190s flew out and made interceptions. 12 Group Spitfires were tasked to fly patrols when possible but it was often difficult due to weather or other commitments.

However, it was the Ju88s that proved the severest danger to Coastal Command aircraft operating in the Bay. These fighters provided aircover for both outward and returning U-boats, as well as flying patrols farther out over the Bay, seeking Coastal Command aeroplanes. They often flew in any number from five to ten, which were tremendous odds for any lone aircraft or flying boat that were unfortunate enough to run into them.

On the 13th, a Ju88 patrol ran into Pilot Officer Willerton's Liberator. At 3.38 pm, St Eval received a radio message – 'Am being attacked by enemy aircraft – three Ju88s, in position FBCW,0900.' This message was also intercepted by another 224 Squadron Liberator, flown by Warrant Officer E.J.J. Spiller. No more was heard from Willerton's aircraft which was indeed shot down by the 88s. A short while later it was Spiller's turn to be located by Ju88s. One member of Spiller's crew was Sergeant Frank Holland (WOP/AG):

'On 13th May we were attacked by a formation of Ju88 fighters about three hours out into the Bay. Cloudless sky. I was duty wireless operator at that time and was occupied sending our position back to base, while we had a ten or fifteen minute battle. We climbed to 8,000 feet, with engines on full boost before they caught up with us. We were saved eventually by a large patch of cloud which suddenly appeared, and also the evasive manoeuvres of our pilot who threw the Liberator around the sky as each one came into attack. I think Flight Sergeant Denny was in the mid-upper turret, Flight Sergeant Mackin in the rear turret and Flight Sergeant Humphrey, the navigator, went back to man the beam guns.

'We suffered a fair amount of damage. One engine was put out of action, holes in the wings and fuselage which had put the hydraulics out of action, but incredibly, apart from Jock Thompson having a small metal fragment in his leg we had no serious casualties. I'm sure our gunners gave a good account of themselves, as one Ju88 at least was damaged. I was never quite sure how many of them there were but I think there were eight. It was a miraculous escape in retrospect. We had to wind the undercarriage down by hand and do a no-brake landing, eventually running off the runway, across the perimeter, through a hedge, across the public road and came to rest in an arable field, but the aircraft still in one piece. All four engines had to be replaced but they had lasted longer than they should have done – giving us extra speed which made it difficult for the Ju88s to catch up after each attack was made. I think our speed and manoeuvres made by the Liberator must have baffled the German pilots.

'The trip had lasted 6 hours, 45 minutes. Usually a patrol lasted twelve hours in the Liberator, as compared with eight hours in the old Whitleys in which I started with 58 Squadron. While with Flying Officer Hartley's crew we were twice attacked by Arado 196 seaplanes which used to sit on the water waiting for us to appear and then take-off and attack. One of these we shot down I remember.

'At the time of the Ju88 attack there were a number of our 'planes shot down over the Bay. Quite frequently we were out on searches for dinghies.'

Sergeant F.T. Holland, 224 Squadron.

The weather hadn't improved much by the 14th when Flight Lieutenant E.C. Smith took his 461 Squadron Sunderland away from Pembroke Dock just before 4 am. He was about 100 miles north west of Cape Ortegal at 10.52, in the Derange area when they too were intercepted by Ju88s.

Smith had met 10/10ths cloud at 200 feet and visibility was almost nil. He decided to cut short the patrol just as four Ju88s were observed 2,000 yards away crossing from starboard to the front of the Sunderland. At the same time two more 88s came in from astern. A couple of 88s attacked from the sun, opening fire at 1,000 yards, scoring hits on the Sunderland's windscreen, port wing and tailplane as well as the hull near the astrodome. The waist gunner was wounded in the thigh while Sergeant J. Barrow suffered a flesh wound as he manned the nose gun. Finally Smith escaped into cloud and turned for home.

Peter Stembridge's and other crews of 172 Squadron had had a 0.5 Browning machine-gun fitted in the nose of their Wellington. His navigator Peter Dene was keen to use it for it had been specifically installed in order to fire at U-boats on a run-in now U-boats were staying up to fight. The gun fired mostly tracer bullets more in the hope of upsetting a U-boat's gun crew than doing any real damage. The man who fired this 'scatter' gun on night operations had to stand astride the crew member operating the Leigh Light controls, prone in the nose.

On this cloudy day, a radar contact was made and Peter Dene got to the gun. He was waiting eagerly for the U-boat to appear out of the cloud and when suddenly the Wellington let down through the cloud a shape appeared. Dene opened fire on the dark shape only to find it was the lead ship of a British convoy heading for Barry. HQ had not told them of this convoy's position but fortunately he did little or no damage.

Flight Sergeant D. Kneale, 228 Squadron:

'This was about the time when U-boats were having additional armament fitted round the conning tower and ordered to remain on the surface to fight it out with attacking aircraft which, sooner or later, had to level out in order to bomb. We also at this time decided, very much unofficially, to add to our armament not only for the purpose of attacking U-boats but also to defend ourselves against 88s which were now beginning to pop up here and there in ever increasing numbers, in two's, four's, sixes, eight's and so forth, attacking from all directions several at a time. Without reference to any authority our skipper, Flight Lieutenant Corrie, bribed, borrowed, or stole a free mounted 0.5 and had it installed in the forward hatch beneath the nose gunner. That was for use by anyone who happened to be spare. We also had four additional Browning .303s fitted, two either side of the fuselage to the rear of the front gunner and fired by the second pilot. We also fitted a further three Browning .303s, one each in the port and starboard galley hatches which were opened up during an alarm, and one on a specially constructed cross bar at the rear door!

'In this manner we had fifteen Browning .303s and one 0.5 and could attack or defend ourselves from any direction. If the original Sunderland with its eight guns was called the "Flying Porcupine" [usually by the popular press] what would you call U-Uncle by the time we finished with it? It was some time before officialdom caught up with us,but by the time it did quite a number of Sunderlands and other types of Coastal aircraft had taken a considerable bashing, both from defending U-boats and ever increasing air attack. This included the quite outstanding combat on 2nd June between Flight Lieutenant Walker and his crew of N/461, attacked in the early evening by eight Ju88s. The manner in which the enemy aircraft divided up and attacked for almost an hour indicated that a great deal of thought and rehearsal had gone into the question of destroying Coastal Command aircraft to ease the pressure being put on the U-boats. Three 88s were claimed shot down and two damaged. Fortunately none of the Australian crew were lost and Walker was awarded the DSO, another the DFC, and the tail gunner the DFM. Unfortunately just several weeks later this crew, flying with another pilot, failed to return from another mission. If Walker's original crew managed so well against eight 88s what could they have achieved if they had been as well armed as we had made U-Uncle? It is an interesting conjecture!

'There was also Flight Lieutenant Arthur Finucane who shortly after the period under review was attacked by four 88s. This combat lasted over half an hour and they claimed one probable and two damaged. Finucane was 228 Squadron. There was also Flight Lieutenant Bert Grimshaw, 228 Squadron. He was attacked by eight 88s over a half hour period and claimed two probables.

'These were the sort of events taking place when our additional armaments came to light due to an armourer speaking out of turn. Much to our surprise we received nothing more than a rocket after the aircraft had been thoroughly inspected for airworthiness. We could have told them it was, having already done several operations in it since installing the extra shooters. Needless to say, it came as no surprise when, in view of the frequent happenings over the Bay, similar modifications to all squadron aircraft became the order of the day. It made sense.'

The Ju88s were active again on the 15th, but so too was Coastal Command, as the weather had improved. At 9.32 am, Flying Officer J.R. Weeds' crew of 224 Squadron found a U-boat on the surface. Pilot Officer Mann, the second pilot, saw her without binoculars, her bow wave clearly visible around eight miles away. As Weeds was up-sun, he decided to attack at once but found he was unable to reduce height (they had been at 5,300 feet) in time so was compelled to make a 180° turn to port and attack up-track from the U-boat's stern. Even so complete surprise seems to have been achieved as the boat did not commence to dive until the Liberator (FL960 'O') was a mile away. As it began to dive the U-boat began to turn starboard. Four minutes after sighting, six D/Cs set at 25 feet, fell away from a height of 75 yards, just 15 seconds after the target had disappeared. As the Liberator flew over, the rear-gunner saw the D/Cs explode parallel with the boat's track. As Weeds circled a patch of oil, 50 feet wide, was seen, but nothing more definite. They flew on, returning to the scene an hour and a half later but the sea remained empty.

The boat had been U-168 (KL Helmut Pich) inbound for Lorient, having been damaged by D/C attacks while attacking convoy ONS 5.

This was the first of a number of sightings and attacks on U-boats in this general area. At 11.27 Flight Sergeant Brookes of 10 OTU found a surfaced U-boat in position 4649/1156 and dropped five D/Cs from 50 feet. One fell close but the other four all fell some way to the starboard of the boat. The nearest explosion lifted the boat, then she went down, leaving just a brown scum on the surface. The Whitley's gunners had fired a number of rounds at three or four men seen on the bridge. This had been the inbound U-648 (Stahl). Two hours later Brookes was still in the general area and found U-591 on the surface at 4615/1150 – only about twenty miles south of the first attack. She was ten miles away when seen and Brookes attacked. As he closed in the U-boat's gunners began to open fire on the approaching RAF aircraft. The Whitley's gunners replied, scoring hits on the conning tower and hull, and wounding the commander – Kapitänleutnant Hans-Jürgen Zetzsche. Brookes dropped his one D/C (this had hung-up in the first attack), that exploded 150 feet on the submarine's port beam. As the Whitley flew over U-591, it was hit by gunfire, but then the U-boat submerged, albeit slowly.

U-591 was a former member of the Arctic Flotilla, but since transferring to St Nazaire, had completed two patrols. This, her third, began on 12th May, but Brookes had ended it by wounding Zetzsche, forcing an abort back to harbour, which she reached two days later. Another U-boat was attacked by Sergeant Thomas of 10 OTU around 1.15 pm further out in the Bay without result (this was U-305 KL Rudolf Bahr – outbound). 45 minutes or so later Sergeant Lambert also of 10 OTU found yet another U-boat in the act of surfacing (4620/0958) but six D/Cs forced her below (outbound U-211 KL Karl Hause).

Meanwhile, ranging Ju88s had already netted another victim. Flight Lieutenant G.A. Church had left for a patrol at 11 o'clock, flying out initially with another squadron Sunderland of 228 Squadron, flown by Flying Officer W.M. French. When they neared their respective patrol areas at 1 pm, they parted company. Flying with French was the Squadron's commanding officer, Wing Commander N. F. Eagleton DFC. It was the last anyone saw of Church and his crew, who were shot down by KG40's fighters.

> 'I clearly recollect Flight Lieutenant Church and his crew who were lost on 15th May. They were flying in V/228 and the following day we went out on a search for survivors. Unfortunately it was a negative result – didn't even see an oil patch. There was one member of his crew with whom I was very friendly – Flight Sergeant D. "Smarty" Smart. He was a grand little fellow. There was a friendly rivalry between us at table tennis. I was good but he was just that little bit better and always managed to beat me, until just before he took off on that last trip. We were in the Mess just an hour or so before take off when he said, "Come on, I'll give you another hiding before I go." But he didn't. For the first and only time I beat him! His parting shot was, "I'll give you a thrashing for that when I get back," but of course he never did come back. That is why I remember so well our search for him and his crew the next day.
>
> 'All the time I was willing them to hang on and be picked up – even if it meant being thrashed by him at table tennis a hundred times over. Somehow playing table tennis in the Mess was never quite the same again. Another member of this crew had been Sergeant C. Sheppard who had earlier been in my crew, so another pal had gone.'
>
> *Flight Sergeant D. Kneale, 228 Squadron.*

The major success of the day went to Wilfred Oulton, Commanding Officer of 58 Squadron. He had taken off at 12.08 pm and six hours into the patrol, while at 6,000 feet well south of the area of the day's earlier excitement (4528/1020) he spotted a wake which turned out to be a U-boat. Oulton made a run-in from the submarine's rear port quarter. As he did so his navigator opened fire with the nose gun, scoring hits on the conning tower and hull. The U-boat was U-266, commanded by Kapitänleutnant Ralf von Jesson. She had sailed from St Nazaire on 14th April.

Six D/Cs went down from around 100 feet, the rear gunner spraying the bridge as the Halifax flew over. As the explosions subsided and the U-boat came into view, her forward hull was lifting clear of the sea. Seconds later a sudden jerk put this forward part into a near vertical position from where she slowly sank, sliding beneath the waves two minutes later.

The last sighting of the day was Flying Officer J.M. Hartley of Oulton's squadron. They sighted a 570 ton U-boat three to four miles away but she crash-dived and only the swirl remained when they reached the spot.

It was another full day on the 16th. Never before had so many U-boats been seen. 224 and 58 Squadrons' aircraft saw boats early in the day. Then at 9.27 am a Beaufighter patrol of 248 Squadron from Predannack were out looking for Ju88s. On his line patrol, Flight Sergeant J. Duncan and his navigator Flight Sergeant T.R.Weaver spotted a surfaced U-boat in position 4600/0834, some miles to the east of the Musketry area. Duncan saw her in the act of diving and went into the attack with a long burst of cannon fire. Hits registered all over the conning tower but moments later the submarine was gone. The boat had been U-591 again (Zetzsche) – undamaged.

No 10 OTU and 224 Squadron made further sightings in the early afternoon, then at 4.42 pm Flying Officer R.V. Sweeny of 224 Squadron was given a S/E contact. The Liberator was at 1,500 feet and began to reduce height when Sweeny saw a large bow wave ahead. Checking through binoculars he saw a U-boat with waves and spray going right over the conning tower. Down to 50 feet, Sweeny took the Liberator into the attack, but when attempting to let go six D/Cs only No. 1 charge fell, the other five hanging-up. The lone D/C was on target but nothing was seen to indicate any success. This was quite correct; U-662 (KL Heinz-Eberhard Müller) was unharmed.

It was a disappointment. Bob Sweeny was an American in the RAF. He and his brother Charles formed the famous Eagle Squadron in 1940 composed of American volunteers. He became the squadron adjutant in the early days, then left to train as a pilot. He was also famous as a golfer in England and America. Educated at Oxford, he became British amateur golf champion in 1937.

*

The final action of the day brought success. Flying Officer A.J.W.Birch of 58 Squadron began his patrol at 2.30 pm, in company with another Halifax. At seven minutes past eight they saw a surfaced submarine when on a course of 212°, the evening sun to their right. The U-boat was off to their left heading due west – course 270°. Both aircraft began a curve to port but as they turned the submarine could be seen beginning to dive.

Tony Birch was the inside aircraft so was able to make the attack. He made an 'S' turn to bring the Halifax onto a head-on approach. Seated in the second pilot seat was Pilot Officer R.H. 'Dick' Collishaw:

> 'The submarine was sighted well within the derestricted area (commonly known as the "Free For All") on the port bow. The crew went to "Action Stations" and commenced the attack. We reduced height to 50 feet on the radio altimeter, with bomb doors open and depth charges selected. This was normally six D/Cs on the first run.

The attack was made almost head-on to the submarine, just on its starboard bow, with the aim of straddling the hull. By this time, the German policy was to mount a large gun on U-boats, manned by two or three men. This gun may have been used but I did not see any explosions and the aircraft was not hit.

At about one mile distance from the submarine, its captain decided to dive. The conning tower was just submerging when we passed over it. The D/Cs exploded and although we still had to "stay on the ball," the tension of the attack relaxed. The position was marked with smoke floats and we started "Baiting Procedure", which was to fly down-wind for 15 minutes and then return. On our return oil could be seen just as we expected, as the submarine was only partially submerged when we hit her.'

Pilot Officer R.H. Collishaw, 58 Squadron.

The submarine was U-463, commanded by Korvettenkapitän Leo Wolfbauer. She had sailed from Le Verdon-sur-Mer on 10th May for the central North Atlantic, and had been on her fifth patrol. All 56 crew perished.

The second Halifax saw Tony Birch's attack, and confirmed good straddle. Later a Sunderland from 10 Australian Squadron saw the oil streak one mile long and a $1/4$ mile wide. A body was also floating nearby together with some debris.

This was the sixth enemy submarine killed since the beginning of May, plus two others damaged. This was more than the total for the first four months of 1943. It was now obvious that sightings and attacks were definitely on the increase and that German tactics had changed dramatically in the Bay. If it continued on this scale, a major victory over the U-boats was in the offing.

CHAPTER THREE

FIGHTS AND RESCUES

As things were obviously hotting up, Flight Sergeant Jim Powell of 224 Squadron was finding some excitement over the Bay on the afternoon of 16 May. He was on a Derange sortie from St Eval in Liberator FL948, M-Mother:

'It must be remembered that until the spring of 1943, every U-boat sighted in the Bay, crash-dived at once. We had in fact been briefed to expect their new tactic of staying up to fight it out, but never having experienced this we made an immediate "standard" attack when we spotted a surfaced U-boat on our port bow at 4-5 miles. Turn and dive and level out at about 50 feet (when the waves really do seem to touch the props), bomb-doors open, thumb on bomb tit on the wheel, but ... it didn't crash dive but engaged us with gun and machine-gun fire as we ran in. We were hit several times but the one that did the damage was a shell from the deck gun that burst between the port-inner and the cockpit. The explosion blew me sideways (and incidentally burst ear-drums are still a problem) and inadvertently I pressed the tit. So our first stick undershot and I pulled out and up while our turret guns peppered away at the U-boat and at least one of the deck gun crew went down and overboard.

'I was weighing up the pro's and con's of a different approach when suddenly, whatever the orders were, the damned U-boat crash-dived, so we went in hell-for-leather and dropped our second stick across the wake. We circled for some time but sadly saw no trace of a hit. I was pretty dizzy and probably a bit concussed, but "Lennie" West who was my co-pilot took over for a while and after checking there was no material damage I decided to carry on with our patrol, despite having no D/Cs.

'One sighting was usually about a month's ration, but about twenty minutes later we saw another U-boat steaming away on the surface. It too stayed on top as we closed, and we circled while all our guns were brought to bear and they hammered back at us. But then, be damned, I thought we'd pull a bluff – standard approach and bomb-doors open ... and it crash-dived to avoid the non-existent depth charges. Our guns gave it a real pasting as it went down, but again no positive results.

'Within half an hour of resuming patrol, our totally disbelieving eyes spotted a third U-boat and this adopted exactly the same tactics, exchanging gunfire while we circled and crash-diving as soon as we made our mock D/C attack. The fire of the second and third boats was fortunately not so well directed as that of the first. When you're at 50 feet and throttled back for the bomb-run it's remarkable how vulnerable you feel as a 4-inch gun plus twin-Oerlikons open up at what seems like point-blank range.

'In fact, although I had previously been involved in other sightings, for the rest of my time on 224 I never spotted another U-boat. Funny, isn't it? They all turned out to be Ju88s in future for me.

'In the context of our hectic couple of hours, it must be remembered that while our main job was of course to kill U-boats, it was nearly as important to make them dive; to keep them down, to use up their batteries and fuel and to constantly remind their crews that crossing the Bay was an unendingly nerve-racking business these days.'

Flight Sergeant J.S. Powell, 224 Squadron.

For his determination and perseverance on this day, Jim Powell was rewarded with the Conspicuous Gallantry Medal. His opponent had been, once again, the inbound Oberleutnant Peter-Artur Stahl's U-648.

* * *

If there was any euphoria at the recent successes against the U-boats, it was dispelled the next day. Obviously the loss of two boats with a third being forced to abort its mission through damage, galvanised the Germans into more aggressive action. Coastal Command aircraft were gaining in strength over the Bay and so needed to be deterred. The Ju88s of KG40 were out in force on 17th May and got amongst the anti-submarine aircraft.

Derange missions were flown in strength on this day. One of the first away was aircraft 'Z' of 10 Australian Squadron, which left its watery base at 5.17 am. Piloted by 27-year-old Flight Lieutenant M.K. Kenzie from Melbourne, the Sunderland (W4004) failed to return and all twelve men aboard were lost. V/KG40 had struck again.

The Whitleys of 10 OTU were out again in force and suffered losses. Sergeant S J. Barnett, who had attacked a U-boat on 6th May, took off from St Eval at 9.35 am and headed south-west. Some time later base received an emergency SOS call from the crew's wireless operator, who said they were under attack by two Ju88s – then silence. They too failed to return but they were luckier than Kenzie and Co. Crippled by the 88's fire, their Whitley (BD260 'P') crashed into the sea 80 miles north-west of Cape Finisterre at mid-day. They were picked up by a fishing boat and put ashore at Vigo on the Spanish coast. Later Barnett and his crew were all repatriated to England via Gibraltar.

Two U-boats were seen and attacked mid-morning, by Sergeant Lambert of 10 OTU but his D/Cs were off target and went into the sea nearly half a minute after the boat had dived. 10 Australian Squadron also saw a U-boat but this too was quickly gone. Then at 11.48 am, Sergeant J.H. Casstles of 10 OTU took his Whitley out from St Eval, and they too fell foul of the enemy, this time the still inbound U-648 (who had damaged Powell's Lib the previous day), and were shot down and killed in the Derange area.

Thus by the early afternoon, three aircraft were missing, giving some anxious moments at 19 Group HQ. Other aircraft were out and so too were more Ju88s. At almost two o'clock, Flight Lieutenant W.S.E. Dods of 461 Australian Squadron was attacked by a Ju88, but the Sunderland evaded into cloud. Surprisingly this Ju88 approached when the Sunderland was in position 5019/0721, which was forty odd miles north-west of the Scilly Isles – a long way from the Bay and obviously planned to engage the RAF crew when they had begun to relax. It was essential for all crews to be vigilant from the moment of take-off if they were to avoid surprise attacks by these marauding long ranging German fighters.

* * *

Flight Lieutenant Dods of 461 Squadron had now flown into his patrol area following the skirmish with the Ju88 north-west of the Scillies. At 4.44 pm they spotted a U-boat on the port bow while flying at 3,500 feet. Bill Dods approached up-sun but when four miles away the U-boat look-outs must have seen the Sunderland for she submerged. Shortly afterwards they were ordered to make a search for any signs of a dinghy, probably in the estimated area of one of the three lost aircraft, but all they found was two Spanish fishing vessels that might or might not have picked up survivors if there had been any. Dods called off the search and resumed his patrol.

Meanwhile, Squadron Leader H.R. Lawson of 58 Squadron (HR742 'D') had attacked a submarine shortly after she submerged, his rear gunner seeing their D/Cs fall just forward of a light green streak visible beneath the surface, but nothing else was seen. U-628 had a lucky escape.

At 5.30 pm another 461 Squadron Sunderland was located by Ju88s, 200 miles north-west of Cape Ortegal. Flight Lieutenant J.G.P. Weatherlake was flying at 500 feet when six Ju88s appeared. Three came into the attack, beginning a 30 minute chase and combat. The Sunderland rear-gunner got in one telling burst at 150 yards range at one 88, which broke away in a dive to starboard before levelling out. Black smoke trailed from its port engine as it flew off. The other two 88s did not press home their attacks and shortly after 6 pm they flew away. None of the Sunderland crew were injured but the flying boat received 200 bullet and four cannon shell hits in the battle. Weatherlake sensibly ended his patrol and flew home, landing at 10 pm. He reported seeing some Ju88s circling two Spanish fishing vessels at one time.

There was a strong feeling by the men of Coastal who flew and fought over the Bay during the war, that some Spanish fishing boats were suspect. With the number of such boats out in the Bay, it was inevitable that some would be seen in the locality of air battles. The RAF men were certain the fishing boats called up the Ju88s, giving them the positions of the Coastal aircraft.

> 'Spanish fishing vessels with radio masts were reported and it became apparent that with German wireless operators on board, sightings of Coastal aircraft were being passed direct to Ju88 bases in France. To counteract this we dropped leaflets on all Spanish fishing vessels seen above a certain latitude, warning them to fish nearer their own coast. From 1st June 1943, our usual depth charge load of eight was reduced to six plus two 250lb surface fused bombs. To my knowledge these were never used against Spanish fishing vessels – I gather the leaflets did the trick.
>
> 'On the lighter side, when patrolling the Northern Spanish coast one often came across the motor vessel *Kerlogue*, registered in Dublin and carrying 'Eire' prominently displayed on each side. She was about 750 tons. As soon as one approached her everyone on board disappeared, even the wheelhouse was deserted. Yet she carried on course, with a speed of about eight knots, heading either for San Sebastian or back, presumably to Lisbon. We jokingly called her the *Marie Celeste* for we never saw a living soul aboard on any encounter.'
>
> *Flight Sergeant G.D. Williames, 228 Squadron.*

Flight Lieutenant Dods' third enemy encounter of the day came at 9.20 pm. They were at 2,500 feet as his gunner saw a Ju88 at 3,000 feet. It began to circle the Sunderland out of range. A minute later more Ju88s arrived, obviously homed in by their companion. They joined up with the first Junkers astern of the flying boat. Four of them made one pass, then flew off, the Australians giving a sigh of relief.

Dods had been an accountant in Brisbane before the war but joined the RAAF in 1939 as an administration officer. By 1941, when he was 32 years old, he applied for aircrew, and reverted to the ranks. Training to be a pilot in Canada, Dods came top of his course, was commissioned and joined 10 Squadron RAAF before joining 461 Squadron. By September 1942 he was once again a flight lieutenant.

May 17th came to an end. Three aircraft had been lost, one damaged and another engaged twice. The Junkers of KG40 had been exceptionally active – a portent of things to come.

* * *

By comparison, the 18th was quiet, only one U-boat sighting being made by 10 Squadron without result. 502 Squadron made the first sighting of the 19th at 7.21 am, but an attack was not made. At 9.52 Flight Sergeant N. Earnshaw of 612 Squadron found a surfaced U-boat but she went under before they could attack. Baiting tactics failed to produce any further signs. Later they found a dinghy, made contact with base, helped obtain a fix, then had to return to base. A Sunderland of 10 Squadron was also in attendance, piloted by Flight Lieutenant Rossiter, who may have been responsible for the loss of U-663 on the 7th.

He had been forced to evade a Me110 fighter earlier, but had later found the dinghy. Two men were in it. They turned out to be the sole survivors of the 224 Squadron Liberator shot down by Ju88s on the 13th. One was the pilot, Pilot Officer George Willerton, the other Pilot Officer R.G. Barham, WOP/AG.

Rossiter dropped emergency supplies as he circled, awaiting permission from 19 Group to make a landing. Permission was eventually given and Rossiter made a superb landing and picked up the two men. Both were in a serious condition and Barham later died in Devonport Hospital. Willerton survived and later received the DFC.

* * *

Another event that occurred on 19th May was that Grand Admiral Dönitz's son was lost aboard U-954. It was this U-boat's first war cruise, having left Kiel on 8th April for a patrol in the North Atlantic. She was sunk south-east of Greenland by HM frigates *Jed* and *Sennon*, near convoy SC130. There were no U-boat men now who did not believe Dönitz knew exactly what they faced beneath the seas of the world. He knew now too, personally, what the loss of a loved one meant, and how that felt.

* * *

With the increase in combats between Coastal Command aircraft and the Ju88s of KG40, HQ Coastal Command had to bring long range fighters into the new conflict to give the anti-submarine aircraft some measure of protection. The A/S aircraft could not, of course, have fighter escort, that was impossible due to speed, range and numbers. But they could fly patrols in direct support.

Coastal Command had its own fighters – Beaufighters from the Strike Wings, and Fighter Command sent Mosquito day fighter squadrons to help out. These units were to provide small detachments to RAF Predannack, situated on the southern most tip of Cornwall, over the next few months. 235 Squadron sent one such detachment down from Leuchars in Scotland on 19th May and were ready to fly patrols the next day.

The 20th did not start well. Flight Lieutenant D. Saunders of 10 Squadron took off at 5.08 am to fly a Derange patrol. The Sunderland only got four miles north-west of the Eddystone Light. At 5.20 the coast guards reported a huge flash and explosion as the Sunderland disappeared off the radar screens. All ten men aboard died instantly. Later a Royal Navy destroyer found wreckage on the sea and recovered two bodies.

Two U-boat sightings were made in the morning patrols, by 502 and 224 Squadrons, and two more the same afternoon by 224 and 172 Squadrons. It was on this day that the Wellingtons of 172 and 407 (RCAF) Squadrons, that normally flew night Leigh Light sorties, plus the Leigh Light Catalinas of 210 Squadron, were switched to day operations. Since the beginning of May there had been virtually no night sightings whereas daylight sightings had multiplied considerably.

> *Pilot Officer P.E. Stembridge, 172 Squadron:*
> 'My crew continued to fly mainly night sorties from late May to July 1943. We flew only three daytime sorties but, on the first (20th May 1943) we detected a U-boat; we saw it visually – fully surfaced – at about seven miles. Unfortunately, it was a beautiful sunny day; there was no cloud cover to use on our run in to the target and the visibility was excellent. The U-boat look-outs armed with very powerful binoculars, had obviously spotted us, probably before we had seen the U-boat, and it was already starting to dive. By the time we arrived there, although at full power, the U-boat had fully submerged and we knew there was not much chance of sinking it or even causing significant damage. However, as we were almost at the end of our patrol time, I dropped our stick of six D/Cs diagonally across the estimated course of the submerged U-boat and ahead of its estimated position. I reckoned the crew would at least hear the explosions, not so far away, and that their nerves would not be soothed thereby. Having watched that fascinating German film Das Boot on TV, I am even more convinced that those D/Cs were not wasted and, at the very least, contributed to the pressure on U-boat crews.'

> *Pilot Officer E.E.C. Goodman, 172 Squadron:*
> 'We had another U-boat attack but this time we'd taken off at two o'clock in the afternoon, as we had begun to be switched from night to day operations. We left a large oil patch, having picked up the contact at 20 miles. Up to this time each crew had its own aircraft and we used to fly it until it was due for a major service. Then we'd go on

leave. But at this time the system changed and we flew whatever aircraft we were allocated.'

Flight Sergeant D.H. Hobden, 172 Squadron:
'Our flights from Chivenor were very long, some up to 13 hours. We would fly down to Predannack to be fuelled and then fly on down to the Bay.

'These trips were mainly searches using the radar and we would eagerly scan the screen to pick up blips and then investigate to see what the contact was. Sometimes it was shipping, and if we were near the Spanish coast there were lots of Spanish fighting boats. We were sometimes allowed to gun these boats on a nod and wink principle. We had so many losses we would tend to get jittery and blame the boats for passing on our positions.

'Day flying after night operations was very enjoyable for it was more of a strain at night. The day time brought more danger of enemy air attack and we were often able to take evasive action from an unseen visual contact through our radar screens.'

Note: Despite aircrew worries that Spanish fishing boats were reporting aircraft back to KG40, there is no evidence that this was the case.

On the afternoon of the 20th, 235 Squadron flew its first patrol over the Bay. At 1.09 pm Squadron Leader A.F. 'Tony' Binks and his navigator Flying Officer Marsden, took off in company with Pilot Officer H.S. Vanderwater and Flight Sergeant A.D. McLachlan. 264 Squadron, equipped with Mosquitos, were also at Predannack and over the Bay. Squadron Leader Binks saw a 264 Squadron Mosquito and recognition signals were exchanged. Shortly after 2 pm, Binks and Vanderwater spotted three Ju88s. Two of the German aircraft made a line astern attack on the two Beaufighters as the Beaus made a tight turn to starboard, meeting the third Ju88 head-on. Tony Binks fired at the Junkers and saw pieces of cowling fall off its port engine. The 88 returned fire but failed to hit either Beaufighter; then it nosed down and dived into the sea in flames. One of the other Ju88s followed his companion down and circled the crash, as the third 88 made a pass on Binks, Marsden firing a short burst at it from his rear gun. Binks, whose intercom had now gone U/S, pulled round tightly to attack the 88 but saw no hits. As the two Beaufighters flew away, both 88s were circling the wreckage but they could see no sign of any survivors.

The lost aircraft was a Ju88C-6 of 13/KG40, its three-man crew being killed.

* * *

Enemy activity was still maintained on the 21st, several Ju88s, Arado196s and Me210s, being seen but no RAF aircraft were lost. Several sightings of

U-boats were made and some attacks achieved, but for the next three days little of note took place in the Bay.

There was still a good percentage of U-boats that simply crash-dived when aircraft were observed, but some fought back. Sergeant Fletcher of 10 OTU found a surfaced U-boat just before mid-day on the 22nd and came into the attack from the rear. At 200 yards the U-boat opened fire, hitting the Whitley, but Fletcher pressed home his attack though his D/Cs undershot. His gunners had fired on the U-boat and it was thought that some of the six men seen on the conning tower were hit.

Three hours later, at 2.52 pm, Flight Sergeant D.W.Brookes of 10 OTU was in action with a U-boat that also fought back. As the Whitley ran into the attack, shells kicked up the water around the approaching bomber, then a cannon shell exploded under its nose, knocking the bomb aimer off his seat, and dropping his bomb toggle. He yelled to the pilot to release but he was not heard in all the noise and excitement. The rear gunner opened fire as they went over the submarine, and one man was seen to fall overboard.

The boat was U-103 (KL Gustav-Adolf Janssen), returning home, and carrying officer prisoners from a British ship sunk by another submarine on the 18th.

* * *

It was a 10 OTU Whitley, flown by Sergeant S.C Chatten, that got into the action on the 24th. He was airborne at 7.15 am and at 2.52 that afternoon surprised a U-boat on the edge of the Derange area. The Whitley was at 6,000 feet when the tell-tale wake was seen three to four miles away. Chatten used cloud cover as he made a gradual left-hand turn to bring his aircraft astern of the U-boat, emerging at one mile. At 2,000 feet, the front gunner opened fire as soon as they were in range. Several men on the conning tower were seen to be hit and fall, then the rear gunner fired as the Whitley flew over the boat. Chatten got a good straddle with six D/Cs. As they circled they could see the submarine was not moving forward, then it submerged.

This boat was U-523, commanded by Kapitänleutnant Werner Pietsch. She had left Lorient just two days earlier on her second war patrol. She was forced to abort her cruise, limping back to her base on the 26th.

When this attack was made, Sunderland 'L' of 228 Squadron had been airborne for an hour. It was to meet U-441, commanded by Kapitänleutnant Götz von Hartmann. Since his 'fight back' dictum, Dönitz had had his U-boats' defensive armament increased, but with U-441 he had gone a step farther. This was a Type VIIC boat with a crew of 67 – sixteen more than the usual crew number. The extra men comprised a ship's doctor, two scientists whose job it was to investigate the ways the RAF were detecting the U-boats, and a specially trained gun's crew. U-441 was in fact an Unterseeboot-flugzeugfalle – (Submarine-aircraft-trap). This Type VII had been converted to something of a flak-ship. She had lost her 88 mm deck gun, replaced with two armoured 'bandstands', one fore and aft of the conning tower. In these had been mounted two quadruple 20 mm guns and one 37 mm semi-automatic gun. Von Hartmann's cruise mission was to be located and attacked, in order that her formidable armament would trap the RAF aeroplane and shoot it down.

She sailed from Brest on 22nd May, her fifth war patrol, but first as a flak-boat. It was Flying Officer H.J. Debnam of 228 Squadron who spotted U-441 and brought his Sunderland into the attack. The RAF crew would be half expecting the U-boat to stay up and shoot back for Coastal Command was now well aware of this apparent German tactic. What they did not expect was the veritable wall of fire that suddenly greeted them. However, the Germans found that the salt sea water had affected a weld on the after 20 mm gun mounting, effectively making this gun useless. Nevertheless, the Sunderland was hit, staggering away severely damaged, crashing into the sea shortly afterwards. But Debnam had released his stick of D/Cs that had in turn damaged U-441. A leak had been caused and her steering gear was damaged. U-441 was forced back to Brest for urgent repairs.

Two further sightings were made on the 24th but attacks did not take place. Flight Sergeant N.C.C. Luther (in Wellington MP542 'C') of 407 Squadron, at 2.30 pm, then Flight Lieutenant Dods, 461 Squadron at 7.28 pm.

Bad weather again curtailed operations over the next two days, although U-boats sailed from base ports, grateful for the weather to get away unobserved. U-440 left St Nazaire on the 26th, for instance, for the last time; she was sunk five days later.

Flying began again on the 27th, but a Whitley of 10 OTU went into the sea. Just before mid-day a 58 Squadron Halifax intercepted a radio message from Pilot Officer Hugh's aircraft – "S.O.S., am down in position ...." Any call of this nature put Coastal crews on full alert for rescue bids, but first the men, who had hopefully managed to climb into their dinghies, had to be found. The sea is a big place and even given locations might prove inaccurate. The aircraft went out – the search was on.

Flight Sergeant J.S. Edwards, flying 'T' of 224 Squadron had been on an escort to convoy SL129 (slow convoy from West Africa to Britain) on the 27th, and picked up a contact during the return flight over the Bay. The Liberator was above cloud and Edwards began to lose height. At 9.58 pm they broke cloud and John McMahon in the rear turret saw a fully surfaced U-boat for a fleeting moment. The cloud was very low with visibility almost nil. Edwards turned the Lib round and they picked up the U-boat again at about $3/4$ of a mile. At one minute past 10 pm the Liberator attacked, Edwards attempting to drop his D/Cs but they hung up. McMahon opened fire from his rear position, hitting the conning tower and hull, then the mid-upper gunner commenced firing, but then they were swallowed up again in thick cloud.

Edwards made another turn but it was difficult at such a low altitude to do so safely with the sea only feet below. Almost immediately they broke cloud again and in the poor light, with both cloud and haze, finding the U-boat proved both difficult and hazardous. Then she was seen again, still on the surface, and Edwards made another run and this time the D/Cs went down, McMahon again strafing the submarine as they flew over her. Return fire from the German boat hit the Liberator, damaging the engine nacelle on the No.2 port engine, undercarriage well and severing a hydraulic line, as well as smashing five holes through the bomb bay compartment. The mid-upper gunner also had a bullet smash through his turret perspex but he was not hit. The D/Cs fell too far astern to cause damage, and although other attempts were made to attack the boat, the cloud and visibility thwarted their efforts. They had to be content with one U-boat shaken up, John McMahon having fired some 2,000 rounds at her during their attacks through the cloud. They had been in action with U-594 (KL Friedrich Mumm), outbound for the Atlantic.

Fog did not help the air and sea search on the morning of 28th May, but aircraft were out. Then in the early afternoon a Whitley of 612 Squadron twice found the same U-boat but was unable to make an attack. This was followed at 3.30 by the crew of Flying Officer A.J. Davey flying a 502 Squadron Halifax. In the outer Bay the Halifax came under gunfire from a U-boat the RAF crew had not even seen. As Davey reacted and began a turn, the enemy submarine was hidden in a patch of low cloud, and thus protected, took the opportunity to dive. In fact this was U-594 again.

Meanwhile, Flight Lieutenant Dods of 461 Squadron (JM675 'O') had been out since 1.34 pm on the search for the missing Whitley crew. At 4.30 they spotted them, in the northern part of the Derange area. With the Sunderland, the rescue crew had the opportunity of being able to land on the sea to pick up any downed flyers but permission had to be sought from Group HQ. After circling to assess the situation, Dods had his wireless operator signal to HQ: 'May I land?' The reply came: 'Land at discretion.' Dods turned into the wind and came down for a landing.

The sea was far from perfect for a landing, and the Sunderland hit a swell. It bounced three times as Dods fought with his controls, then on the final bounce it stalled and dived into the cross-swell. The impact caused the front part of the fuselage to break away to just behind the cockpit. Dods was killed instantly and the acting co-pilot, Flying Officer R. DeV Gipps, badly injured but rescued by Flight Sergeant W. Mackie. Gipps was in fact floating away but Mackie swam to him, supporting him for half an hour until the one and only dinghy to survive intact, was paddled over to them. The rest of the Sunderland crew scrambled into this dinghy and later they joined up with the Whitley crew, lashing their dinghies together. Sergeant Mackie later received the BEM for his courage.

Fate had been against the unfortunate Dods, but his crew had been lucky.

HQ knew their position, and when they failed to report in, guessed that something had befallen the Australians. It was now late in the day but aircraft were once again sent out to the spot. One of these was a Wellington of 172 Squadron, piloted by Peter Stembridge. They located the dinghies, remained in contact and dropped flame floats to make certain of the survivors' position. A great comfort to the men, wet, cold and anxious, in the dinghies.

'My final recollection of operations over the Bay concerns our location, during the night of 28/29th May 1943, of a dinghy, illuminated with the Leigh Light. It had survivors of one of our aircraft and was at approximately 48°N 10°W. We circled it for some 3³/₄ hours, transmitting the appropriate W/T messages to the controlling authority and to other aircraft and ships that might be in a position to assist.'

Pilot Officer P.E. Stembridge, 172 Squadron.

The morning of 29th May did not fare well for Flight Sergeant Norman Earnshaw and his Whitley crew of 612 Squadron. They took off from base at 5.50 am to fly a Derange sortie. At 8.30 a message was received asking for a check on their position and saying they had engine trouble. Ten minutes later this was followed by an SOS but with no position. As time went by, Group tried to make contact with the Whitley but the radio remained ominously silent. At base the time of their return came and went. Finally the time came when they had to be down somewhere – their fuel would have run out.

Meanwhile, Pilot Officer G.O. Singleton of 461 Squadron was over the two dinghies of the previous day. Three of the men were injured. Flying Officer Raleigh Gipps, the co-pilot of Dods' Sunderland, and Sergeants Rodwell and Brizell of 10 OTU.

Cloud base was just about 100 feet with visibility down to less than a mile and deteriorating. Singleton decided to land at once in case he lost sight of the men in the water. This he accomplished successfully and the survivors were taken aboard. However, the sea was rough and with sixteen extra men inside, the Sunderland was too heavily laden to take off. More aircraft appeared overhead. Flight Lieutenant N.C. Gerrard of 10 Australian Squadron, Flight Lieutenant Corrie of 228 Squadron, then Flying Officer Sharwood of 279 Squadron. Because the Sunderland was unable to take off, a French sloop (L.19) *La Combattante* was called up and homed to the position. Gerrard spotted the sloop at 9.48 am, and by 10.35 the ship's lifeboats were taking off the extra men and then took Singleton's Sunderland (T9114 'E') in tow, now with just a skeleton crew aboard. They removed the depth charge pistols making them safe for jettisoning.

Four and a half hours later the tow line broke in the heavy sea, but

Singleton did not give up and starting the engines decided to try for a take-off. For three miles the Sunderland gained speed as it crashed, bounced and bludgeoned its way over and through the waves and spray. Singleton finally got it away, staggering into the air, but with a seven foot hole torn in the hull, it was not going to be able to land on water back at base. He was ordered to put the flying boat down at Angle airfield near Pembroke Dock. They could not bale out for flying boat crews did not normally carry parachutes. The D/Cs had already been jettisoned, and when he arrived over Milford Haven at 8 pm, he jettisoned all excess fuel and equipment. Singleton made a successful crash landing alongside the runway, cutting a 150 yard furrow, but only damaged one float and a wing-tip as the aeroplane gently laid over. Surprisingly, Singleton received no decoration for his gallant rescue.

* * *

Despite some bad weather over the Bay, patrols were flown during the day and some sightings made. Flight Sergeant A.W.J. Hazell and his navigator Flight Sergeant E.C.G. Hurle were flying a patrol in their Beaufighter. Coastal Command had been experimenting with rockets for attacking U-boats, and Hazell was carrying eight 25 lb RPs (Rocket Projectiles) on an anti-submarine sortie. At 11.24 they had the good fortune to spot a U-boat and immediately attacked.

Only the periscope and wake were visible and all eight rockets went into the sea in a salvo but nothing resulted from the attack. A 228 Squadron Sunderland also had a sighting towards late afternoon but no attack could be made before she disappeared. Flying Officer H.A.L. Moran, an Australian with 59 Squadron, was on his way to escort a convoy and while on the north-west edge of the Bay, his crew spotted a U-boat (position 4815/1405). It was 5.30 pm as Moran released four D/Cs over the submerging boat, the explosions lifting her bows out of the water at an angle of 45°. Now on the surface, Moran brought his Liberator (FL984 'S') round for a second attack. Four more D/Cs went down and exploded near the submarine. German sailors appeared on the deck and began exchanging fire with the Liberator, which had now expended its cargo of D/Cs. The battle went on for fifteen minutes, the U-boat steering an erratic course before she finally submerged. The U-boat – U-552 – on her way back to base, was badly damaged and did not put to sea again until 2nd October 1943.

Although not strictly within the scope of this book, this damaging attack on U-552 has to be mentioned as being in the general area and was a boat that was about to run the gauntlet across the Bay.

'H.A.L. Moran was another of our Australian captains of aircraft; another splendid fellow. He came of a wealthy family and was very far from being a rough type. Good-looking, socially secure and justifiably self-confident, he – like many others – was a first-rate captain of aircraft, and got results.

Wing Commander G.C.C. Bartlett, OC 59 Squadron.

Another RAF casualty of the day was another Whitley of 10 OTU. Airborne at 9.25 am with Sergeant McAlpine at the controls, it ditched off the south-west coast of Wales at 9 pm after circling a British coaster. All the crew got out and were picked up by the coaster and put ashore.

Better weather on the 30th brought much activity over the Bay. Ju88s were seen during the day and had some success against anti-submarine aircraft. The long suffering 10 OTU lost Sergeant L.O. Slade from a dawn patrol. Shortly after mid-day Group received a message that they were experiencing engine trouble. At 12.55 the message was more urgent: 'I require immediate assistance– position 4648/0900.' – bang in the middle of the line Cape Finisterre-Scilly Isles.

In fact, Slade and crew had attacked U-459, inbound for France. In the exchange the Whitley (Z9440 'Z') was hit, which was the cause of the reported engine trouble. The Whitley was not an aircraft to go very far on one engine and shortly afterwards Sergeant Slade had to put down on the sea. However, they were picked up and ended up as PoWs.

There were a number of sightings of submarines during the morning, the first at 9.55 am. Flight Lieutenant D.W. Eadie of 210 Squadron attacked a U-boat which fought back. She inflicted severe damage on the Catalina, killed the front gunner, Sergeant H.Roper, and wounded two other crewmen. Eadie flew back to base but the hull was so badly holed that the flying boat sunk after landing but the rest of the crew clambered out safely.

It is probable that the U-boat involved was U-418 commanded by Oberleutnant Gerhard Lange. As she was sunk on 1 June (see later) there had been no time to make a report about shooting down the Whitley. David Eadie later received the DFC while Sergeant J.A.Dick collected a DFM for staying at his post on the radar despite having been wounded. He assisted his pilot to get home before telling anyone he had been hit.

Aircraft of 58 and 206 Squadrons had sightings mid-morning. Flight Lieutenant Elsworthy of 224 Squadron fought with a U-boat just before 1 pm (this was U-459 again) and three more were attacked that afternoon by 206, 502 and 10 OTU aircraft, while Flying Officer Baird of 461 Squadron spotted another around 7 pm but this too went under before he could do much about it.

At 8.47 pm a message was received from Flight Sergeant H.V.Archer's 224 Squadron Liberator (BZ713 'S') that they were under attack by Ju88s but nothing further was ever heard from them, the grey waters of the Bay keeping the secret of their last watery resting place. However, we now know that KG40 had notched up another kill.

There had been another dinghy episode on this day when a 248 Squadron

Beaufighter (Flying Officer R.G. Worth and Flying Officer A.E. Stoker) sighted four men in a dinghy, all waving furiously. As they circled, they sent a radio message to HQ, then returned to base. Changing aircraft, Worth and Stoker flew back to the position and located the dinghy again. This time they counted eight men, as apparently four others had been lying in the bottom of the dinghy.

At 7.13 pm a Fortress from 220 Squadron, piloted by Flying Officer C.F. Callender (FK201 'T') arrived at the scene, now counting five men in the dinghy. Callender dropped a raft and rations to the survivors, some being picked up by them. Flight Lieutenant R.Drummond of the same squadron (FK212 'V') also arrived and dropped emergency rations that were picked up by the men. As the aircraft's PLE was reached, two Spanish fishing vessels were seen about two miles away and heading for the dinghy. These men were Sergeant L.O. Slade and his crew of 10 OTU who had gone down after mid-day. The fishing boats later rescued them and landed them all at Marin.

A better fate befell Flight Sergeant Earnshaw and his crew of 612 Squadron who had ditched the previous morning. After Earnshaw brought the Whitley down, the impact caused the large dinghy to be thrown out and the attaching line worked loose. The dinghy drifted under the tail of the Whitley and sank with it. The emergency dinghy was also thrown out and its line too became detached. However, the crew managed to cut the lacing and the dinghy inflated after operating the CO_2 bottle by hand. Only the K-type dinghy functioned properly and inflated on its own. The Verey cartridges [$1^1/_2$ inch signal cartridge] were saved but the pistol lost in the ditching. The food supply was, however, taken into the dinghies.

All through the 29th and 30th the men had continually to bale out the water from inside the dinghies and fluorescine was trailed. No less than twelve aircraft were seen before a Beaufighter finally sighted them. It directed a Hudson of 279 Squadron to them which dropped a Lindholme dinghy. They were finally rescued 36 hours after coming down. The only casualty was the navigator who injured his knee climbing into the rescue craft!

The last day of May saw less activity but far more success. The day did not, however, begin well, 407 Squadron RCAF losing a Leigh Light Wellington flown by Flight Sergeant H.C. Collins (MP542 'C'). Only one body was ever recovered from the sea.

At 11 o'clock Wing Commander Wilfred Oulton took off for a patrol. Three hours later he saw two twin-engined aircraft but no contact was made. In the meantime it was a 201 Squadron Sunderland that had the first success of the day. Flight Lieutenant D.M. Gall took off at 10.34 am. Although a squadron within 15 Group of Coastal Command, it was one of a couple of units which had aircraft attached to fly operations within 19 Group's area of operations. Douglas Gall had been with 201 Squadron since October 1941 and prior to this day had flown 732 hours on the unit's Sunderlands.

'We were on a routine anti-submarine patrol to the south-west; for once the weather was beautiful, and we were able to fly at our optimum height of 5,000 feet. (We had radar, but it was very rudimentary, and we preferred to fly below cloud and use our eyes. On this day, however, there was no cloud.)

'I should say here that we disliked A/S patrols, as compared with convoy escort work. With the latter, at least we had something to look at, but on the patrols we had to suffer the extreme boredom of flying mile after mile with nothing to see but sea for something like fifteen hours at a time. We got to the stage of thinking there were no U-boats to be sighted.

It therefore came as a tremendous surprise to us when the submarine was sighted visually in the distance. It was some way away – I wouldn't like to trust my memory to say how far (eight miles) – but we headed straight towards it, making our best speed, which was something in the region of 150 knots – downhill!! And, of course, we were going downhill, as we wanted to get to our depth-charge dropping height of fifty feet as quickly as possible. I'm afraid I didn't even think about refinements such as coming out of the sun. I just wanted to get there before it dived, because of course that's what it was going to do – any second. And, in any case, this was our first sighting.

'Now I am not sure how early this was in the period of "fighting back"; all I know is that, if there were previous incidents, I was not aware of them, and we all expected the boat to dive. Indeed, when he did not, I asked the navigator to check whether we were near one of the "free lanes" for our own submarines. I was pretty sure we were not near one, but I had to be absolutely certain.

'As we approached, I still had this haunting fear that it might be one of ours, and when it began to flash at us, I had the navigator check the recognition letter of the Day. Of course I do not remember what it was, but it was certainly not an "H" or "S", which was what was flashing.

'It was my Scottish rear-gunner who eventually put my mind at rest by calling on the intercom: "He's no' flashin' skipper; he's firin'." There was a bit of a swell running, and the U-boat's gunners may have been inexperienced, for we did not feel a tremor.

'Here I must pause to say that we were fortunate enough that day to have the squadron gunnery officer as a "guest" crew member, a Pilot Officer Martin. Luckily, too, he was manning the front turret at the time, using the "pea-shooter", as we called the one forward-firing Browning. And he used it to great effect, as witnessed by the dead bodies I saw in the conning tower as we passed over.

'We dropped our stick of four depth charges from about 50 feet above the water. The dropping in these days was done visually by the pilot, and I must admit that I missed by yards! But it was to be my lucky day, for the U-boat captain decided to turn at the last minute. I was amazed at the speed with which he turned through ninety degrees, but delighted to see that he made the turn the "wrong way" right into the middle of the stick.

'As we turned round, we saw a shimmering explosion over the surface of the sea, the bows came out of the water to a vertical position, and then slid slowly down. There was much jubilation and cheering on board R of 201 but even in the excitement then, I couldn't help feeling, as I have felt so often since – the poor devils!'

Flight Lieutenant D.M. Gall, 201 Squadron.

The U-boat was U-440 and under her commander, Werner Schwaff, was outward-bound from St Nazaire to the Atlantic, having sailed on this her fifth war patrol, on 26th May. Gall circled the spot for fifteen minutes watching a large patch of oil spread over a two mile area, before resuming patrol. On board the Sunderland was Squadron Leader N.L. Smith, a newly arrived flight commander replacement. Flying to gain first hand experience, he certainly chose the right day and the right crew.

Then at 3.51 pm Oulton and his crew found the enemy:

'We were on a planned offensive patrol, running north-south roughly parallel with the Biscay coast of France and creeping westward. My squadron practice was to use the H_2S only intermittently, because of the effective U-boat search receivers, and to make the maximum use of any cloud cover below about 5,000 feet. So we were lolloping along just in and out of the cloud base, when we spotted an irregularity in the pattern of waves and "white horses" about ten miles ahead, as far as I can remember. So back into the cloud, up to 2,600 rpm and maximum boost, dipping out of the cloud about once a minute, and about three minutes later we identified the U-boat, proceeding about 12-14 knots on the surface, and we went into the attack. We had been trying out a technique to get some help from the mid-upper turret, ie. approaching quite high, then at about 1,000 yards diving quite steeply down to the surface, which allowed the mid-upper gunner to spray the target to put the U-boat gunners off their job a little, and flattening out at the last moment at about fifty feet for the final run in. This seemed to work out all right and we laid a stick of six depth charges across the boat from her starboard quarter to her port bow, just ahead of the conning tower.

'As we came round in a tight turn and the explosions sank away, the

U-boat had lost way and was turning slowly to starboard. With only three depth charges left, we made another attack, coming under some flak but suffering no damage. My rear gunner reckoned we had bracketed the stern, and the U-boat was obviously in bad shape, but still turning slowly to starboard.

'We reported the action and state of play to 19 Group, asked for reinforcements and set up the standard W/T homing procedure,uncomfortably aware that we might have visitors other than the RAF. The first to arrive after about 20 minutes was another Halifax of my own squadron J/58 who had found us but didn't see the U-boat; so we formated on "J" and led him down into the attack, then pulling off about 200 yards on his starboard beam and giving him covering fire to keep the flak-gunners' heads down a bit. Alas, he was a young pilot and over-anxious and dropped his stick of D/Cs about 100 yards short. He did the same again on his second attack, which one could understand and sympathise with. It must have been a bit unnerving.

'So back to the homing procedure and presently a Sunderland, E/10 of the Australian Squadron based at Mount Batten, turned up, obviously not knowing what was going on and not knowing what we wanted him to do. I couldn't raise him on voice radio and we flew in circles for several minutes on close formation, while I made signals with my hands and my wireless operator tried to pass a message by Aldis lamp. Eventually I shepherded him down to the crippled U-boat, and as soon as the Australian saw it, no more time was wasted. Once again, we formated and gave covering fire during the run in, but his D/Cs weren't close enough to administer the *coup de grâce*.

'A few minutes later, another Sunderland arrived, X/228 who evidently by now had understood the tactical situation. He went straight into the attack and laid his first stick across the U-boat midships. Before the gouts of water from the DC explosions had half fallen away, there was a great sheet of blue and orange-coloured flame with a great deal of white and some black smoke. When this cleared, the U-boat was gone, but the sea was littered with wreckage and bodies, some of whom were still alive.

'Meanwhile, 19 Group had warned us of considerable Ju88 traffic in our area, so we thought it prudent not to linger. At that point, I felt very sorry for those poor devils in the water. They had only been doing their duty as they saw it and were as brave as any other combatant. So we flew down over the mess and dropped our two rubber dinghies and a couple of Mae Wests, in the hope that some of them might survive and be picked up by one of the RN hunter-killer groups operating in the area.

'Then we climbed for the nearest cloud and beat it for St Eval.'
Wing Commander W.E. Oulton, OC 58 Squadron.

Oulton's rear gunner later said: 'The U-boat was obliterated in the plumes of the explosions. As the plumes died away I saw the boat and stern again, then the remainder of the U-boat, wallowing in the depth-charge pool.'

The other aircraft that joined in the attack on U-563 was the 58 Squadron Liberator flown by Pilot Officer Eric L. Hartley, then the two Sunderlands, one from 10 Squadron – Flight Lieutenant Maxwell S. Mainprize. They saw men in life jackets come onto the deck as the other Sunderland, of 228 Squadron, went in – Flying Officer W.M. French. As their D/Cs exploded, bodies were seen to be flung into the air. Then the U-boat seemed to shudder and go down.

U-563 had left Brest on the 29th for her eighth war patrol, commanded by Oberleutnant Gustav Borchardt. It was a Type VIIC submarine heading for the Atlantic. As the aircraft left the scene some 40 bodies were seen in the sea. As Flying Officer French continued to patrol, he found another U-boat at 7.25 pm. With no D/Cs left he attacked with his gunners. The U-boat fired back but as no serious threat developed, the submarine took the opportunity of diving. This had been U-530.

Not far from the position of U-563's demise, another submarine was spotted by Flying Officer Bob Sweeny and crew of 224 Squadron at 6.48 pm. She was fully surfaced and opened fire on the Liberator as it emerged from cloud at 3,200 feet, Sweeny having used the cloud to approach from eight miles. They were right over the U-boat, flak bursting and passing all about them. Sweeny circled, 1,500 to 1,000 yards away as his own and the German gunners exchanged gunfire. Then the submarine – it was U-621, returning to Brest from her fourth patrol, having been cruising around the Azores – began to alter course. Sweeny pulled the Liberator round and went in, the German gunners momentarily silent – probably waiting for more ammunition to be passed up to them. The Liberator went over at 50 feet, the second pilot seeing four sailors manning a gun on the submarine clearly, their white faces looking up at them. The rear gunner sprayed the conning tower as it appeared below him and saw the six D/Cs overshoot slightly. However, as the explosions subsided oil could be clearly seen behind the U-boat.

Sweeny circled and came in again, but U-621 was submerging. As six more D/Cs went down she had disappeared but the stick appeared to land across the U-boat's track only seconds after she went under. Nothing more was seen, but Krushka's U-621 had been damaged and limped back into Brest on 3rd June.

In Bob Sweeny's crew was Flight Sergeant E. Cheek. Eddie Cheek was to be involved in three U-boat casualties during the Battle of the Bay:

'The tactics of anti-submarine warfare took on a more decisive role in the spring of 1943. Prior to this anti-submarine operations were either in direct support of convoys or flown over areas where U-boats could be a threat to approaching convoys or where they were known to be operating. The absurd requirement of the Dönitz system, which required that each U-boat should make regular daily contact, by radio with their headquarters, enabled our shipborne and shore-based direction finding services [and ULTRA intercepts. Ed.] to establish their whereabouts. It was soon realized that the limited submerged range of the U-boat (which are now described as just submersibles, not submarines) should make it possible to define an area west of their bases in France, in which they must surface to recharge their batteries. Having established this area, in the Bay of Biscay, it was only necessary to concentrate our anti-submarine aircraft in this area. This ploy was soon detected by the Germans, and they sensibly decided to arm their craft with anti-aircraft weapons, after all, it should not be too difficult to shoot down the slow ponderous search aircraft. When this became apparent to us a simple solution presented itself, the aircraft which first detected a U-boat would broadcast the position, and wait for other aircraft to arrive so that a concerted attack could be made. German reaction was predictable, they introduced formations of Ju88 aircraft into the Bay, to apply the coup de grâce to the lumbering A/S aircraft. Right, said the RAF, we will introduce formations of Beaufighters and Mosquitos to put fear and dread into the "beastly Hun". I think we managed to hold the edge until the Schnorkel appeared on the scene. The concentration of A/S effort in the Bay, coupled with the increased presence of German fighters had a predictable effect on aircrews, in that lookouts spent more time scanning the skies above, than the sea below. These patrols were code-named "Derange" and we were convinced that the code reflected the mental state of the staff officer(s) responsible for their inception.'

Flight Sergeant E.S. Cheek, 224 Squadron.

The month of May ended with a tally of eight U-boats sunk and five others damaged. Of these, two had been sunk and a third damaged on 31st May. However, two days earlier, on the 29th, the Germans took a major tactical decision.

In order to make it difficult for RAF aircraft in the Bay area to locate U-boats, and if found to enable them to fight back more effectively, Dönitz instructed all U-boats returning across the Bay, west of longitude 16° West, to continue passage in company, in groups of up to four boats.

Rendezvous points for these crossings were given for 31st May and 1st June. The same procedure would also be introduced for outward sailing

boats which would assemble at pre-arranged rendezvous points in groups of
three to six, and put in command of the senior U-boat commander. These
would leave the French coast in daylight on the surface, with strict orders
not to dive if attacked by aircraft, but to fight back with all defensive guns.
The groups would dive at night at prescribed speeds, then surface at dawn,
reform and proceed on the surface once more. Groups would disperse at
longitude 15°W. Air cover by Ju88s of KG40 would be provided as far out
into the Bay as possible, but especially over the rendezvous points by the
French coast.

These orders were not however implemented before the month ended. In
the last two days, twelve U-boats were sighted, and ten attacked. As already
mentioned, two were sunk and another damaged.

Thus ended a definite phase during the Bay offensive. Centimetric ASV
and Leigh Light successes had forced Dönitz to change his comparatively
safe night surface passage for his U-boats, forcing him to begin one
mistaken tactic after another. These resulted in the losses the U-boat arm
could ill-afford at a time the Atlantic battle was at its height. The next two
months continued to cost him dearly as he pursued his course of action.

* * *

Meanwhile 19 Group's aircraft, assisted by 15 Group, kept after the U-
boats. At this time the daily round is recalled by John McMahon who was a
WOP/AG with 224 Squadron:

> 'We spent the time on operations as either convoy escort, or anti-U-
> boat patrol. We did about one trip every four or five days.The
> duration of each trip was eight to ten hours or more. The WOP/AGs
> worked in two-hour shifts which relieved the monotony somewhat.
> The rear turret was the loneliest place – after two hours seeing
> nothing but water and sky it was a relief even to watch the radar PPI
> endlessly searching for a blip which so rarely appeared. The
> navigator also had a lonely vigil but at least he could see where we
> were going. All the other crew members were situated on the flight
> deck and could see each other. Later we got a flight engineer which
> meant we had someone available to man the beam guns. These were
> 0.5-Brownings free mounted on each side of the fuselage and were
> belt fed from a wooden box high up on each side.
>
> 'It was my allotted position on our first encounter with Ju88s. From
> what I remember the rear gunner yelled something about enemy
> aircraft – the skipper put the nose down and we dived to safety in a
> bank of low cloud. I finished in a heap beside the chemical toilet with
> the huge belt of ammunition on top of me.
>
> 'Our first encounter with a U-boat wasn't much of a success; we
> picked him up on the radar at about 15 miles and homed in. We

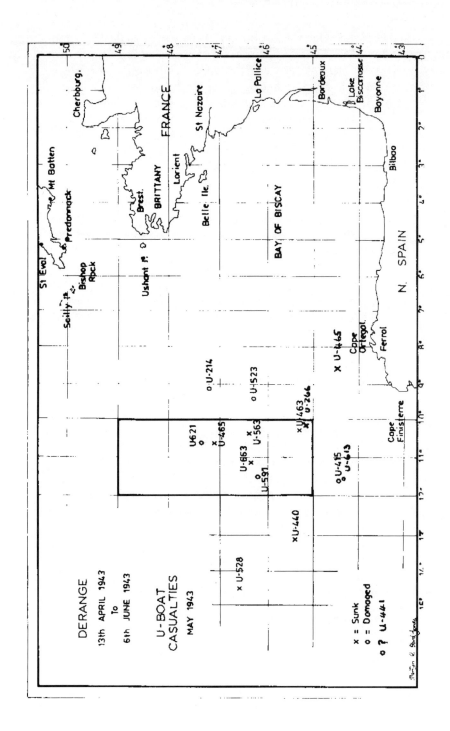

DE RANGE
13th APRIL 1943
To
6th JUNE 1943

U-BOAT
CASUALTIES
MAY 1943

x = Sunk
o = Damaged
o ? U-441

FRANCE

BRITTANY

BAY OF BISCAY

N. SPAIN

Cherbourg.

Mt Batten
Predannack
St Eval
Scilly Is.
Bishop Rock
Ushant I.

St Nazaire
Lorient
Brest
Belle Ile.

Lo Pallice
Bordeaux
Lake Biscarrosse
Bayonne
Bilboo

Cape Ortegal
Ferrol
Cape Finisterre

x U-465

o U-214
o U-523

U-621 o
x U-465
x U-563
U-663 x
o U-591
x U-463
x U-266

o U-415
x U-613

x U-440

x U-528

spotted him through a break in the low cloud and turned for a perfect run in. Unfortunately the depth charges hung up. We tried a second run but the weather was closing in and as we released the D/Cs from the bomb bay, they missed him as we were banking slightly. We then discovered the flak he was throwing up had damaged the release mechanism in the rear bomb bay. What we did not know was that one of his shells had burst the tyre on our starboard landing gear. On touch down, the aircraft left the runway and, fortunately for us, eventually came to a halt without hitting anything.

'From what I can recall of life on the squadron – we never really worried very much about it. The Ju88s took a heavy toll and we had a few picked up from the Bay by the Navy – one instance, a pilot and WOP/AG, were picked up by a Sunderland flying boat after being adrift for six days in a dinghy. Unfortunately the WOP/AG died in hospital which left the pilot as the only survivor (Willerton and Barham).

'On the lighter side we had the skipper who returned safely after being attacked by ten Ju's. His classic remark was when they had spotted five above them and another five below: "I didn't want to start anything." He had dived into cloud and brought his damaged aircraft and crew home safely.

'During this period we were billeted at Newquay – the RAF had taken over some of the hotels. We were in a hotel at Porth Bay. We spent the off-duty time on the beaches or in the pubs. Other "perks" were the rum ration before debriefing on return from operations and after debriefing the mixed grill – ham and eggs, etc. which was a luxury in those days few people enjoyed. We also had 14 days' leave every three months with a handsome 6/– per day extra while on leave from the Nuffield Foundation or some such establishment.

'On another occasion we were on anti-U-boat patrol when we picked up a couple of German warships on the radar. At least that is what they turned out to be when we got closer. I think they were destroyers but I cannot remember. However, we reported to base and circled at a safe distance as every now and again puffs of black smoke appeared too close for comfort. After an hour we got a signal back from base which said, "Do not, repeat, not attack, return to base immediately." This caused some amusement as attack was the last thing we had in mind.

'On our way back we had a grandstand view as the Royal Navy was engaging a German merchant cruiser, which was making for the French coast and the two German ships we had spotted had been coming out to escort her in.'

Flight Sergeant J. McMahon, 224 Squadron.

CHAPTER FOUR

THE TACTICS CHANGE

The German submarine U-418, commanded by Leutnant zur See Lange, had sailed from Kiel on 24th April for her first war patrol. She had spent May in the North Atlantic but rather than returning to northern Germany, Lange had been ordered to a Bay port. At 11 o'clock on 1st June she was travelling towards the French coast, on the surface, her bridge-crew keeping a sharp look-out for hostile aircraft.

Two hours earlier a Beaufighter of 236 Squadron's detachment at Predannack had flown out on an anti-submarine patrol, piloted by Flying Officer M.C. Bateman and his navigator Flight Sergeant C.W.G. Easterbrook. On board too was Lieutenant-Commander Francis J. Brookes of the Royal Navy, who was a naval specialist in U-boat warfare.

The squadron detachment had commenced anti-submarine patrols at the end of May, and as already mentioned, Flight Sergeant A.W.J. Hazell had found and attacked one on 29th May. The squadron had only just begun to practise with their new weapon – the 25 lb rocket projectile, and flying over the Bay in search of German submarines was as good a way as any to start using the new R/Ps. It would not be until September 1943 that the RAF were allowed to use them over enemy-held territory in case an unused one fell into enemy hands. Mark Bateman, and the other members of the squadron, had spent just three or four days practising with the new rockets, having had explained to them the need to make an attacking dive at a 20° angle. They were told to keep the Beaufighter steady for if one pulled up when they were fired, the R/Ps went down, and if one nosed down slightly, the rockets went up. Bateman himself had flown his first Bay patrol on 29th May, flying out on a similar patrol to Flight Sergeant Hazell. Indeed, on 1st June, Hazell had also flown out from Predannack, but, on both occasions, the Beaufighters had headed into quite different patrol areas. Flight Lieutenant Hugo 'Mike' Shannon, had led the detachment to Cornwall. Lieutenant-Commander Brookes had recently been engaged on a lecture tour of Coastal Command stations, and was now taking the opportunity of actually flying with an operational unit to see for himself how anti-U-boat missions were conducted in order to gain more practical experience.

It was in fact Brookes, sitting close behind Mark Bateman in the somewhat cramped cockpit area, who first sighted U-418. He had been scouring the grey waters of the Bay with his binoculars when he spotted the boat some ten miles off. Lowering his binoculars he tapped Bateman on the shoulder, pointed and yelled, "U-boat! Can you see it?"

Bateman quickly picked her out and headed straight for her, beginning a descent from 3,500 feet. He selected four rockets, in pairs. Then the German look-outs saw him and the boat began to dive. When he was 800 yards from the diving submarine, the conning towers and stern were still above the surface. He fired the first pair, then the second a moment later. He did not aim directly at the boat but at the sea, about 25 yards his side of the target, as he had been shown. The four R/Ps streaked ahead, leaving a trail of bluey-white smoke. The R/Ps hit the sea by the side of U-418, striking the hull a devastating blow, puncturing the metal hull. The warheads broke off and penetrated right through the boat and out the other side. Water poured into the doomed vessel, the weight of which took the U-boat straight to the bottom.

Bateman circled but could only see a green patch of disturbed water amidst the swirl left by the diving submarine, followed later by a larger patch about 100 yards ahead. Whether he had made a kill he could not tell, but he had been on target. Returning to Predannack he could only claim a possible kill, and because the R/Ps were still secret a report added that the attack had been made with depth charges.

It was not until September that Mark Bateman received a letter from Coastal Command, stating that following the receipt of additional information, his attack on a submarine on 1st June had been reassessed by the U-boat committee and had up graded his 'seriously damaged' to U-boat destroyed. By this date he had already received the award of the DFC and promotion to flight lieutenant. He completed his tour with 236 Squadron in November, being posted to No 2 Coastal OTU.

Two other singleton U-boats, making for France, were sighted by Flying Officer G.A. Sawtell of 58 Squadron on the 1st, but both dived before attacks could be made.

After the losses sustained by the U-boats on the last day of May,the Ju88s were more active on the 1st, and they had some success. At 2.27 a civil Douglas DC3 KLM/BOAC airliner from Gibraltar was shot down by 14/KG40, in position 4630/0937, almost mid-way between Cape Finisterre and the Scillies. The famous British actor Leslie Howard was on board and he, along with the crew and other passengers, all died.

Sergeant Jackson of 10 OTU saw a Ju88 flying 2,000 feet below his Whitley but the German crew failed to see them. Not so fortunate was Flight Lieutenant F.W. Gilmore of 58 Squadron. They had flown on patrol at 3.18 pm. A brief position message was received at 7.11 pm but the Halifax failed to return, shot down by Ju88s.

Junkers 88 fighters were active again the following day and it was another 58 Squadron Halifax that had the first encounter. Shortly before 10 am, Flying Officer A I Sladen's crew saw the fighter and fired at it as Sladen dodged into nearby cloud.

The weather on this day was fair to cloudy with occasional thundery rain showers but some bright intervals. Four Beaufighters of 248 Squadron from Predannack flew an anti-fishing vessel patrol in the afternoon and at 3.41 pm, Sergeant P.T. Wilkinson and his navigator, Sergeant S. Bartram, spotted a U-boat on the surface. It was two miles ahead, crossing the aircraft's track. So fast did this happen, that Wilkinson was unable to sight his guns, but the U-boat's gunners managed a burst of fire as the Beau flashed overhead. Wilkinson pulled round in a steep turn, then attacked from dead astern. He fired one long and one short burst (160 rounds of 20 mm), scoring hits on the conning tower while splashes of other shells churned up the water on either side. The U-boat (she was U-455 outward bound) crash dived.

An hour later outbound U-172 was spotted, again on the surface, by Flight Sergeant Johnson of 58 Squadron. He flew his Halifax over the submarine after she submerged and dropped a stick of depth charges but saw no results.

Then at 7 pm, Flight Lieutenant C.B. Walker of 461 Squadron, flying in the Derange area, was intercepted by eight Ju88s. They were spotted by his rear gunner Flight Sergeant R.M. Goode, six miles off, at which time the navigator, Flying Officer K.M. Simpson, took up the fire control position in the astrodome. Crew members not on watch took up position to fire guns through the Sunderland's galley hatches, guns that had been recently installed as a special modification by the Australians.

Obviously in for a battle, Walker jettisoned the DCs, while the wireless operator sent a message to base, as the 88s positioned themselves about the flying boat. Three went out to the port side, three to starboard and one at each beam. As one Ju88 came in from each beam, Walker swerved his Sunderland steeply down to the right, then over to the left. However, one burst of gunfire set the flying boat's port outer engine on fire and the aircraft's compass was shot away, splashing burning alcohol over the 25-year-old pilot. Putting out the fires, the two pilots (Flying Officer W.J. Dowling was the second pilot) had to wrestle with the controls for 45 minutes as twenty successive attacks were made by the German fighters. Simpson, still in the astrodome, was wounded but continued to direct the pilots and gunners as attacks developed. Then when the intercom was smashed he passed notes by hand. One Ju88 was hit and crashed after receiving a burst from a mid-ships gunner. Then the rudder and elevator trimming wires were severed, the tail turret damaged and Flight Sergeant Goode knocked unconscious. The midships and front gunner shot down a second Ju88 but the starboard galley gunner, Sergeant E.C.E. Miles, was fatally wounded, being replaced by the second engineer. A third 88 went into the sea, hit by the midships gunner and the now conscious rear gunner who was operating his turret by hand. The attacks lasted till 7.45 pm when only two Ju88s remained. After a final half-hearted pass, they flew off.

The Sunderland had been riddled, 500 bullet holes later being counted, one crew member was dead and four others wounded. 'Col' Walker struggled home over the last 300 miles, finally having to put down at Marazion near the shore off Cornwall. Walker received the DSO for this epic fight, while Simpson received the DFC. Flight Sergeant R.M.Goode and Flight Sergeant A.E.Fuller both received DFMs. There were no KG40 losses.

* * *

Beaufighters and Ju88s clashed on 3rd June. Just before 11 am Flight Lieutenant 'Mike' Shannon and Pilot Officer I.S. Walters, nearing the second hour of an anti-submarine patrol (in JL819 'W') from Predannack, were suddenly attacked by the now usual number of eight Ju88s. They approached down-sun and formated on Shannon's Beaufighter, three on either beam, 1,500 yards away, and 1,500 feet above. The two other 88s positioned themselves one at each quarter, at same height and distance. Very similar tactics to the 88s that attacked Walker's Sunderland the previous day.

Aboard the Beaufighter was Lieutenant-Commander Brookes who had been with Mark Bateman when they attacked U-418 on 1st June. Just as on that occasion, Brookes was positioned behind Shannon. Once positioned to their satisfaction the Ju88s made attacks in pairs, one fighter from each side diving down, attacking, then reforming on the Beau's beam in order to repeat the manoeuvre. Walters was wounded in one of the first passes and therefore was unable to operate the rear gun. Shannon dived the Beaufighter to sea level, taking violent evasive action as each pair of 88s came in. He then felt a bullet pass close to his head. Although it missed him it hit Commander Brookes in the head mortally wounding him. Another Ju88 came at him head-on. Shannon blazing away with his cannon but saw no hits. The Beaufighter was now going flat out north, the 88s chasing. One 88 repeatedly attacked from dead astern, Shannon believing the German's intention was to make him turn so that the other 88s could close in, formate and continue with beam attacks. The sky was clear of cloud, leaving Shannon no option but to try and out run his attackers. After about eight minutes the 88s gave up the chase. Shannon radioed to base and struggled back to Cornwall. His inner starboard fuel tank and both wings had been hit, also the hydraulics had been damaged. Reaching base he found his wheels and flaps would not operate but he made a creditable belly landing and was congratulated on a tremendous effort against odds.

In November 1943, Shannon was wounded in a strike on a convoy off Den Helder and flew back to make another belly landing. This time he received an Immediate DFC.

* * *

The only U-boat attack of the day came at 12.45 pm. A 407 Squadron RCAF Wellington (MP541) piloted by Flying Officer G.C. Walsh D/C'd a submarine that had just crash-dived. Bubbles and oil were seen in profusion but this inbound U-boat reached port safely.

There was now, and suddenly a complete lack of sightings for ten days. Singleton U-boats continued to arrive back at their Biscay ports until 9th June. This was because it was difficult for the commanders to comply with Dönitz's orders to join into groups when the individual boats were well spread out and their known positions to each other were only approximate ones. However, two small groups were successfully brought in. U-161 and U-229 crossed the Bay together between 3rd and 7th June, U-575 and U-731 between the 6th and the 11th. This was in accordance with Dönitz's standing order No 13. This was issued on 30th May, and made reference to the earlier May directive for all U-boats on passage through the Bay (or from Germany through the Iceland Channel). They were to proceed submerged surfacing by day in order to charge batteries and to ventilate the boat. Long surface runs by day were only permissible in good visibility when surprise by aircraft was less likely.

Another difficulty the U-boats faced off the Biscay coast line was sea mines laid by Coastal Command. When inside the 100 fathom line, U-boats must proceed on the surface and only dive if threatened by aircraft. As the 100 fathom line was only 100 miles or so out from the French coast (north from La Pallice to the Brest peninsula) it was very rare to see RAF aircraft this near inside the line.

U-boats were also required to leave harbour in the mornings or enter during the evenings so that port approaches could be patrolled by German fighters during daylight hours to provide extra cover. With the now scheduled group sailings, the task was fairly simple. The first such group left La Pallice on 2nd Jun – U-333 and U-572 – and successfully completed the crossing by the 7th.

Following this, further groups of three or five boats began leaving ports regularly between 7th and 12th June. Lorient-based U-135, U-508 and U-759 all crossed safely and so did U-571, U-590 and U-618 from St Nazaire on the 8th. However, U-185 and U-564 from Bordeaux were spotted after they had joined forces with U-134, U-358 and U-653, which had sailed from La Pallice on the 10th. They were lucky in that the sightings were made by unarmed aircraft on transit flights. The U-boats were seen on the 12th in position 4500N/0840W – about 90 miles north-west of Cape Ortegal. The leader ordered all boats to dive and when they surfaced some hours later, continued undetected through the Derange area. They reached the outer bay (and safety!) at longitude 15°, late on the 13th.

* * *

During the period 4th – 10th June very little of note happened in the Bay. Some bad weather was the main problem and to an extent, recent Ju88 encounters proved worrying. In the early evening of the 5th, a group of eight Ju88s harassed two Coastal aircraft within a quarter of an hour. A 206 Squadron Fortress was engaged at 6.05 pm but escaped; then at 6.20 Flying Officer Curtis of 58 Squadron was attacked. The 88s made several passes, one fighter coming in head-on, opening fire at 600 yards, followed by a second 88 attacking from the port beam, but this broke away as soon as Curtis turned his Halifax (HR744 'O') towards it. The 88s remained above and behind, allowing Curtis to reach the safety of cloud.

Fred Hall had begun flying operations over the Bay with 10 OTU, prior to a posting to an operational bomber squadron. He remembers:

'After briefing for operations we were issued with rations which consisted of canned orange juice, sandwiches, chocolate and coffee in thermos.

'I found flying in the Whitley warm over the Bay so usually flew in shirt sleeves with Mae West. It was also necessary to use the sunglasses provided by the RAF. The first two flights were uneventful, but on our 3rd patrol on 5th June, we sighted a U-boat in the afternoon on the return leg to base at approx. 4925N/0815E. We dived and raced immediately towards the U-boat which was fully on the surface but by the time, which was $1\frac{1}{2}$ minutes, there was no sign of the U-boat. They had soon spotted us and had submerged very fast. We dropped a sea marker and then flew a triangular course for 40 minutes, arrived back over the marker, but were out of luck so resumed course for base.

'We carried leaflets which we were instructed to drop on any fishing boat lying to. On one trip we spotted one boat, washing draped over lines, so we showered them with leaflets, which instructed them to get moving. After showing no signs of movement we flew around the boat and the rear gunner let fly a few rounds of ammo. This had the desired effect and the crew jumped about and the boat sped off pretty smartly. It was feared that Spanish fishing vessels were transmitting signals as to movement of aircraft and vessels in the Bay.

'Whilst on one Operational Sweep we sighted out to starboard an Arado flying on a parallel course. As he took no notice of us we decided to do likewise and he eventually moved away further to starboard.

'I had occasion on returning from one trip to reprimand the skipper who although a flying officer and I a sergeant, was 21 and I was 30, for flying dangerously low over the waves. I told him if we were ordered to fly low so be it, but if in future he wished to indulge in his bit of fun he was to tell me before we took off because I didn't want to risk my neck unnecessarily.

'I was to recall this warning on 3rd November; when he flew into a hillside and killed all on board during an air test.

'I enjoyed the challenge of navigating out of sight of land for nine to ten hours using simple aids, i.e. wind drifts, loop bearings, sun shots – all not exactly reliable – then seeing the Bishop's Rock coming up where it should be and on time.

'It was easy to be off track to port and go flying up the Irish Sea or off to starboard and up the English Channel. Then start running short of fuel and not knowing whether to turn to port or starboard.

'I consider I owe a lot to my continued existence because of the fact that I had flown from St Eval over the Bay and obtained confidence in my dead reckoning navigation.

Sergeant F.P.G. Hall, 10 OTU.

Fred later flew with 76 Bomber Squadron, but his crew were all killed on the air test on 3rd November 1943. He was not with them as he was on the ground preparing maps and flight plan for that night's operation.

A sad casualty of the 5th was the Commanding Officer of 612 Squadron, Wing Commander J.S. Kendrick. His squadron was busy converting from Whitleys to Wellington XIIs. Taking off in MP656 'E', Kendrick was in the circuit at Chivenor, flying at roof top height. The Wellington was observed suddenly to make a steep diving turn and its port wing hit a tree. The aeroplane crashed into the River Taw and burst into flames. Kendrick and two others were killed but two others miraculously escaped injury.

Finally on 11th June came the first U-boat sighting in more than a week. Sergeant Linsell, flying a Whitley of 10 OTU, saw the submarine eight miles away, while he was about 100 miles south-west of the Scillies. Linsell turned towards her but she dived before an attack could be made. This was at 2.50 pm and twenty minutes later Linsell saw the enemy again but this time it was a Ju88. However, Linsell flew into the sanctuary of cloud.

* * *

Another squadron detachment had arrived at Predannack to support Coastal Command aircraft, 25 (night-fighter) Squadron sending three Mosquitos from Church Fenton to be attached to 264 Squadron. Flight Lieutenant J. Singleton led the detachment and they had arrived on the 6th. They were in action on the afternoon of the 11th. Joe Singleton (DD757) with his navigator, Flying Officer W.G. Haslam, led six Mosquitos – the three of 25 Squadron with three of 456 Squadron. One of 456 developed engine trouble and returned to Predannack, leaving five Mosquitos.

'Geoff Haslam and I had teamed up in March 1943. On 5th June we took off to do a night flying test in preparation for a Ranger sortie that evening. During the flight we were recalled to base and on landing the Commanding Officer (Wing Commander Simon Maude) told us to report to Predannack, taking two other aircraft and crews from "A" Flight. Pilot Officers Jack Cheney and J. Dymock and Pilot Officers Jimmy Wootton and J. Mycock were selected. We left Church Fenton under strict security, not knowing what our duties were to be.

'Next morning we were briefed about Instep Patrols, that our primary targets were Ju88s. Secondary ones were trawlers, within a defined area, which were understood to be reporting air movements to the enemy. With Geoff, I led a patrol of four aircraft later that day. With us were Jack Cheney and two aircraft from No 456 Squadron. Cheney spotted a trawler which we duly shot up as briefed. Later we saw some Coastal Command Beaufighters deep in the Bay – which we had been told to watch out for. We returned without further incident.

'By next morning, 7th June, the weather had closed in with a damp sea mist making all flying impossible for the next four days. This was a very frustrating period.

'On 11th June the weather cleared and in the afternoon I led a patrol of five aircraft flying in a loose vic at sea level – Wootton No 2, Cheney No 3, Flying Officer Newell No 4 and Flight Sergeant Richardson No 5. When near the end of the outward leg, Wootton sighted five Ju88s through broken cloud, flying at 5/6000 feet and almost directly above us. I closed up the formation and commenced climbing, telling Nos 3 and 5 to operate as a section apart. (It later transpired that Cheney's R/T was unserviceable and in consequence neither he nor Richardson engaged the enemy aircraft).

'The 88s went into a climbing orbit (defensive circle) in line astern and fired off flares to which we replied with our Vereys, hopefully to confuse and so delay action whilst we gained more height and a better position up sun. When the enemy aircraft were about 2,000 feet above us I told the section to break and pick their own targets at the same time as co-ordinated tracer was fired at us. The necessity to call the break was that the 88s were climbing and tightening their circle whilst we were trying to keep inside theirs. At the point of break it was clear to me that no further advantage could be gained by delay. Even so, in order to obtain the necessary deflection I had to pull into a very tight climbing turn and was literally "hanging on the props" and if I fired any bursts longer than the $1/2$ second given, would have stalled the aircraft. I had selected the most rearward enemy aircraft and my first burst scored hits. With further bursts the 88 went straight into the sea leaving a pool of oil. With no other aircraft in sight and the patrol scattered, I put out a general call for any aircraft receiving me, to return to base independently. Geoff gave me a seaward dogleg course to avoid the Brest area and all aircraft landed without further incident, within ten minutes of each other.

'I understand the Ju88 we destroyed was a C6, 360288: FB+HZ of V/KG40. When later looking at our combat film we could see the head of the dorsal turret gunner and also the flash from his gun as he returned our fire. At that particular stage in the engagement, the combat was nearing completion and although this man must have realised the plight of his aircraft he carried on firing at us. I do not know whether he was one of the two crew members we saw bale out but I do know he was a very brave chap indeed and deserved to survive. The next day I was told that I was "tour-ex", and posted to TFU Defford and ordered to return to Church Fenton. Flight Lieutenant "Bill" Baillie ("B" Flight) with Pilot Officer Burrow ("A" Flight) took over at Predannack and Geoff and I returned to our parent station.

Flight Lieutenant J. Singleton, 25 Squadron.

Joe Singleton had fired three bursts of cannon – his machine-guns failed to fire. Flames and black smoke had passed back from the 88's port engine and oil sprayed back over the Mosquito's windscreen which made sighting difficult. Being so close and his forward vision obscured, he had rapidly to peel away to the right to avoid a collision. With the 88 now in a steep dive, Joe gave it a fourth burst from about 150 yards. Bits of cowling from the starboard engine flew back. As the Mosquito passed above and behind the 88, two of its crew were seen to bale out, one exiting through the top hatch, being struck a glancing blow as he passed by the port elevator. Moments later the Junkers hit the sea.

* * *

The 'fight back' policy was not confined to the Bay area as evidenced by the new Commanding Officer of 206 Squadron, Wing Commander R.B. Thomson. He was patrolling the north transit area to the east of Iceland. The submarine he found, U-417, fought back and although the Fortress's D/Cs destroyed the U-boat, her return fire brought down the aircraft. All the crew got into their dinghy being rescued by a Catalina three days later.

Further U-boat group sailings took place on the 12th (a second group on the 10th had been U-84, U-306 and U-732 from Brest). U-68, U-155, U-159, U-415 and U-634 sailed from Brest and Lorient, while U-257, U-600 and U-615 went out from La Pallice. During this period of few sightings, eight groups of U-boats and ten singleton boats had crossed the Bay unseen. While Dönitz might have been congratulating himself on his new tactics, it was short-lived.

The sighting of five U-boats in one group by the transit aircraft on the 12th, was the first evidence for the RAF that the U-boats had changed to a new tactic for traversing the Bay. As it happened the tacticians of the anti-U-boat war, aided by Admiralty Intelligence had assumed that some sort of tactic like this might develop. A meeting on 7th June of interested parties from Coastal Command and the Admiralty discussed what policy should be followed if in fact the U-boats did sail in groups. It was concluded:

(1) That patrolling aircraft should work in pairs.

(2) That the aircraft making the first sighting of a group should shadow and report until a striking force of aircraft arrived.

(3) That an air striking force should be maintained in the patrol area in readiness. (This was discarded as requiring more aircraft than could be made available.)

(4) That [there should be] a comprehensive follow-up procedure either from base or by aircraft already in the area.

(5) That a surface craft striking force be introduced into the area.

(6) That an escort carrier be attached to the surface striking force. This was not considered justified in view of its vulnerability both to submerged attack and to enemy shore-based bombers.

At Coastal Command HQ at Northwood the following day, recommendations were decided upon. The Command was keen to make every effort to induce the Germans to continue their group procedure as it would be far easier to deal with them by day. Additionally it was far better to know where a group of, say, five boats were, rather than finding only one, while at least four others were spread out somewhere in the Bay. It was obvious too that if an aircraft sighted a group whose intention was clearly to stay and fight, it would be highly dangerous for the crew to attack. It would be safer if the sighting aeroplane called up other Coastal aircraft within easy reach of the U-boats. In order to make this effective, it would be essential to fly the maximum number of aircraft within the general search area. These would need to be staggered throughout the hours of daylight so that at least two aircraft could be available to respond to the sighting reports.

It would also seem logical that if group sailings did develop the Germans would increase their fighter cover. Thus RAF fighter interception patrols would need to be strengthened. It would, however, be advantageous to place the Command's main search area as far as possible from German air bases.

If aircraft were to attack groups of U-boats whose intentions were to remain surfaced and use their combined defensive fire to ward off attacks, the question then arose as to the best method of attack. Coming down to 50 feet to drop Torpex depth charges would present the U-boats with a good target. It would perhaps be better to bomb them from height. This limited the choice of available weapons to the 600 lb anti-submarine depth bomb. Another weapon might be the rocket, coming into use with Beaufighter squadrons. Experiments were already being made to use these on larger aircraft such as Liberators. Nevertheless some aircraft would need to carry depth charges in case singleton U-boats were found that crash-dived. It would all need some fine balancing of times, coverage and weaponry.

The final recommendations were:

(1) That every effort be made to increase the density of Leigh Light Wellingtons flying south of latitude 4730N and west of 0700W and that Leigh Light Catalinas be operated west of longitude 1500W until such time as Leigh Light Liberators were available.

(2) That all No 19 Group aircraft be concentrated in the Derange area and as many of Nos 19 and 15 Group long range aircraft as possible in the Orderly area.

(3) That fighter patrols be accompanied by AI fitted aircraft.

(4) That all aircraft [crews] be conversant with and practised in the homing procedure by D/F loop.

(5) That the AOC No 19 Group be asked to consider the practicability of keeping a small strike force available to take advantage of sightings upon which a follow-up attack from base could be effected. General discussion and planning along these lines were continued over the next few days. This produced a new scheme of patrols to meet the possible increase in group U-boat tactics.

Late on 12th June, the AOC-in-C Coastal Command, Air Marshal Sir John Slessor CB DSO MC, keen to take full advantage of the current German tactics, sent a signal to all Groups acquainting them with the new situation. Until further notice, the maximum effort of both 19 and 15 Groups must be directed to the Bay offensive. Minimum air cover would be directed to convoys.

The Derange and Orderly patrol areas were changed and substituted by Musketry and Seaslug. The Musketry area stretched between latitudes 4730N and 4330N and longitudes 0930W and 1130W. This area would, weather permitting, be swept by seven aircraft at a time, flying on parallel tracks and carried out three times daily during daylight. As it was reasonable to assume that U-boats would continue to submerge at night to avoid the Leigh Light aircraft, they would need to surface and reform at first light. Therefore the first sweep aircraft had to be well into the Musketry area by dawn.

Should a group of U-boats in fact be spotted, it was left to the aircraft captain's discretion as to whether he should make an immediate attack or wait until he had homed in support aircraft. This might depend on his weaponry and on sea conditions. If the sea was calm the U-boat's gun platform would be far steadier for good defensive gunfire.

In any event, before attacking the sighting crew must break radio silence and send the code number '465', followed by a numeral indicating the number of submarines seen, then their position, course and speed. If the captain decided to call up reinforcements, he would then switch over to M/F homing procedure to enable other aircraft to make rendezvous. As a back-up, 19 Group HQ would broadcast the given position to ensure all available aircraft received the message. Once a pack had been found they had to be hunted to exhaustion to the exclusion of the rest of the area until all had either been sunk or had definitely escaped.

On the fighter side, three RP Beaufighters were kept at readiness during daylight hours and would fly to a sighting area immediately one had been found. Additionally 10 Group Fighter Command would provide sections of Mosquitos to give air cover in case long range Ju88 arrived on the scene to interrupt the anti-submarine aircraft.

The Seaslug area was situated further out to the west, between latitudes 4730N and 4400N and longitudes 1300W and 1500W. Seaslug would be patrolled by VLR (Very Long Range) and LR (Long Range) aircraft from 15 Group during the day when convoy situations permitted aircraft to be released and be used. The patrols would be co-ordinated by the AOC 19 Group, in conjunction with his Group's own patrols.

During the hours of daylight Leigh Light Wellingtons would cover Musketry, Leigh Light Catalinas Seaslug. As it was known for certain now that U-boats could detect ASV Mark II emissions, aircraft using this radar were to keep their sets switched on during their patrols so that U-boats could be surprised by aircraft using centimetric radar, in conjunction with intercepted Enigma intelligence information.

The scene was now set for an even greater concentration of effort in the Bay. John Slessor wanted to kill U-boats and by a combination of circumstances was suddenly presented with more than a better chance of doing so. The danger was that he might increase his own casualties, but the loss of an aircraft against that of a U-boat must be worth it.

CHAPTER FIVE

GROUP SAILINGS BEGIN

The new scheme of things did not come into operation until 14th June 1943. The group of five U-boats first seen on the 12th were through the Derange area by the end of the 13th. On the 13th, however, a number of other actions occurred in the Bay.

The Mosquitos on detachment at Predannack, forming a unique cosmopolitan composite squadron from a number of different units, flew four aircraft early that morning. Two of 151 Squadron and two of 157 Squadron were out and at 10.20 am way down in the Bay and westward when they found a large FW200. It was flying south-west, out to seek Allied convoys and it appeared just to starboard and slightly behind the four Mossies at 500 feet. The two 151 pilots curved round and began blasting huge chunks off the four-engined monster. Flying Officer Boyle/Sergeant Friesner and Flying Officer J.D. Humphries/Pilot Officer H.J. Lumb had then the satisfaction of seeing the Focke Wulf crash into the sea in flames. Sunderlands of 228 Squadron were out on the 13th. At 10.58 am, Flight Lieutenant G.D. Lancaster (DD834) took off, followed at 1.30 pm by Flying Officer L.B. Lee (DV967). Both were to find the enemy.

Meanwhile, at 3 o'clock that afternoon 264 Squadron sent out four Mosquitos, although one had to return with an engine out of action. The other three had a brush with three single-seat FockeWulf 190s, and Flight Sergeant W. Kent/Pilot Officer A.C. Turner (DD633) scored hits on one of them.

Three Mosquitos of 25 Squadron plus one of 410 also flew a patrol. They found patchy cloud at 5,000 feet and a continuous cloud layer three thousand feet higher. Between the two they ran into four Ju88s. The German fighters broke formation when they saw the Mosquitos, climbing towards the higher cloud layer. Flight Lieutenant A.S.H. Baillie, who was leading, followed the 88s but lost sight of them in the cloud. Reducing height into the clear air again he saw one Mosquito, then the other two, right down at sea level. He tried to close with them but finally lost sight of all three. Baillie flew on alone and eventually landed at Predannack at 5.50 pm.

Prior to this, however, base received a radio call from Flying Officer Jimmy Wootton, asking for an emergency homing to base, then a further message reporting that they were being chased by FW190s. None of the three Mosquitos returned. The 190s were probably the same aircraft encountered by 264 Squadron, which were in fact from 8/JG2 based at Brest. They claimed all three RAF aircraft shot down.

The detachment from 25 Squadron speculated on the loss of their companions. Undoubtedly they were low on ammunition, having already been in action with Ju88s, and having been flying for over four hours when their first transmission was heard they must have been low on fuel. This being the case they most probably had been forced to fly closer to the Cherbourg peninsula than they would normally have done. They would therefore have to risk interception by FW190s rather than make a long detour.

Everyone understood that in an even combat between FW190s and Mosquitos the odds were heavily loaded against the Mosquito and most probably the 190s had been under radio control and been positioned for an interception, having picked up their transmissions. Although 10 Group Spitfires were asked to support Coastal Command aircraft when flying close to Cherbourg, this very much depended on other commitments and priorities.

* * *

By the late afternoon, 228's two Sunderlands were well out from England. At 6.48 pm, Flight Lieutenant Lancaster spotted a lone U-boat, dropped six D/Cs ahead of the swirl made by her crash dive,but only three were seen to explode, bringing no results.

Flying Officer Lee's aircraft went to the extreme edge of the Bay area, to position 4430/1500, finding, at 8 pm, the five U-boats. Apparently Flying Officer Lee courageously went straight into the attack, singling out U-564, but the Sunderland met a hail of gunfire and was shot down into the sea. Nevertheless, his D/Cs damaged the U-boat to such an extent that she was unable to dive. U-185 was assigned the task of escorting her towards the Spanish coast while the other three boats carried on out into the vast areas of the Atlantic. The Germans then sent out a destroyer from Le Verdon to meet the two submarines, while KG40 flew air cover sorties from dawn on the 14th.

Early on the 14th, operations began in the Musketry and Seaslug areas. At 9.30 am a patrol of four Mosquito aircraft on a fighter interception patrol sighted another group of U-boats in position 4450/0800, some 45 miles due north of Cape Ortegal. This was additional evidence that the Germans were using the expected group sailings tactic. These were U-68, U-155, U-159, U-415 and U-634 that had sailed from Brest and Lorient on the 12th.

The Mosquitos, three from No 307 Polish Squadron and one from 410

RCAF Squadron, were led by Squadron Leader S.Szablowski and his navigator, Sergeant M. Gajewski (HJ648). When Szablowski spotted them they were manoeuvring into a tight formation and immediately they all opened up with intense defensive fire on the Mosquitos. Szablowski ordered his aircraft into line astern and led an attack upon the second U-boat. He saw strikes on its conning tower and then he attacked the No 3 boat, seeing more strikes from his cannon fire. However, Szablowski's port engine was hit by the U-boat gunners and promptly stopped. Flying Officer J. Pelka/Flight Sergeant M. Zakrocki (HJ658), attacking second, found his guns wouldn't fire. Mosquitos 3 and 4 did not attack because of the intense fire and because their leader was clearly in trouble, his smashed engine leaving a trail of smoke.

Szablowski coaxed his machine back the 500 miles to Predannack and because his hydraulics were powered by the port engine, he was forced to belly land, which he did successfully. What he didn't know was that his cannon fire had inflicted so many casualties among the men on the bridge and at the guns of both U-68 and U-155, from Lorient, that both had to abort their cruise and return to base. Both were Type VIIC submarines, on their seventh and sixth patrols respectively. The Commander of U-68 was Albert Lauzemis and of U-155 Johannes Altmeier, holder of the Knight's Cross.

The remaining three U-boats carried on but following up 307 Squadron's attack report, they were found at 3.58 pm that afternoon by Sergeant Manson in a Whitley of 10 OTU. The pilot began circling two miles off as a sighting report was sent but then the U-boats were seen to be going under. The Whitley pilot went in to attack, aiming his D/Cs at U-415, but they undershot and the submarine escaped damage.

While this group had been under attack the group of three submarines that had sailed from La Pallice on the 12th, U-257, U-600, and U-615 were spotted by a Sunderland of 10 Squadron flown by Flight Lieutenant H.W. Skinner. He circled eight miles away and homed in Flight Lieutenant G.O. Singleton of 461 Squadron at 9.30 am. The same homing message was picked up by a third Sunderland (JM678), Flying Officer S. White of 228 Squadron. He arrived at 9.47 in position 4524/1025 – 160 miles north-west of Cape Ortegal. As White arrived he made an immediate attack. Either this, or the mere fact that there were now three Sunderlands to contend with, convinced the senior U-boat commander that enough was enough and he ordered the boats to dive. Seeing this the two Australian pilots quickly headed in but the attack proved fruitless. Their having been in the area so long obviously attracted the Luftwaffe, as Ju88s began sniffing around. Singleton saw some and White was attacked by another but he evaded then turned for home. Later another Ju88 came to within 500 yards. As White climbed towards some cloud, his rear and mid-upper gunners fired at it; they then gained the safety of the clouds.

Shortly before four o'clock that afternoon, the U-boat group resurfaced and were sighted by a 10 OTU Whitley flown by Pilot Officer Orr. One of the U-boats was out of formation so Orr decided to make an immediate attack. The U-boats opened fire on the approaching Whitley, its gunners replying. At the last moment the U-boat changed course and the D/Cs only straddled the extreme bow. U-600 was the target and it was seen to be turning in a tight circle. Some gunfire was exchanged before Orr had to break off to return home.

Twenty minutes later another OTU Whitley arrived flown by Sergeant Manson. This crew had, as already related, used its D/Cs to attack the group 307 Squadron had strafed, 40 minutes earlier. Now without any anti-submarine weapons, they could only join in a gun duel. U-257 and U-615 had circled back to reform on U-600 that had received some slight damage from Pilot Officer Orr's attack, and when Manson found them were in fact on a south-easterly course. The Whitley and the U-boats exchanged fire while a homing call was made, but then Manson had to begin his trip home, having reached his PLE.

At 8.15 pm, a Fortress of 220 Squadron apparently found a U-boat. This was FK212 'V' flown by Flying Officer C.F. Callender from St Eval. His radio operator called in a sighting report as Callender went into the attack. However, the Fortress failed to return and it was thought it was downed by U-boat flak but in fact it was later intercepted by Ju88s from KG40 and shot down.

Half an hour had passed since the three U-boats had last been encountered. Wellington 'H' of 547 Squadron had picked up the sighting reports, and Warrant Officer J.W. Hermiston brought his aircraft into the area. At eight minutes past 9 pm, Hermiston made a visual sighting on the U-boats at three miles while coming in at 2,000 feet. The U-boats were roughly parallel at about 500 feet apart. Hermiston circled to the left, ahead of the submarines. Immediately all three boats opened fire and began to veer to port. As they did so, Hermiston went in to attack the right hand submarine that had lagged behind in the turn – U-615. Sergeant Bill Owens was aboard the Wellington:

> 'The 14th June attack on U-257, U-615 and U-600 was our second operational trip. I was in the front turret during this attack. We had sighted the U-boats dead ahead from a long distance off. It was a beautiful summer evening, blue sky, calm sea. We had all the time in the world to prepare and plan the attack. Hermiston was a seasoned pilot with many flying hours in the RCAF. He decided to attack out of the setting sun. We came in low and opened fire from a distance of about two miles. I could see splashes in the water leading to the conning tower of the nearest U-boat. At the same time I could see flashes from the deck guns of the U-boat as they fired at us. It was a perfect attack and the depth charges completely straddled the U-boat.

My bullets were on target and I could see the tracer bullets bouncing off the conning tower and the deck of the U-boat. If my memory serves me right I think we made either one or two machine gun attacks after we had dropped our depth charges. Davies (Sergeant L.Davies) the rear gunner and myself had a great time hosing the poor devils with .303 bullets.

'The U-boats made no attempt to submerge but remained on the surface popping off at us. There was blue smoke coming from the U-boat we had attacked and we firmly believed we had badly damaged it. Their return fire was getting very hot and Hermiston decided to break off the attack. My machine guns, twin Brownings, had jammed, which was another good reason for getting out of range of their guns. We climbed high and radioed details and position of the attack to our UK Control Station. This had been a perfect attack in every detail and I have always believed our depth charges must have caused serious damage to the U-boat, that is until I read your letter telling me otherwise.'

Sergeant W. Owens, 547 Squadron.

In their first attack, at 2,000 feet, Hermiston dropped two 100 pound anti-submarine bombs that exploded on either side of the conning tower. Coming in again, with Bill Owens blazing away in the front turret, Hermiston toggled six D/Cs from 50 feet across U-615's bows, four to starboard, two to port. As the Wellington pulled up, smoke was indeed seen to come from the U-boat and it began to slow. Hermiston circled for over half an hour, carried out homing procedure until finally the U-boats dived – U-615 having, in the final analysis, not been damaged to any great degree.

* * *

Meanwhile, the two submarines heading for their French base, the damaged U-564 and her escort, U-185, were not far off the Spanish coast. It will be remembered that U-564 had been damaged on the 13th by Flying Officer Lee of 228 Squadron when in company with U-145, 358, 653 and 185.

Early on the 14th these two boats had sighted a flying boat but were not themselves detected. At 9.40 am two friendly FW200s had approached but quickly sheered off when the jittery U-boat gunners had opened fire on their 'air escort'.

The day passed slowly for the two U-boat crews, but their luck finally ran out at 2.39 that afternoon. By this time they were in position 4417/1025 – 85 to 90 miles north-west of Ferrol off the Spanish coast. It was a 10 OTU Whitley, flown by an Australian, Sergeant A.J. Benson, aged 23, that found them.

The U-boats were travelling at 10 knots and put up a barrage of gunfire. Arthur Benson circled out of range as his wireless operator put out a sighting call. Two hours later a 415 Squadron Hampden arrived, both aircraft shadowing the U-boats until 4.45. At this time Benson received permission to make an attack.

Because of her damage, U-564 was unable to take any avoiding action as Benson flew in. He straddled the submarine with his six D/Cs, which ruptured U-564's hull. The Whitley, however, had been badly hit by the defensive gunfire, Benson struggling away northwards.

He reported the attack, also that his aircraft was badly damaged and his hydraulics hit. At 7.20 Benson reported his starboard engine U/S, then ten minutes later he reported being at position 4730/0810, followed at 8 pm by an 'SOS.' From D/F bearings this was about 80 miles south-west of the Scillies but an air-sea-rescue search failed to find any survivors.

Benson had brought his crippled Whitley down onto the sea and he and his crew all got into their dinghy safely. They drifted for three days, and three nights until they were about 100 miles south-west of Brest (4843/0655). They were then picked up by a French fishing boat and landed at Morgot where they were handed over to the Germans to become prisoners of war. Benson later received the DFM and promoted to warrant officer.

U-564 went down, but U-185 succeeded in rescuing nineteen of her 46 crew, including the Commander Oberleutnant Fiedler, then continued toward their destroyer escort rendezvous. A flight of Ju88s also came out and found the still shadowing 415 Squadron Hampden which was quickly shot down. Meeting finally the destroyer, U-185 transferred the survivors of U-564 then turned to continue her patrol out into the Atlantic.

* * *

The group of five U-boats attacked by the Polish Mosquitos and the 10 OTU Whitley on the 14th, had been reduced to three after U-68 and U-155 had been forced to return to France. U-159, 415 and 634 had continued their outward journey and were sighted just before 8 am on the 15th, by 502 Squadron. Flying Officer A.J. Davey had flown his Halifax out from St Eval at 3.44 am, carrying three 600 pound anti-submarine bombs. When he and his crew spotted the three U-boats they circled for fifteen minutes under intense but inaccurate flak. Sergeant Harry Barrett, the flight engineer, looked out as Johnny Davey[1] made an approach. They circled at 1,000 feet, watching as the U-boats zig-zagged to distract the next bomb attack. Harold Archer, the rear gunner, sent a few rounds at them, then Davey entered cloud. He worked his way round in order to make an approach out of the sun behind the U-boats. Coming out of the clouds two miles away, the U-boats began evasive action again and the Halifax crew was unable to use its Mark XIV bomb sight. This was a serious disadvantage not

---

[1] Flying Officer A.J. Davey received the DSO for his work with Coastal Command but was killed flying as a passenger from the Azores in 1944.

envisaged. From about 700 feet a jinking submarine was an impossible target for a high level sight such as the Mark XIV. After several tries, Davey saw that the U-boats were beginning to dive and at last having a steady target, three bombs were dropped from 2,000 feet. They overshot slightly about twenty seconds after the U-boats had submerged, the target boat, U-415, escaping unscathed.

These three U-boats were seen again on the 16th by Flying Officer E.E. Allen of 59 Squadron (FL973 'C') in the Seaslug area. Allen attacked the centre boat with six D/Cs despite intense return fire. The D/Cs overshot the target and the Liberator was hit four times and most of the instruments were knocked out. The rear-gunner fired 120 rounds at the conning tower, then Allen made a second attack but two boats had gone down and the last one, on the starboard side, was also submerging as he flew in. The D/Cs went into the sea thirty seconds after the boat went under. Flying Officer A.R. Neilson DFC of the same squadron (FL989 'L') searched for these boats but made no contact. At 4.18 Sunderland 'G' of 422 Squadron saw them again but intense flak forced the aircraft to sheer off. Fog patches then came to the U-boats' aid and the Sunderland eventually lost them. They finally sailed out of the Bay area after two days of attacks and high tension.

* * *

The experience of the last few days was almost exactly what had been expected. Groups of U-boats had been encountered but overall the defensive fire had not been as deadly as some had feared. It had frustrated some attacks and upset the aim in others, so obviously co-ordinated attacks by more than one aircraft was desired. On 16th June Coastal Command ordered that a leader should be detailed at briefings for each group of aircraft patrolling the Musketry area. This was amended on the 27th to the captain of the sighting aircraft. He would take the leadership role over those other aircraft that were homed onto a single U-boat or a group sighting. He would then concert the efforts of all aircraft in order to divide the U-boats' fire before an attack was carried out.

Due consideration was also given to forward gunfire from the attacking aircraft. The gunners too needed to be instructed on when to open fire. Until now, RAF gunners were not encouraged to open fire before 600 yards, for generally the inaccuracy beyond this distance was a waste of ammunition. However, it was felt now that opening fire at 1,000 yards would help to keep the U-boat gunners' heads down and put their aim off during the vital run-in. Some squadrons, as mentioned earlier, had fitted .5 guns to their aircraft but generally the .303 guns were quite effective, as it was the volume of fire that was most useful.

* * *

This mid-June period, unknown in detail at the time, had netted some good results. Seven anti-U-boat aircraft had been lost and another damaged, while three Mosquitos had also been lost and another damaged. However, one U-boat had been sunk and two more damaged sufficiently for them to return to port. A number of others had been harried and delayed and their crews shaken up. The Ju88s had not interfered too much with Coastal Command aircraft – only one Hampden and a Fortress were actually lost to KG40 – which permitted the Seaslug area to be moved further eastwards. This happened on 21st June, Seaslug moving between longitudes 14° and 12° West.

* * *

Further success came on 17th June, but it was achieved by a 15 Group aircraft flying in support of 19 Group's Bay offensive.

Submarine U-338 sailed on her second war patrol from Bordeaux, on the 15th, commanded by Kapitänleutnant Manfred Kinzel, for an Atlantic cruise, and met Flying Officer L.G. Clark DFC (who had made an unsuccessful attack in FA703 'A' on 31st May on a fully surfaced U-boat). Clark took off from St Eval in Fortress FL457 'F', at 3.36 pm, to fly a Musketry patrol.

At 7.22, Sergeant W.E. Pollard, the front lookout, spotted U-338 on the surface, six to eight miles away. The U-boat was on a course of 250°, the Fortress on a 186° track with the sun on right rear quarter, Pilot Officer G. Niven, the second pilot, being at the controls. Due to a temporary failure in the intercom transmitter box, Pollard was unable to attract Niven's attention, but the navigator, Pilot Officer J.D. Ackerman, yelled the sighting report and Clark took control. The Fortress had been sighted, for the submarine began to take evasive action to port and then to starboard. Clark began to lose height, diving at between 230 and 240 mph, as the U-boat opened fire. Flak was intermittent until the range closed at which time red tracer from aft of the conning tower passed close to the port side of the Fortress, a piece of shrapnel hitting the leading edge of the starboard wing.

Clark came in at 30° to the U-boat's starboard bow, and levelling out, he reduced speed to 200 mph. Six D/Cs went down. Two were released by Clark, while the other four, on outside racks, were released by the navigator using the Mark 6 distributor. In consequence there was probably a time lag between the first two and the last four, but all six seemed to overshoot.

Clark hauled the Fortress round to the left in a climbing turn and came round for a second attack along the U-boat's track. However, Kinzel was taking U-338 down and by the time Clark came in, the submarine had all but disappeared. Five D/Cs went splashing into the swirl and as they flew over, Warrant Officer A. Garnham, looking through the bomb bay doors, saw part of the submarine still visible. The D/Cs exploded alongside the boat but then nothing could be seen. They continued to circle for a quarter of an hour until a recall to base signal was received. U-338 however, had been damaged and Kinzel had to put back to port, arriving on the 21st.

This U-boat finally went to the bottom on 20th September 1943, on her third war patrol, sunk by a Canadian ship, HMCS *Drumheller*.

Bad weather restricted much aerial activity during 17th and 18th June, but on the 18th, a 59 Squadron Liberator, flown by Flying Officer G.B. Lynch on a Seaslug patrol, found U-450 and U-645 sailing on an easterly course. U-645 was in fact escorting U-450 that had been damaged by a 220 Squadron Fortress in the Northern Transit Area on 6th June. Seven of her crew were wounded and temporary repairs had been effected. They made rendezvous with U-645 that had a doctor on board, then both boats headed towards a Biscay port.

Flying Officer Lynch approached the two U-boats, one of which submerged, the other sending up defensive fire. As Lynch began a homing call, the second U-boat crash dived. With improved weather on the 19th, came a sudden flurry of Luftwaffe activity. Shortly after 11 am a 10 OTU Whitley, piloted by Flying Officer Price, was attacked by a Ju88, south-west of the Scillies. The Whitley was damaged in the tail before Price reached cloud cover.

At 12.23 pm a patrol of three Mosquito aircraft from 307 Polish Squadron and another of 410 Squadron RCAF, found a German Blohm & Voss 138 – a three-engined flying boat. The leader of the Mosquito patrol, Squadron Leader S. Szablowski/Sergeant Gajewski (HJ657) ordered the Mossies into line astern, but Flying Officer E.A. Murray of 410 Squadron (DD757) did not understand the order and turned sharply into the attack – too sharply to be effective. The Blohm & Voss climbed towards some cloud but Szablowski and Flying Officer J. Pelka/Flight Sergeant Zakrocki (HJ658), were able to attack it from head-on. The flying boat began to smoke but it was still climbing. Szablowski flew above the German, ordering Pelka to remain below. The crippled 138 just about reached the cloud as Pelka delivered the *coup de grâce*. The German fell away and crashed into the sea, bursting into flames as it did so. Three of the five-man crew were seen to reach a dinghy and they were only about 60 miles due west of the Brest peninsula, so might be rescued. The flying boat came from 1(F)/129 (KL+MA).

Later that afternoon 264 Squadron flew patrols over the Bay. They had a brief skirmish with Ju88s at 3 pm, and an hour and a half later another combat took place with Ju88s – probably out looking for the survivors of the Bv138. The result was one Ju88 damaged by Flying Officer E.A. Turner/Flight Sergeant W.D. Holden in DZ680.

The final clash came just after 7 pm. Three Mosquitos of 151 Squadron with one of 456, found a trawler off the Spanish coast near Ortegal, with eight Ju88s circling above it. The four Mossies attacked, the 88s making for cloud. The leader of 151, Squadron Leader B.D. Bodien DFC, shot down one Junkers in the melée while Warrant Officer G.F. Gatenby/Flight

Sergeant J.M. Frazer (DZ299) of 456 Squadron, damaged another. Both Flying Officer Boyle and Pilot Officer Humphries of 151 also claimed Ju88s as damaged but Boyle had to make a crash landing at base with undercarriage trouble. The Ju88 crew downed were later rescued by a Spanish fishing boat two days later.

It was 236 Squadron and 248 Squadron's Beaufighters that spotted the two submarines U-450 and U-645 in the early afternoon of 20th June, which had last been seen on the 18th. The damaged U-450 and her escort quickly dived out of sight knowing (or perhaps hoping) the fighters would not be carrying depth-charges.

Later that afternoon two Whitleys of 10 OTU found and attacked a submarine just over 100 miles north-west of Cape Ortegal. This was the Italian boat outward-bound for the Far East, the *Barbarigo*. Pilot Officer Orr made the first attack, dropping his six D/Cs from 75 feet but they undershot. Then Sergeant H Martin attacked as the submarine slewed 90°. His D/Cs also undershot but the defensive fire put up by the boat hit the Whitley. The whole aircraft became enveloped in flames and the other Whitley crew had to watch helplessly as it crashed into the sea. Moments later the submarine dived beneath the waves. The boat was later reported missing – cause unknown. Whether any damage had been inflicted which later proved fatal is not known.

This drama was also observed by Flying Officer T.H. Minta of 58 Squadron (HR746 'M') out on patrol in company with two other Halifaxes of the same squadron – Flying Officer A.l. Sladen (BB279 'Q') and Flight Sergeant l.S. Dunbar (HR744 'O'). The section had just turned to investigate the wake when they saw the two Whitley aircraft attack. As Minta flew over the crash area, all that could be seen was some wreckage and an empty dinghy. A Beaufighter patrol from 264 Squadron, consisting of four aircraft, made contact with Ju88s during the afternoon. Flying Officer W.K. Moncur and his navigator, Sergeant F.W. Woodruff, (DZ291) shot down one Ju88 C-6, which was claimed as a probable. However, V/KG40 lost F8+AX in this action.

* * *

Supply submarine U-462, commanded by Oberleutnant Bruno Vöwe, sailed from Bordeaux on Saturday 19th June on her fifth war cruise. A Type XIV submarine, its vital task was to supply boats already in the Atlantic and short of fuel and torpedoes. By mid-day on Monday the 21st, U-462 was just over 100 miles north of Ortegal.

Four Mosquitos, three of 151 Squadron and one from 456 Squadron, were led by Squadron Leader Joe Bodien DFC, who just two days earlier had shot down a Ju88. They had been out from Predannack for just on two hours, flying a zig-zag line patrol when at 12.13 pm they spotted U-462 on the surface. Bodien led his men in, each blasting the submarine with cannon fire, strikes being seen all over the conning tower. The vessel was badly damaged and suffered casualties amongst her deck crew, forcing Vöwe to abort his vital mission and return home.

That evening four Mosquitos of 264 Squadron were in action on a mission in support of Bay operations. Wing Commander W.J. Allington DFC AFC (flying HJ652) took off at 8.15 pm on Instep Patrol No 184. At 9 pm, flying at zero feet, Bill Allington and his navigator (Flying Officer R.G. Clark) spotted a Blohm & Voss 138 heading west at 600 feet. Allington attacked, aiming for the starboard engine and fuselage, which produced flames from both. Squadron Leader L.T. Bryant-Fenn/Flying Officer L.H. Hayden (HJ646) and Allington attacked again as the 138 dived into the sea, although Bryant-Fenn's Mosquito was slightly damaged by flying debris.

Reforming, Allington led the Mosquitos towards the German flying boat base at Biscarosse. They were there at 10.27, Allington pulling up to 1,500 feet. Below he saw four Bv138s in a line on the water at the north-west end of the lake. A huge Bv222 floated at anchor between these and the shore-line, with two more Bv138s farther out. The Mosquitos attacked claiming three Bv138s set on fire and the Bv222 badly damaged – a small fire started in a port inner engine. Flying Officer J.L. Mason/Flying Officer R.J. Roe (HJ656) also fired into the open end of a large hangar. Flak was heavy but only one hole was found in one elevator.

As the Mosquitos headed out to sea, a huge explosion lit up the sky behind them. They flew towards Ushant but Mason flew two miles west of the Ile de Sein, and spotted three mine-sweepers. He strafed the western most ship from bow to stern. Bryant-Fenn had one engine give out and had to make a belly landing at base, but otherwise the raid had been a great success. From a later report from a German prisoner, two Bv138s and two Bv222s of 1(f)GR129 had been completely destroyed. (Bv138s 310160 and 311019; Bv222s 0439 and 0005.)

At 8.30 the next morning a Ju88 attacked aircraft 'U' of No 1404 Met Flight over the Bay. Flight Sergeant Davis saw the 88 diving down out of the sun and he headed for the clouds. A burst of gunfire damaged the Hudson but after an exchange with the rear gunner, the 88 pilot discontinued the action.

The only other incident of note on the 22nd occurred at St Eval. Sergeant A.F. Hildebrant, when landing his 415 Squadron Hampden after having engine trouble, swung and crashed into another Hampden. A depth charge exploded, damaging two further aircraft.

CHAPTER SIX

THE SECOND ESCORT GROUP

Item No 5 of the list of proposals from the meeting between the Admiralty and Coastal Command Anti-U-boat Divisions on 7th June read: 'That a surface craft striking force be introduced into the area.'

When Sir John Slessor had commenced the new scheme of air patrols on 12th June, he also sent a signal to the Admiralty suggesting that now was a good moment to employ a surface hunting group to work in co-operation with Coastal Command's anti-U-boat aircraft.

The Admiralty agreed and as attacks on Gibraltar convoys had not developed as expected, the Commander-in-Chief Western Approaches and Plymouth was asked to detail the support group assigned to this route into the Bay area. This was agreed and so the 2nd Escort Group sailed from Liverpool on 16th June to sail to position 4530N/1200W in order to act as an anti-U-boat striking force in conjuction with air operations in the Seaslug and Musketry area. It arrived on station on the 20th and comprised HM ships *Woodpecker*, *Wild Goose*, *Wren* and *Kite*. HMS *Starling*, carrying the senior officer and group commander, Captain F.J. Walker, joined up on the 23rd, having been delayed in Liverpool to complete repairs. This group was supported by the cruiser HMS *Scylla* in case of interference from at least four *Narvik* (Z class) destroyers the German Navy was known to have based at La Pallice.

The 2nd Escort Group achieved two successes within days. An 86 Squadron VLR Liberator, on its way to carry out a convoy escort on the 23rd, spotted three in-bound U-boats in position 4449/1350. The aircraft was carrying two Mark 24 mines which were released near the swirls produced when all three submarines dived. A few minutes later a brown patch was seen on the water.

The three boats were U-119, 449 and 650, and it was 650 that received damage in the attack and her steering was affected.

On its way home after completing the escort duty, the Liberator again saw the three U-boats still heading for the Bay. The damaged U-650 dived, covered by anti-aircraft fire from the other two which forced the Liberator pilot to sheer away. The two boats then dived and although one 600 lb anti-submarine bomb was dropped, no further damage was inflicted.

The contact, however, was followed up by Captain Walker's group and an asdic contact was made early on the morning of 24th June. Depth charges forced one submarine to the surface which was promptly rammed. Continuing the asdic contacts, D/Cs sank a second U-boat that afternoon. U-119 and 449 had been the victims, the damaged U-650 escaping to limp into St Nazaire on the 28th. There were few sightings in the Bay at this time and in fact there were only two U-boats in the Bay. On 27th June the Musketry area was once again modified, being extended westward to meet Seaslug on longitude 1200W, and southwards to latitude 4330 and the Spanish coast. Seaslug was also extended to the south to latitude 4300N.

The order was for aircraft in these areas to fly individual patrols and attack lone U-boats immediately. If packs of two or more U-boats were located, they were to be reported and then shadowed. Homing procedures would hopefully bring other aircraft to the scene as well as the 2nd Escort Group. 19 Group HQ would broadcast sightings, and all aircraft within 100 miles would concentrate their attentions to the area of the U-boats. Attacks would be under the direction of the sighting aircraft's captain.

* * *

A 151 Squadron Mosquito was lost on an Instep patrol on the 23rd June. Three 151 Mosquitos and one of 456 Squadron were out at 4 pm. At 7.25 they were 120 miles almost due north of Ortegal, flying in line abreast at zero feet. Squadron Leader Bodien, the veteran air fighter who had flown two tours with 151 Squadron, was leading. He had been an NCO pilot flying Defiants in 1941 at which time he and his gunner had destroyed three night bombers. In 1942, now commissioned and flying Mosquitos, he had destroyed another. His fifth victory had been achieved during this detachment, a KG40 Ju88 on 19th June. Pilot Officer J.D. Humphries was flying next to Bodien and seemed to edge towards Bodien's aircraft and go slightly above it. They collided, Bodien's cockpit perspex shattering. However, Humphries' tail was cut off and at such a low altitude, the Mosquito with Humphries and Lumb, went straight in, leaving just a little bit of wreckage on the surface.

There were three brief U-boat sightings made on the 14th, while early on the 25th, Flying Officer B.E.H. Layne of 201 Squadron (15 Group) had a short encounter with a Ju88 in the outer Bay area.

An Instep patrol flown early the following morning by four Mosquitos of 264 Squadron, led by Squadron Leader P.G. Burke (HJ714) also encountered a Ju88. It was attacked and damaged by Flying Officer E.A. Turner/Flight Sergeant W.D. Holden (DZ680) (their second claim of the month) but their Mosquito received damage to the port radiator and the engine had to be feathered. Turner made a successful landing at Predannack, but the patrol had been cut short after the combat in order to escort the damaged aircraft home. Sergeant K .T. Ashfield of 415 Squadron had been out over Musketry but ran into trouble on his return. About ten miles from Predannack both engines of his Hampden cut out. D/Cs and ammunition were jettisoned and Ashfield prepared his crew for ditching, when the port engine suddenly picked up when they were down to 300 feet. Ashfield force landed at St Merryon, with wheels up and although the aircraft was damaged he and his crew were unhurt.

Only one sighting was made on the 26th, by Flying Officer Wallace in a Wellington of 547 Squadron. His front gunner saw a periscope wake dead ahead when at 1,500 feet but the U-boat went down. A marker was dropped and baiting procedure carried out but nothing further was seen.

The next day, Sunday, began a more successful week for Bay operations. At 5.30 am Flying Officer B.E.H. Layne lifted his 201 Squadron Sunderland III off from Lough Erne (W6005 'P') and headed down into 19 Group's Seaslug area. He was on station five hours later but it was another two hours (12.35 pm) before a U-boat was sighted five miles ahead on the port bow travelling at an estimated nine knots. Layne was at 3,000 feet and he turned to the left in order to curve round to the right of the boat to come in with the sun and wind behind him, diving down to 75 feet as he did so.

The U-boat was U-518, her commander, Friedrich-Wilhelm Wissmann, taking her on her third war patrol from Lorient, whence they had sailed on the 24th. They had reached the outer Bay, 200 miles or so due west from Cape Ortegal – so near to getting clean away into the Atlantic. Layne came in dead astern of the diving U-boat – the conning tower only being visible. Two D/Cs were dropped and their explosions seen at the apex of the submarine's swirl. Three or four minutes later the U-boat came back to the surface. Layne had begun a circle to the left and when U-518 came up he pulled round again for an attack, coming in this time square on to the boat's starboard side.

Now on the surface the U-boat's gun crew manned all guns and put up a heavy barrage as the Sunderland thundered towards them. This was returned by the front gunner and then the rear gunner as they flew over U-518. Two more D/Cs went down that fell on the boat's far side. Further approaches were made but each time Wissmann brought his boat round to face the Sunderland and the defensive fire was too much to face. They called for other aircraft but then Wissmann took his boat down and contact was lost. However, U-518 was hurt and Wissmann had to return to base, though Coastal Command hadn't finished with him just yet.

It was fairly quiet for the next couple of days. 612 Squadron,which had begun to exchange its Whitleys for Wellingtons at the beginning of June, became operational on the 28th and began flying night Musketry patrols. The next day, the 29th, U-386 sailed from St Nazaire, but only two sightings of U-boats were made, one by a 10 OTU Whitley shortly after mid-day, and that evening by a 59 Squadron Liberator.

Three Wellingtons of 407 Squadron took off from Chivenor for night patrols at around 10.30 pm, one flown by Flight Sergeant N.C.C. Luther failing to return, (HF142). The two others, one flown by Squadron Leader R.Y. Tyrell, also ran into trouble. Enemy aircraft were seen, the first one successfully evading attention.

Tyrell's crew made several radar contacts but all turned out to be aircraft – night flying Me210s or Me410s according to the gunners. One enemy fighter carried orange and white lights on its wing tips and opened fire on the Wellington at 300 yards, breaking away when only 30 yards distant. Then a second fighter, this one with an orange light in the nose, attacked, but fired out of range, its tracer seen to fall away well short of the Wellington. The enemy aircraft then closed in but a burst from Tyrell's rear gunner caused a flash on the fighter and it broke away trailing a flame. The fighters – there were at least five – began signalling to each other with their lights before making attacks. Tyrell, however, was equal to the task and successfully evaded several attacks while his rear gunner kept a steady rate of fire. Finally the fighters flew off much to the relief of the Canadians.

As that Wednesday (the 30th) dawned, two inbound U-boats, U-180 and U-530, were spotted by Flying Officer C.W.J. Harradine of 53 Squadron (BZ750 'R'), although they only reporting seeing one of the boats. Flak was encountered by the Liberator as it came down out of the sun but the D/Cs failed to release. Before he could attack again the U-boats had dived. U-180 was a 1,600 ton U-Kreuzer and was carrying a valuable cargo of gold and some Japanese officers as passengers. She had been operating off the South African coast during April and May and had picked up her passengers south west of Madagascar after making rendezvous with a Japanese submarine. Dönitz provided a destroyer escort for the two boats on 1st July, and these were to be encountered again.

Meanwhile U-518 was picked up again as she limped towards her base following the attentions of Flying Officer Layne three days earlier. She had now reached position 4422/0951, 100 miles north-west of Ortegal. At 11.12 am 10 RAAF Squadron found her.

Flight Lieutenant H.W. Skinner saw the U-boat four miles away and began to lose height as he circled. The U-boat began taking violent evasive action making a good attack impossible, so Skinner circled round again then came in at 150 feet in the face of heavy gunfire. Six D/Cs went down, one exploding 20 yards from U-518's[1] port beam, but the others overshot. Fire from the Sunderland appeared to hit at least three sailors on the conning tower, but the German gunners also scored hits as the flying boat went over. The rear turret, port elevator, both wings and the rear

---

[1] U-518 was sunk by US destroyers on her 8th patrol, 22nd April 1945.

section of the hull were all hit and the rear gunner, Flight Sergeant J.S. Burnham, not yet 21 years old, was mortally wounded.

With his Sunderland severely damaged, tail gun out of action and a seriously wounded crewman, Skinner broke off the action, the U-boat being seen still sailing eastwards on the surface. She reached Bordeaux on 2nd July.

The last U-boat attack in June came at 4.40 that afternoon, Flight Sergeant R. Bottomly of 547 Squadron attacking a U-boat that had dived after the RAF crew had sighted her periscope and conning tower, 200 miles south-west of the Scilly Isles.

* * *

The 2nd Escort Group under Captain Walker had not been able to follow up any aircraft sightings since the 23rd and on 28th June it returned to Plymouth. It was replaced by Escort Group B5.

At Plymouth a conference took place, Walker wanting to improve communications in order to gain a clearer picture of sightings for his group as well as for AC HQ at Plymouth. It was agreed that in future, the Group Commander (Walker) would have an aircraft attached to him, under his personal control, to provide a direct link with sightings within his reach and upon landing, the crew would give AC HQ exact knowledge of his group's location, future intentions, together with other messages or information. These would be passed to the aircraft from the ships by Aldis signals because of the need for radio silence while the group was on station. 19 Group HQ would also in future confirm to the group all positive sightings so that they would not go chasing after 'suspected' U-boats, or any water swirls seen that were nothing to do with submarines at all.

* * *

Patrols over the Bay took long hours to complete. All the time the crews were on full alert, searching the sea for any signs of submarines or surface vessels. Searching the sky too for enemy long range fighters. The times are revealing in Flight Sergeant J.H.Wright's log book. He was a WOP/AG with 423 RCAF Squadron flying with 15 Group from Castle Archdale. His pilot was Flight Lieutenant P. Frizell DFC RAAF.

Personal

Op. No.	Date	Type of Operation	Duration
No.22	30 May 1943	A/S Sweep – Bay of Biscay	15:20
No.24	7 June 1943	A/S Sweep – Bay of Biscay	15:00
No.25	9 June 1943	A/S Sweep – Bay of Biscay	15:05
No.26	14 June 1943	P/T Sweep – Bay of Biscay	
		Sighted Ju290 – no attack	15:10

No.28   19 June 1943   A/S Sweep – Bay of Biscay
                           Landed at Gibraltar   16:30
No.29   21 June 1943   Convoy Escort – Bay of Biscay
                           Landed at Base   17:45
No.30   27 June 1943   Seaslug A/S Patrol – Bay of Biscay 15:20

During the last 16 days of June there had been 50 sightings in Musketry and Seaslug with 16 attacks, in daylight. There had been no night sightings. These operations had been carried out by 24 anti-U-boat squadrons with a total strength of 307 aircraft. Fighter detachments from one Beaufighter and eight Mosquito squadrons had provided Instep patrols.

Many of the sightings were the same U-boats seen on several different occasions as they crossed the Bay. In this latter period – 13 to 30th June – nine groups and seven singleton U-boats had traversed the Bay (32 boats in total), but only three groups and two singletons (11 boats) had done so without being seen.

One U-boat had been sunk, U-564, (plus two by the 2nd Escort Group) and five others damaged sufficiently to necessitate a return to harbour, U-68, 155, 462, 338 and 518. These successes had cost the RAF fourteen aircraft in this same period, making a total of fifteen for the month. Three of the anti-U-boat aircraft were known to have fallen to Ju88s and one possibly to a night-fighter. Three had been shot down by U-boats; plus two damaged, the others had all been reported missing. Four others had been damaged by Ju88s, and two damaged in U-boat attacks. Of the fighter losses, three had been shot down by FW190s, another simply missing. Two more had been lost to Ju88s, another damaged and one had been damaged in an attack upon a U-boat. Four Ju88s had been claimed as destroyed by RAF fighters.

Although Coastal Command had no real way of knowing the full extent of U-boat casualties in the Bay, it was clear that the Germans' tactics were not achieving the success they'd hoped for.

Sir John Slessor was still keen to maximise on the opportunities still offered and requested AHQ Gibraltar to fly cross-over patrols west of Cape Finisterre whenever possible. He also asked the Americans at Casablanca to assist if possible. At the same time, Slessor re-doubled his efforts to persuade the Americans to deploy some of their anti-submarine aircraft, patrolling long hours over mostly U-boat free areas, into his Bay offensive. It seemed obvious to him to bring the maximum number of aircraft to cover the German bottle-neck in the Bay of Biscay.

Grossadmiral Dönitz was only too well aware of the short-comings of his group sailing scheme and was beginning to consider providing destroyer escorts for his U-boats as far west as possible. He also requested again, increased Luftwaffe support.

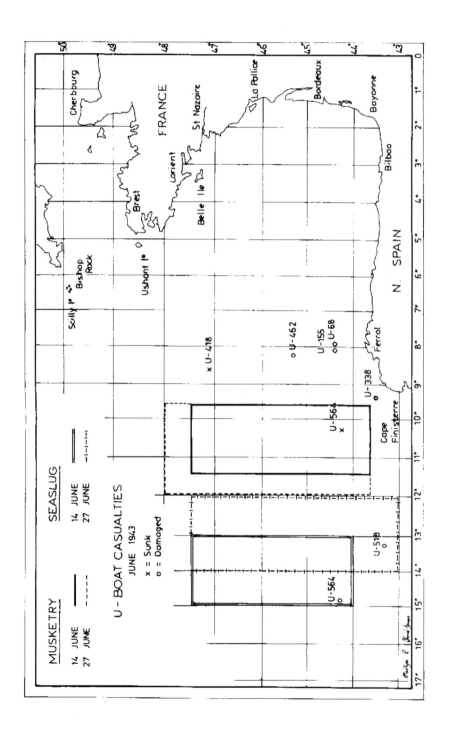

In addition he impressed on his commanders the need to take all precautions against air attack when in the Bay. Lifejackets must be available for the entire crew when in the danger area and no new submarines were to be allowed to sail until quadruple 20 mm flak mountings had been fitted. These fittings were to be hastened for all Bay submarines. Group sailings, which had been suspended on 12th June, were resumed towards the end of June and between 28th June and 1st July, four groups totalling nine boats put to sea. They reached the Musketry area in the first days of July.

CHAPTER SEVEN

THE PRESSURE CONTINUES

Sir John Slessor sorely needed additional squadrons in the Bay, and these could only be provided by the Americans. As early as the end of April 1943 the American joint Chiefs of Staff had been asked to help with six squadrons – 72 aircraft – that appeared on their order of battle as being surplus to their minimum requirements. They replied, under the guidance of Admiral E.J. King, Chief of US Naval Operations, that the total number of squadrons over and above their minimum were not in existence.

This answer amazed the British who decided to check the American levels. So, in the first weeks of May, the RAF delegation in Washington was asked to provide figures on the flying hours flown by American anti-U-boat squadrons from US bases where no Allied ship sinkings were occurring or U-boats had not been sighted. The figures supplied were included in a memorandum compiled by the British Chief of Staff and put to the Combined Chiefs of Staff on 22nd May. The US Chiefs of Staff submitted a similar memorandum, still stating that there were no aircraft spare.

This state of affairs might have continued indefinitely had not Sir John decided, with the approval of the Chief of Staff, to go to America in person for a face to face meeting with Admiral Ernest King. Part of the problem was the antagonism between the American Navy and Army. General 'Hap' Arnold had always been anxious to deploy his Army anti-U-boat squadrons to the Bay, but as long as his squadrons operated from America they came under Admiral King's Naval jurisdiction.

During a meeting between Sir John and King on 24th June, a fair measure of agreement was reached. The despatch of two US Army B24 Liberator squadrons would be expedited and King promised that a further four would be made available as soon as possible. Accordingly the 4th and 19th USAAF Squadrons began operating from St Eval on 13th July and nine days later VP63 Squadron USN, flying PBY-5 Catalinas equipped with Magnetic Anomaly Detectors (MAD) – a method of locating U-boats below the surface – was transferred to Pembroke Dock.

The promised additions to these three units did not begin to arrive until

September 1943, by which time it was too late. The promised total of 72 aircraft never did materialise.

* * *

While these meetings and coercions were in progress, July came. At 6 am on the 1st, U-180, carrying gold and Japanese officers in company with U-530, attacked by 53 Squadron on the 30th June, were met by two Z-class destroyers. Two hours later they were spotted by three Beaufighters of 248 Squadron, led by Squadron Leader F.E. Burton DFC. When seen they were a mile off the Beaufighter's port beam, the destroyers were two miles apart with the submarines between. The destroyers put up a terrific barrage preventing any chance of an attack.

Following Burton's sighting report, Flying Officer R.T. Merrifield of 53 Squadron arrived, the vessels having been picked up by the Mark V ASV at 32 miles. Merrifield edged his Liberator in closer and made visual contact only to be attacked by four Ju88s. A running fight ensued that lasted for 42 minutes, the 88s making persistent attacks from ahead, but the beam gunners operated effectively hitting two of the German fighters which broke off the action both with their port engines smoking. The Liberator was only slightly damaged and nobody on board was injured. Later an Intelligence report confirmed that one Ju88 had ditched and another had crash landed in Spain. However, it seems as if the only casualty was one Ju88 of 13/KG40 which force-landed at Santander, Spain. This action resulted in Immediate awards to three of the crew. Robert Merrifield received the DFC while his beam gunners, Flying Officer Gordon F. Wood received the DFC too and Flight Sergeant Roy Niven the DFM and promotion to commissioned rank.

On Friday the 2nd, the supply submarine U-462, under her commander Bruno Vöwe and escorted by U-160 was outward bound from Bordeaux. It will be recalled that Vöwe's U-462 had been forced back into harbour after being damaged by Mosquitos on 21st June. This time she and U-160 had reached sixty miles west of Coruna before being located by a Liberator of 224 Squadron.

Warrant Officer E.J.J. Spiller DFC, had become airborne at 9.10 am that morning. At 2.02 pm they had picked up a S/E contact nineteen miles distant but at three miles the contact was lost. They continued their patrol and at 3.30 pm another contact was made at eighteen miles and fifteen minutes later, they sighted the two U-boats. Sea conditions were excellent and cloud was fairly low. Spiller came in from the cloud and coming through them at 1,000 feet, ten miles from the contact, the two boats were seen a few minutes later in line astern despite hazy conditions.

Initially Spiller thought the boats were surface vessels, but his second pilot Sergeant R. Pierce identified them as U-boats. Edward Spiller immediately dived down to starboard to attack the leading submarine. This boat began to open fire on the approaching Liberator as the second one began to submerge. Spiller then pulled round to attack the submerging boat while his rear gunner raked the leading one. As he came up to the position Spiller yelled instructions to the bomb aimer and then dropped the six D/Cs. As the bomb aimer didn't hear what was said, he released the anti-submarine bombs. The U-boat had been down 7-8 seconds at the drop. Spiller circled as the other boat also dived. Looking down at the position of the D/Cs and bombs, air bubbles were coming to the surface and gradually an oil patch began to form a circle about 80 yards across. A marker was dropped and Spiller continued to circle, the oil still clearly visible. A second marker was dropped when PLE was reached and they turned for home.

One bomb had, however, hit U-462 forward which so damaged her ballast tanks that she had again to return to Bordeaux. U-160 escorted her part of the way.

> 'We attacked two U-boats with bombs, depth charges and machine gun fire. The first run in they were firing at us on the surface and evasive flying constricted the use of a low level bomb sight which I was using in the nose position, but on the second run in we dropped a stick of depth charges and bombs. I think we were very low and we attacked the leading submarine which was half-submerged. We circled for about ten minutes and noted a large oil slick, but no wreckage and we were told later that we had damaged one of them. I do remember there being an explosion which shot the tail gunner into the roof of his turret, but thankfully he was OK. We returned to base after a twelve-hour trip. I don't think we sustained any damage.'
>
> *Sergeant F.T. Holland, 224 Squadron.*

Later that day these two U-boats were spotted again, this time by a Sunderland of 228 Squadron flown by Flight Lieutenant G.D.Lancaster (DD834). One could be seen trailing oil and both put up a barrage of flak as the Sunderland approached. Lancaster began homing procedure and awaited instructions from base HQ but none were received by 8.15 when both boats, probably aware that other aircraft were undoubtedly on their way, dived. They chose a moment when the Sunderland was some way off, and were under before Lancaster could attack.

* * *

July had started well so far. At 10.39 on the night of 2nd July, Flight Sergeant Alex Coumbis of 172 Squadron took off for a night patrol. They had been out four hours, when his operator picked up a contact on the 10 cm radar screen at thirteen miles to port. Coumbis headed the Wellington round and prepared for a possible U-boat.

At this moment there were a number of inbound and outbound U-boats crossing the Bay. U-126 and U-154 were just two and it had been these that

Coumbis had picked up, although he would only see one of them. When ³/₄ mile from the contact the Leigh Light was switched on which illuminated U-126 with decks awash – she was going under. At 50 feet Coumbis dropped six D/Cs, aimed to straddle to 60° across the submarine from starboard to port. As the aircraft went over the rear gunner saw all six explode, one close to the boat's port side, as he pumped 500 rounds into the midst of the water gouts. Coumbis circled and came back above the spot his automatic flame float sat on the water but that was all that could be seen.

Nevertheless, U-126, returning from West Africa – her sixth war patrol – and commanded by Oberleutnant Siegfried Kietz, went straight to the bottom. The attack was seen by U-154 whose captain reported it to B.d.U., then continued his journey home.

> 'Alex Coumbis was a very personal friend and he and his wife "lived out" in Braunton, North Devon with me and my first wife. He was a Rhodesian and a very charming man married to a Scottish lady. Alex was subsequently killed in an air accident in Wales.' [1]
>
> *Flight Sergeant D. Hobden, 172 Squadron.*

Another two U-boats were picked up by Warrant Officer Brands of 502 Squadron at 7.18 am. These were U-160 and the damaged U-462 struggling for a safe port. The Halifax carried bombs, not D/Cs and the violent actions of the two U-boats confounded attempts to bomb them from high level with the Mark XIV bomb sight. Choosing a good moment when the Halifax was making a turn the two boats went down.

They were later met by two destroyers and U-462 was escorted into the Gironde while U-160 resumed her outward passage.

Shortly after nine o'clock, Squadron Leader P.J. Cundy took off from St Eval at the controls of his 224 Squadron Liberator. Pete Cundy was an experienced Coastal pilot and had damaged U-508 on 26th February. Previous to this, Cundy had flown with 53 Squadron in 1940 (Blenheims) and then with 120 Squadron when this was formed in 1941.

> 'Regarding my own crew, this basically consisted of Flying Officer Fabel (navigator), Warrant Officer Spiller (second pilot), Flight Sergeant Owen (flight engineer), Flight Sergeant Cheek, Flight Sergeant I. Graham and Flight Sergeant A. Graham. Apart from Ronald Fabel and Ian Graham, who were my Blenheim crew in 1940 (53 Squadron), the others joined me when 120 Squadron formed at Nutts Corner in 1941. We were detached from 120 in May 1942, complete with a Mark II Liberator AL507, nicknamed *Dumbo*, for

---

[1] Flying Officer A Coumbis KIFA at RAF Freugh, 18th January 1944.

"special duties" in USA under the auspices of MIT, Cambridge, Mass. We returned with this aircraft to UK in October 1942 but instead of rejoining 120 Squadron which by this time was operating from Iceland, were posted to 224 Squadron who were converting from Hudsons to Liberators at Beaulieu. In my opinion 224's conversion would have been more quickly and efficiently achieved if they had been pulled right out of the "line", so to speak, and not tried to convert to the new type and carry out limited operations at the same time.

'On 26th February, 1943 we were flying at about 6,000 feet in clear blue sky above a calm sea when we spotted a U-boat almost immediately below. U-boats crash-dive in about 30 seconds but we managed to get down somehow and dropped four depth charges across the swirl. Afraid our airspeed was too high but this was not surprising under the circumstances. Shortly afterwards the U-boat's bow appeared and she hung vertically like a fishing float for about four minutes and then sank. We had no more depth charges to release, having unsuccessfully attacked (too late) another U-boat earlier in the patrol. Also as our aircraft on this occasion was *Dumbo*, the Mark II Liberator which did not have gun mountings for the beam positions, (nor self-sealing tanks for that matter) the only further damage we could have inflicted was via the tail turret which for various reasons could not have been very effective. In the event, and to our consternation, approximately twenty minutes later the U-boat slowly came to the surface and eventually got underway and headed eastwards at about six knots.'

With Peter Cundy on 3rd July was Lieutenant-Colonel Farrant:

'The reason for Lieutenant-Colonel Farrant's presence on 3rd July 1943, was that he was trying to promote Coastal Command's acceptance of a new type of anti-submarine bomb. If memory serves me correctly these weapons were dropped at the same altitude and speed as depth charges but in sticks of eighteen at a time and a direct hit was essential.[2] In this particular incident our bomb load consisted of one stick of these little chaps and four depth charges and on the first run-in the bombs were released by Ian Graham whose turn it was at the time to be in the bomb-aimer's position. It was the Command's policy for all wireless operators/air gunners etc. (as well as pilots and navigators) to be trained in the use of the low-level bomb-sight in order that they could be rotated between this position and the radar, rear gunner and beam lookout posts thus creating a variety of tasks leading to greater alertness. All very necessary on these sorties which averaged 12 – 14 hours and sometimes longer.

---

[2] This was the RN *Hedgehog* mortar missile with a hollow charge warhead. Not followed up.

'Colonel Farrant presumably was from some ordnance department and I believe there was also another army officer (Major somebody, can't remember his name) also involved in this project. Anyway one or the other always promised me a bottle of Scotch if we ever clobbered a U-boat with their pet bombs and I am pleased to say that this pledge was honoured.

'We sighted the enemy several miles away and I pushed the stick forward. The U-boat captain was not asleep and saw us coming. He opened fire with all armament, including a 37 mm cannon, while the aircraft was still a mile away and, as the range closed, he scored hits on us.

'My gunners were not idle. They returned a hot fire and one of the U-boat crew was seen to fall overboard. We had stopped a few bullets; there was a hole in a tank and the petrol was flowing over the engine exhaust. I thought there might be a fire at any moment, but we carried on and dropped our depth charges, one of which hit the U-boat abaft of the conning tower and bounced off into the sea.

'As we circled for a second attack we saw the depth charges go off. There was a sudden spurt of water close to one of the enemy's guns, which abruptly ceased firing. I imagine the gun crew got the shock of their lives, if they still lived.

'The enemy started evasive action, but was very low in the water and with little way on. Once again we flew over and our second stick of depth charges straddled it, hiding the U-boat in the huge plumes of the explosions which merged into a single gigantic fountain of water.

'I circled round again and we saw that the U-boat had disappeared. All that we could see was a dark brown patch of oil. Then several bodies rose to the surface. My navigator saw six men who appeared to be swimming. I saw another four, and another member of the crew saw three others. Only one of the Germans seemed to be wearing a Mae West.'

Squadron Leader P.J. Cundy, 224 Squadron.

Flight Sergeant Eddie Cheek was a member of Cundy's crew and had flown with him for some time:

'We joined 224 in October 1942, having just spent six months in USA, working with MIT Boston, developing the first American centimetric ASV, with a PPI display, on the 10 cm wavelength. This equipment then developed into ASV Mark V.

'At this time 224 was based at Beaulieu in Hampshire. (I have since learned that SOE agents were trained on the Beaulieu estate, adjoining the airfield.) In April 1943 the squadron was transferred to St Eval in Cornwall. At this time Peter Cundy was a flight lieutenant having already been awarded the DFC for our exploits while serving with 120 Squadron at Nutts Corner, in Northern Ireland. In May Peter was promoted to squadron leader and assumed command of 'A' Flight. It was at this time the Wing Commander, A.E. Clouston, assumed command of the squadron, vice Wing Commander "Bill" Kearney. Clou was a hardman, certainly not cast in the same kindly mould as Bill Kearney. He commanded us positively, without fear or favour. "Clou" was a New Zealander who had joined the RAF pre-war, and after completing a short service commission became a well known civil aviation personality. He purchased from the RAF a wrecked DH Comet (i.e. DH88 not a DH106) which was repaired and registered as G-ACSS, in which he made many epic flights. He also had the AFC which I believe he earned the hard way, at RAE Farnborough, flying Hurricanes into balloon cables, to test the efficiency of cable cutters!

'Clou was held in awe by most of us, and nobody took chances with him. After assuming command he made it a practice to fly with each of his crews, no doubt to learn the task and evaluate his crews. On one such flight something of interest was sighted, and Clou gave instructions for this to be photographed, using the hand held K20 camera. Such an operation required the port beam gun mounting (carrying 2x.303 Brownings) to be disengaged and swung inboard, so that the guns were now trained down the fuselage. A young Canadian gunner moved forward with the K20 to the hatch, in a position with one .303 pointing across his chest and the other across his back. Murphy's Law now came into operation, the clown holding the guns inadvertently fired a burst. The cameraman was wounded across his arms by a few rounds, which then continued down the fuselage, through a large protective shield of armour plate, through the turret doors finishing in the back of the poor rear gunner; of course, by this time each round was the size of a saucer, and did nothing more than tear the gunner's Irvin jacket, bul no blood was drawn. Clou heard the uproar, raced back aft and quickly sized up the situation. He wrapped a piece of rag round the wounded gunner's arm and said, "Now get back to your post!" As if we needed any confirmation, it was apparent that Clou was no pushover.

'On a lighter note, we were standing in the sun outside our hangar at St Eval when Clou emerged from his office. One of our crew, Archie Graham, said, "Watch this." He then plucked a dandelion and really sidled up to Clou, with his hand behind his back and flagrantly omitting the courtesy of a salute to his commanding officer, proffered the dandelion and said, "I brought this for you, sir." We confidently awaited the explosion which was bound to follow, but no, Clou replied, "Thank you, Archie, how sweet." We now had a suspicion that Clou was partly human.

'Squadron Leader Cundy and crew were briefed to operate J/224 on a Derange patrol in the Bay of Biscay. We were informed that we were to make the first sortie with a new weapon; the 35 lb AS bomb [Hedgehog bombs, Ed.], which were hollow charge weapons based on an anti-tank device, and to be dropped in sticks of 72. At dispersal Peter introduced us to a Colonel Farrant, who had been involved in this new weapon, and was to accompany us. I asked the Colonel why he was bothering to spend many long dull hours incarcerated in a metal tube, and he said that because of his interest in the weapon, he felt he should see it in action. I could only reply that many crews had completed full operational tours without even smelling a U-boat. (I have since read in Norman Longmate's *The Bomber*, that the sinking of a U-boat entailed no less than 7,000 hours of operational flying – this is an extract from a memo from Air Marshal Harris to Winston Churchill on 28th June 1942).

'We made a sighting of a 714 ton U-boat travelling on the surface. Peter pressed straight on with the attack, releasing the stick of 72 lb'ers, and during the attack, we were aware of strikes on our aircraft. After the attack Peter put the aircraft into an orbit about the U-boat, and we could see bodies and wreckage in the water. While this was in progress I went aft to see how things were in the after compartment. The port beam gunner and Colonel Farrant were looking through the hatch at the terrible results of our attack. I noticed that the Colonel was undoing his Mae West, and I felt obliged to ask him what he was going to do. He told me he was about to throw his life-vest down to: "Those poor devils down there." As we had not yet determined the extent of our own damage I was constrained to tell him that there might well be a need for it by these ".. poor devils up here."

'The damage suffered included cannon strikes on the starboard mainplane, fin, rudder and one petrol tank. The aerodynamic qualities of the aircraft were not seriously impaired, and we made an uneventful return to St Eval. Fairly soon after this sortie, Peter was awarded the DSO.'

Flight Sergeant E.S. Cheek, 224 Squadron.

As the Liberator flew off, leaving several men swimming in the sea and other bodies floating lifelessly, there was obviously no doubt about this kill. Cundy flew home on three engines and landed safely, but U-628 went to the bottom.

* * *

There were two other encounters on this successful day. Three inbound

U-boats were sighted in company by Flying Officer Jackson of 423 Squadron at two o'clock. These were U-170, 535 and 536, and all opened fire on the lone Sunderland which sheered away. Then the U-boats went down before an attack could be made.

Half an hour later a Liberator of 53 Squadron flown by Warrant Officer L.L. Esler RCAF found Stahl's U-648, outward bound. Esler found her on the surface, having gained contact at twelve miles. He put his salvo of D/Cs across U-648, five being seen to explode on its port side. The U-boat rolled over and disappeared. Return fire had been experienced from the boat and even one round had been fired from the large gun forward. Large oil patches were seen but no damage had been inflicted. It was previously thought that the boat was U-386 but this is not the case.

Two U-boats sunk and two damaged for no July losses boded well for 19 Group. The 4th was quiet, although another submarine sallied forth into the Bay, U-267 from St Nazaire headed for the Atlantic on its third war patrol.

Monday the 5th began with 10 RAAF Squadron seeing a U-boat but making no immediate attack. Only when the ships were seen diving did Flying Officer R.R. Gray dive but his D/Cs hit the water almost a minute after they had disappeared. The 2nd Escort Group returned to the Bay on this day, still under the command of Captain Walker. They homed onto the area, but it was not one but a group of three U-boats that the Sunderland had found, U-170, 535 and 536 – the same group 423 Squadron had found on the 3rd. Walker's ships searched the area till 5 pm without success.

An hour and a half later a 53 Squadron Liberator found them on the surface. Flight Sergeant W. Anderson RNZAF had left St Eval at 6.26 am and had been co-operating with Walker's group all day. Finally PLE was reached and Anderson had to return to base. No sooner had this decision been made than his crew picked up the three U-boats. Anderson's first attack was spoilt, due mainly to the intense gunfire, maintained by the boats. On his second, two D/Cs hung up but the third brought success. Two D/Cs splashed to the port side of U-535 and six to starboard, just abaft the conning tower. Flak hit the Liberator, damaging the wings, rear fuselage and tailplane, and wounding a beam gunner. As the spray cleared, two boats were seen sailing away, the other that had been attacked was lagging behind. Anderson had now to leave the area quickly and did not have the satisfaction of seeing his kill founder and sink shortly afterwards. Wilbert Anderson was later commissioned having received the DFC as a Warrant Officer. Helmut Ellmenreich and his crew all perished.

This fifth success in five days brought with it the first loss for July. A 10 OTU Whitley flown by Sergeant Clarke failed to return from its morning patrol.

Undoubtedly the recent U-boat losses galvanised the Luftwaffe into action for there was increased air activity over the next couple of days, beginning with an attack on a 415 Squadron Hampden. Flight Sergeant H.R.

Clasper jettisoned his D/Cs and headed for cloud being lucky to escape.

Then an Instep patrol was intercepted by FW190s on the 7th. Three Beaufighters of 248 Squadron took off in company with two 235 Squadron aircraft. Flying Officer P.J. McGarvey RCAF/Pilot Officer A.M. Barnard saw them first and fired a burst to attract the attention of the others. But one Focke Wulf attacked Flying Officer J.C. White/Flying Officer R.C. Arthur and black smoke poured from their fighter. It then turned onto its back and dived flaming into the sea. A patrol of 456 Squadron Mosquitos whose patrol had been delayed saw the end of this action, and the burning Beaufighter going into the sea, about 70 miles south-west of the Scillies.

At exactly the same time, 250 miles further to the south-west, 53 Squadron were again in the midst of the action. Flying Officer Boulter came across U-230, 566 and 709, but only two were on the surface. Boulter attacked and one submarine seemed to disappear, and go down but neither was damaged, although his Liberator sustained damage to its starboard outer engine but Boulter flew it home.

In mid-afternoon Flying Officer Waite of 53 Squadron found a singleton U-boat way down off the Spanish coast, with decks awash but an attack produced no results. However, this U-boat – U-267 (KL Otto Tinschert) – outbound, suffered serious damage from a 210 Squadron Catalina this same day and was later hunted by the 2nd Escort Group, which forced her captain to abort his mission and return home.

* * *

The success continued the next day – 8th July. Just after 8 am a 304 Polish Squadron Wellington piloted by Sergeant Kieltyka saw a surfaced U-boat and attacked. He got a good straddle and saw wreckage but the U-boat – the outbound U-230 – survived with only minor damage.

That afternoon Coastal Command's 'ace' U-boat killer was flying – Squadron Leader Terence Bulloch DSO DFC now with 224 Squadron flying a special Liberator.

Bulloch hailed from Northern Ireland and joined the RAF in 1936. He flew with 220 and 206 Squadrons in the late 1930's and early months of World War Two, and by the end of 1940 had received the DFC. During a 'rest' between tours he flew with the Atlantic Ferry Unit, delivering aircraft across the Atlantic to Britain, bringing a number of the new Liberators across. In 1941 the first RAF Liberator Squadron was formed – 120 Squadron – and one pilot to join its ranks was Terry Bulloch. Over the next year he made several U-boat attacks when other pilots flew patrol after patrol without even a sighting. He damaged U-89 on 16 August 1942, then damaged U-653 two days later. On 12th October he sank U-597, then damaged U-89 for the second time on 5th November. These successes resulted in a Bar to his DFC, then a DSO and Bar.

Bulloch then became an instructor but also tested a number of special installations for anti-U-boat Liberators. These included Leigh Lights and air-to-surface rocket projectiles. To test the latter under operational conditions he was attached to 224 Squadron. One of his crew was Sergeant A.G. Dyer. Alf Dyer had flown with 1407 Met. Flight in 1941 and then with 200 Squadron in West Africa in 1942 until shot down over Vichy French territory on 18th May. He eventually escaped internment and returned to England and was assigned to Bulloch's crew.

Sergeant A.G. Dyer, 224 Squadron:
    'In June 1943 I joined the crew of the "ace" of Coastal Command pilots, Squadron Leader Bulloch DSO and Bar, DFC and Bar, an Irishman and working for Coastal Command Development Unit. We did the experiments on rockets versus the U-boats and then on operations flying Liberators III, V, and VIII attached to numerous squadrons hunting U-boats in the Bay of Biscay, and flying from such bases as St Eval (224 Squadron), Ballykelly and Tain in Ross and Cromalty and Iceland. Tests on the rockets were completed in June '43 (flying from Beaulieu).'

Squadron Leader T. Bulloch, 224 Squadron:
    'I was on attachment to 224 Squadron at St Eval with my special Liberator Mark V, BZ721, equipped with rocket projectiles. I had a roving assignment in those days attaching my crew and aircraft to various squadrons after months of development of this great weapon flying out of the experimental establishment at Boscombe Down.
    'The RPs used were 25 lb solid shot, which when released at the correct dive angle and speed had remarkable ballistic qualities. On entering the water, they would descend to approx. 25-30 feet depth, then level off, travel horizontally a distance, and then re-emerge from the sea. The head would penetrate the pressure hull of a U-boat and come out the other side. A great weapon!
    'Unfortunately, a hamfisted Czech squadron (Liberators) who were equipped with it, used to damage the wings (wrinkling them) on the pull out. A case of not using correct elevator trim!'

At 8.53 am on the morning of Thursday, 8th July, Bulloch took off in his BZ721. The sea was calm and there was slight wispy cloud at 6,000 feet with unlimited visibility. On this patrol they had Flight Lieutenant C. Campbell with them, who was an armaments officer. He was acting as an air gunner and at 1.17 pm was manning the port waist gun position when he saw with the naked eye, a wake – quickly recognised as a U-boat, some eight miles off travelling at an estimated 12 knots. The Mark V ASV picked up the contact at almost the same moment – the delay probably due to interference from a number of fishing vessels in the immediate area. The U-boat was Kapitänleutnant Auffermann's U-514 – a large type lXC/40 submarine out on her 4th patrol going to the Cape, having left Lorient five days earlier. She was in position 4337/0859 – only 20 miles or so off the Spanish coast from Coruna. Bulloch's attack was recorded as follows:

Date: 8/7/43. Time of attack:- 1316. Position:- 43°37'N 08°59'W. Weather conditions: Wisp of thin cloud at 6000 feet; Sea calm to slight. Visibility unlimited; Wind 300° T 12 mph.

Duty: On Musketry Patrol. Nature of initial contact: When flying on track 355° at 6600 feet, a wake and then a U-boat was sighted bearing Red 140°, distant 8 miles. Radar contact obtained almost immediately after visual sighting, delay being probably due to interference from a number of fishing vessel contacts. Course and speed of U-boat: 240°, 12 kts.

Direction of approach: Pilot circled to port losing height and attacked from Green 110°; the U-boat took no evasive action and did not open fire.

Details of 1st attack: The 1st pair of RP was fired at a distance of 800 yards, at an altitude of 800 feet, the 2nd pair at 600 yards at 600 feet, and the salvo at 4 RPs at 500 feet with the angle of dive estimated 17°, IAS 265 mph. The front gunner fired 30 rounds, rear gunner 200 rounds and port waist gunner 60 rounds, estimating hits on conning tower and forward of it.

Time of release: While U-boat was still on the surface.

Surface evidence: The navigator in the front turret saw splashes of entry definitely between the U-boat and its bow wave slightly abaft a point midway between the conning tower and the bow. The splashes were about 30 feet wide. The rear gunner observed 1 RP emerging from the sea beyond the U-boat which was seen to dive $\frac{1}{2} - 1$ minute later with tail up at least 15° to 20°.

Squadron Leader T. Bulloch, 224 Squadron:
'You probably are not aware of what occurred after our D/C attack! It's not mentioned even in the official report. I did a quick turn and ran in at a very low level, and dropped (which was then a top secret weapon) one Mark 24 mine (our crews nicknamed it "Wandering Annie") – actually an acoustic torpedo which was designed to follow the U-boat's propeller noise after submerging and home on it.[3] However, it was without doubt the RPs which killed U-514. The technique used was a 20° dive with cruise power set, and firing the RPs as described in the report. Thankfully we were equipped with a special radio altimeter and on the pull out were less than 100 feet above the sea.'

---

[3] Colin Campbell, the armament officer aboard the Liberator, informed this author.

Sergeant A.G. Dyer, 224 Squadron:

'My memories of the 8th July 1943 trip was that about 1.15 pm on a fine sunny day, a U-boat surfaced very near to us indeed and there was a saying in Coastal Command squadrons that U-boats just "popped up" when Bulloch was around whereas other pilots could fly for hundreds of hours without sighting one. I was just changing position with Flight Sergeant Larkin – him to replace me on wireless – me to take station at starboard window with .5 Browning – and Larkin actually transmitted the sighting-attack messages to base. I believe we were in close radio contact that day with Captain Walker DSO and Bar of the "Little Ships" and he was pretty quickly on the scene and hoisted black pennant to confirm the kill while we were doing continuous circuits round the point of attack.

'So far as I can recollect the rockets undershot the U-boat (as they were intended to do), went right through the U-boat and soared in the air on the other side. We all flew down to Coastal Command HQ Northwood on 10th July to give our accounts of the attack.'

'To clarify: the Mark 24 mine circled until picking up popping noise of cavitation from a propeller – (collapse of vacuum). Bull's 20° dive technique showed on training runs this could be achieved as he explained above.

'Bull strongly advised HQ Coastal Command to develop R/P attacks by Liberator units as compliment to the Mark 24 mine – ignored despite a high success rate from Hudsons and Swordfish.'

The day ended with seven Ju88s finding a 53 Squadron Liberator (BZ716 'B')180 miles north of Coruna. Flying Officer J.F. Handasyde was on a Musketry patrol but was diverted to hunt for a reported U-boat, then set course northwards from Sisargas Island, just to the west of Coruna, when PLE was reached. They had been heading home across the Bay for an hour, flying at 500 feet, at the time the 88s picked them up.

Two Junkers attacked, closing to 300 yards, their fire killing the port beam gunner, Flying Officer J. Witts and wounding his starboard partner Flight Sergeant H.A. Pomeroy in the left leg and scrotum. The Liberator's starboard outer engine was smashed and shut down, reducing the aircraft's speed to around 180 mph. All the while Handasyde was taking violent evasive action, climbing, diving and pulling round into tight turns, forcing the 88s to breakaway or fire low. Only three of the attackers came in close but all seemed to be trying to force the Liberator eastwards. Perhaps the German pilots had orders to try and force a capture in the hope of discovering the secrets of Coastal Command's aircraft and their ability to home in on their submarines with apparent ease.

Finally, at 5.10 John Handasyde managed to reach cloud cover. It was estimated that 30 to 40 attacks had been made upon them, and damage had been inflicted to two or three of the 88s, having been seen to fly off with smoking engines. At 6.40 a twin-engined aircraft shadowed them two miles astern for an hour but finally flew off. Handasyde landed at Thorney Island without brakes and with a burst tyre, but it was a good landing. Cannon and machine-gun fire had riddled the wings, fuselage and tailplane. Handasyde was awarded an Immediate DFC, Flight Sergeant Harold Pomeroy an Immediate DFM.

Three of KG40's aircraft had received damage and four members of the aircrew were wounded in this action. They claimed the Liberator as shot down.

* * *

It was relatively quiet in the Bay over the next three days, only a 59 Squadron Liberator making a 'no result' attack on a surfaced U-boat early on the 10th.

In response to Slessor's request to Gibraltar and Casablanca for their patrols to be spread further north to help with the Bay battle, success had been achieved. Between 7th and 9th July, fifteen sightings and twelve attacks were made by aircraft from Gibraltar or Port Lyautey. These had sunk three and damaged three more off the west coast of Spain, off Finisterre.

U-232   sunk by 2 USAAF Squadron.
U-435   sunk by 179 Squadron (Flying Officer E.J. Fisher 3948/1438).
U-951   sunk by 1 USAAF Squadron.
U-603   severely damaged by 202 Squadron
       (Flight Lieutenant Dowell 4210/1340).
U-267   severely damaged by 210 Squadron (Pilot Officer
       J.A.Cruickshank* 4145/ 1136), but it is also thought that his attack
       was upon U-183 which suffered minor damage, in which case
       D/53 Squadron damaged U-267.
U-183   slightly damaged by 1 USAAF Squadron.

(*A year later Cruickshank was to win the Victoria Cross for his gallant attack upon and the sinking of U-361.)

In addition, the 1st USAAF Squadron had attacked U-953 (light damage) and U-211, no damage.

This activity and the losses sustained by his U-boats caused Dönitz to signal those boats using the north, north-west and west of Spain, to avoid the area. He also told his commanders that according to the Luftwaffe crews flying air cover, they had seen U-boats diving when 'surprised' by their aircraft so late that they were still visible when their Junkers arrived above the spot. They were reminded that they were in the greatest danger if they dived too late. They should only dive if they had not been spotted or if they were confident they could reach at least 320 feet before an attacking aircraft could reach them. At this time Dönitz was very well aware of the organised offensive being waged against him. He was aware too that the RAF's efforts were making heavy demands on the U-boats' battery capacity so they were frequently forced by batteries urgently needing to be recharged, to surface and fight it out with no immediate chance of diving. He had also noted the presence of the 2nd Escort Group with all the implications that entailed. He therefore required that every effort be made:

1. To pinpoint the surface forces by organised air reconnaissance so that U-boats could be given evasive routes.
2. To attack the surface force with the few German destroyers available.
3. To attack the surface force with all FW200s available.

Dönitz also noted that the Ju88s had not wrested any sort of superiority over the Bay, nor forced the RAF to lessen its activities. It seemed the only concession achieved was that Allied aircraft did not operate east of the 8°W line, so that his boats were relatively safe there against surprise attacks. The Luftwaffe was bringing Me410s in to try and combat the Mosquitos in the northern sectors, allowing Ju88s to operate further south in formations of less than eight aircraft. In this way more sorties could be flown in support of U-boat groups.

* * *

After three quiet days, activity increased on the 12th, and several German aircraft were seen during the day. Ju88s gained an early success against 228 Squadron. Sergeant R. Codd took off at 7 o'clock that morning in Sunderland DV977 'Y'.

They had completed half their patrol by 2 pm and had reached Spanish territorial waters. Several fishing vessels were seen and some photographs were taken of the Spanish coast. Near Coruna some white puffs were seen, taken to be AA gunfire, warning the RAF aircraft not to enter territorial waters. Codd turned away and entered cloud. Half an hour later they flew into some clear air at 500 feet. Suddenly a number of Ju88s appeared from all directions and attacked. The Sunderland replied with all guns. One engine was hit and began to leave a trail of smoke. Then the rear gunner reported his turret U/S just before the intercom was knocked out. Two or three minutes later, Sergeant E. Davidson, the flight engineer operating the mid-upper turret, heard an appalling crash and the Sunderland dived into the sea. Davidson escaped through the mid-upper hatch but his Mae West did not inflate. Once in the water he saw a dinghy still in its valise, floating nearby and swam towards it. After a long struggle the dinghy half inflated and he climbed in. He then saw the navigator who had been badly injured about the face, and tried to pull him into the dinghy but found it very difficult. After a long struggle he had to abandon his efforts but by then it appeared to Davidson that his companion had died.

Shortly afterwards he found the bellows and managed to fully inflate the dinghy. Some two hours later two Halifax aircraft circled him, then one flew off. Some time later a Catalina and a Sunderland arrived, the former also circling with the Halifax. After $8^1/_2$ hours in the sea, at around 11 pm, he was picked up by a RN sloop. His watch had stopped at 2.35 pm; he was the sole survivor.

On another 228 Squadron Sunderland, flying a Musketry patrol that afternoon, piloted by Flying Officer Bill French, they had no less a personage than Air Chief Marshal Sir Edgar Ludlow-Hewitt K.C.B. C.M.G. D.S.O. M.C. L.d'H. (Inspector General of the RAF), as a passenger. They were out for a full twelve hour patrol.

The weather was fair over the Bay on this day, but with occasional showers. At 10.30 am, three 248 Squadron Beaufighters, led by Flight Lieutenant C.R.B. Schofield/Sergeant J.A. Mallinson, went out on patrol. At 2.05 they sighted a U-boat two miles off to port and the Beaus turned, flying into a line astern formation. As they came in they could clearly see fifteen to eighteen men standing on the deck and conning tower, watching the three RAF aircraft. As they closed, the U-boat opened fire with a light gun aft of the conning tower. Tracer shells zipped by, just above Schofield's port wing. Schofield returned fire with a long burst of cannon shells. The U-boat was now firing with a heavy gun forward of the tower and Schofield saw something the size of a cricket ball pass over his cockpit. Lieutenant G.C. Newman (Free French)/Flying Officer O.C.Cochrane then attacked, firing long bursts and seeing hits on the conning tower.

The U-boat – it was U-441 (flak-trap), out again after being damaged on 24th May – was now firing continuously, the Beaufighters breaking away to take evasive action, but then the third Beau was coming in. Flying Officer P.A.S. Payne/Flying Officer A.M. McNichol, opened up, their fire falling short but then Payne crept it up and then it began to splatter around the conning tower.

U-441, up against three hard hitting, nimble fighters, rather than a hoped for lumbering anti-submarine aircraft, was now taking violent evasive action and the men on deck had now all disappeared. One man was seen in the water, a second lying on the deck. All gunfire had now ceased, allowing the Beaus to press home their attacks. Flight Lieutenant Schofield saw more of his cannon shells blasting upon the submarine, then an explosion, followed by flames, as if something had caught fire aft of the tower. More attacks followed, even the navigators spraying the boat with their rear guns as each Beau flew over. Finally the submarine began to dive out of sight.

The supposedly deadly aircraft trap – U-441 – had again been damaged. The explosion on the deck had been ammunition, and of the crew, ten had been killed and thirteen wounded. Included amongst the later was her CO,

Kapitänleutnant Götz von Hartmann. He was forced to order a return to harbour, escorted finally into Brest by a destroyer sent out by Dönitz. All the boat's officers had either been killed or wounded, the ship's doctor taking over and bringing her home.

The Luftwaffe was galvanised into action once again as a result of this action, resulting in the attack and destruction of the 228 Squadron Sunderland already mentioned, and a Whitley of 10 OTU. This was attacked by five Ju88s which sent Sergeant C.T. Rudman and his crew into the sea where they all perished. The air gunners, however, shot down one Ju88, its crew later being rescued by the Royal Navy.

* * *

It was 228 Squadron that was in the action on the 13th. Flying Officer R.D. Hanbury – a former Imperial Airways pilot – took his Sunderland off home base waters at 3.04 am and headed out towards the Musketry patrol area as dawn came up. Thirty-six minutes earlier, Flying Officer A.R.D. Clutterbuck of 58 Squadron had also left base, flying his Halifax into Musketry.

At 7.58 am Clutterbuck's second pilot, Flying Officer A.R. Burns, sighted three surfaced U-boats on a course of 140°, in 'vic' formation. These were U-607, 613 and 445 . U-607, commanded by Oberleutnant zur See Wolf Jeschonnek (half brother of the late General Hans Jeschonnek of the Luftwaffe) had left St Nazaire on 10th July with U-445 commanded by Oberleutnant zur See Rupprecht Graf von Treuberg leading. They were preceded by a 4,000-ton Sperrbrecher (heavily armed and specially re-inforced anti-mine vessel) and a mine-sweeper on each quarter and a U-boat on each quarter of U-607. An air cover patrol of four Ju88s should have been overhead but only one actually turned up. At 11 pm they submerged, resurfacing at 7.30 am on the 11th. Half an hour later a radar contact, believed to be an enemy surface vessel was picked up, and they submerged. They resurfaced at 2 pm, charging their batteries for three hours. That evening they were joined by U-613 commanded by Kapitänleutnant Helmut Köppe from La Pallice.

They arranged between themselves that each should take a turn at being guard boat for a 24-hour period and that the guard boat commander would decide whether to dive on the approach of hostile aircraft. If it was decided to fight it out, the green signal flag, waved in a figure-of-eight, would denote this course of action. Any intention to dive would be signalled by lamp. Each submarine would keep GSR watch but on different wavelengths. When surfaced the three boats would proceed in line abreast, U-607 being furthest to port. At 9.04 pm, U-607 submerged reaching 130 feet, but Jeschonnek went deeper, to 260 feet, for an exercise.

The 12th July proved uneventful, the three boats remaining in company, on the surface throughout the day, submerged at night. At 00.01 on the 13th, a bottle of champagne was opened and a toast drunk by the officers to acknowledge Jeschonnek's birthday. As events turned out, his birthday was to be far from happy.

At 7.55 am the boats surfaced, U-607 again taking up the port position. Köppe was guard boat for the 13th. Three quarters of an hour later, Clutterbuck's Halifax was spotted by the man of the watch. Almost immediately a Sunderland came into view. Reader Hanbury had arrived.

Jeschonnek turned his boat in order to present a narrow target to the Halifax, but in doing so he became a little separated from the other two U-boats. Nevertheless, Jeschonnek and his crew were confident that the combined fire of the three boats would drive off the aircraft. So confident that he and his first Officer, Leutnant Egon Horsemann, aged 21, lit cigarettes and waited for the aircraft to come into range.

Clutterbuck flew close to Hanbury's Sunderland, signalling to him that he intended to circle in an anti-clockwise direction. This should force the U-boats to break formation and attempt to cover both aircraft. The two captains later related:

'When they break formation we'll both attack,' signalled Clutterbuck.

'We headed back on the opposite course,' said Clutterbuck.'Then we heard a brief interchange of German sentences. I don't understand German, but I knew something was up. The U-boat leader was obviously giving his other two boats some order.'

The orders were soon clear. The starboard U-boat broke away from the formation and began to submerge. It was immediately attacked by the Sunderland.

'We cracked right in,' said Flying Officer Hanbury, the Sunderland captain.

'There was heavy flak fire but I came in so low I had to jink over the conning-tower. "One of our depth-charges fell plumb on the conning tower and another three close alongside the starboard bow," added the rear-gunner Flight Sergeant Lacy.' [4]

Clutterbuck came in from ahead while Hanbury came in from astern, the sun behind him. The boats opened fire at 1,000 yards and U-607 continued until its two single 20 mm guns jammed but the quadruple 20 mm, that had been specially fitted at St Nazaire after their last (fourth) patrol, remained in action. They had every intention of staying on the surface to fight it out.

As the two aircraft came in, there were two different views on what happened next, one from the air, another from the sea. Arthur Clutterbuck saw that the two outside U-boats were beginning to submerge, covered by the centre boat. As the one that had become slightly separated from the others was attacked by the Sunderland, Clutterbuck flew right across the other outside U-boat that was beginning to go down. He dropped eight D/Cs, three of which fell short, two on target and three overshot.

---

[4] *Coastal Command Leads the Invasion*, M. Wilson and A.S.L. Robinson. Quoted by courtesy of Century Hutchinson Ltd.

Meanwhile, Reader Hanbury went down over the separated boat and released seven D/Cs. However, according to survivors from U-607, they felt deserted by the two other boats and at their interrogation stated they had no intention of submerging but the other two did, leaving them at the mercy of the Sunderland. Certainly they saw no signal indicating that the others were going to dive:

Flight Sergeant G.D. Williames, 228 Squadron:
'At 7.30 am our flight engineer, Flight Sergeant McFarlane was in the front turret of "N for Nuts" and he reported on the intercom: "Three U-boats approx three miles, starboard bow." U-boats fully surfaced, bristling with guns, fresh out from St Nazaire bound for the Atlantic shipping lanes.

'The position and strength of the enemy force was radioed to Command HQ and to our nearest supporting patrol, and as we circled the U-boats they circled clockwise to direct their main fire-power at us. In turn we effectively maintained our position just outside their anti-aircraft barrage and although one or two bursts came uncomfortably close we remained intact. The gunners had a double job to advise the skipper of the nearness of these bursts and to keep a close watch for the Ju88s who most certainly would have been advised of our presence.

'Reinforcements arrived almost immediately in the shape of another aircraft, which according to our orders now joined the circuit on the opposite side to us. The U-boat gunners now had a problem, two targets to concentrate on and as hoped our tactics paid off. The U-boat that had been maintaining the outside left station suddenly lost way and started to turn anti-clockwise.

'This was the pay off. "Attacking now," the skipper's voice came calmly over the intercom as he pushed the aircraft down in a steep dive levelling off just over the wave tops, jinking left then right to confuse the enemy gunners. Heavy flak coming at us now, a curtain of red hot metal, the odds were shortening fast, the surprise element had been overcome, the U-boat gunners were getting on target. Then we were within a 1,000 yards of them. Despite the evasive action the aircraft was taking, "Mac" adjusted his fire and raked the conning tower and gun platform killing and maiming the gun crews. Then we were on them so low that it was necessary to pull the great aircraft over the top of the conning tower. The attack was a classic of its type for two depth charges fell along the starboard stern, the third actually hit the conning tower and the fourth and fifth alongside the port bow. Out of the holocaust and exploding water, the U-boat reared in mortal agony, the bow broke off at the conning tower and somersaulted over, in the brief seconds that we climbed and turned, all that remained of

Top: Wellington VIII of 172 Sqn (HX379 WN-A) in October 1942. Note the ASV aerials and Coastal camouflage.

Bottom: Wellington 'G' (MP539) of 172 Squadron with its crew, l to r: F/O Peter Dene, F/Sgt Peter Stembridge, F/Sgt Dennis Hobden, P/O Jimmy Boyd, Sgt Bob Webb, and P/O Eddie Goodman.

Top left: F/Sgt John Brooks, 224 Squadron.

Top right: Sgt G D Williames, 228 Squadron.

Bottom: Watergate Bay Hotel, 224 Squadron's officer's mess (St Eval, Cornwall).

Top: 'The Baird Boys', summer 1943. L to r: standing – A Petherick, R V Stewart, R McKeller, K C B Field, G M Watson, T. P Williams. Seated – F/O J Dobson, S/L R Baird, F/O D Hughes, R Watts. Kneeling – H V Weeks and J D Temple, 461 Squadron RAAF.

Bottom left: Sgt Geoff Watson, 461 Squadron RAAF.

Bottom right: Flight Lieutenant Fred Hall DFC, flew as an NCO with 10 OTU in the early summer of 1943.

Top left: F/Sergeant Doug Kneale, 228 Squadron.

Top right: Sergeant Frank Holland, 224 Squadron.

Bottom left: Wing Commander W E Oulton DSO DFC, OC 58 Squadron in 1943.

Bottom right: Spiller's crew after the fight, 13 May 1943. L to r: F/Sgt Mackin, Sgt Pearce, W/O Spiller, F/Sgt Humphrey, F/Sgt Denney, F/Sgt F T Holland, Sgt Thompson. Starboard inner engine feathered and Liberator has run off the runway.

Top left: Cannon shell hit on Lib's starboard wing, 13 May, during Spiller's encounter with Ju88s.

Top right: Flight Sergeant Jim Powell of 224 Squadron, won the CGM for his actions on 17 May 1943. Photo taken after being commissioned.

Above left: French fishing vessel in the Bay, along with Spanish boats, were regularly encountered both day and night by Coastal crews.

Above right: F/Sergeant John McMahon, WOP/AG 224 Squadron.

Left: P/O Jack Edwards and Sgt Sid Whiter, 224 Squadron.

Top: Boulton Paul rear turret on 224 Squadron Liberator.

Bottom left: Flight Lieutenant D M Gall DFC, 201 Squadron, sank U-440 on 31 May 1943.

Bottom right: U-563 under attack by Wilfred Oulton, 58 Squadron, 31 May 1943.

Top left: Flight Lieutenant Mark Bateman DFC, 236 Squadron, sank U-418 with R/Ps on 1 June 1943.

Top right: Flight Lieutenant Joe Singleton

DFC and Flying Officer Geoff Haslam DFC, 25 Squadron.

Bottom: Mosquito of 264 Squadron (W4081 PS-R).

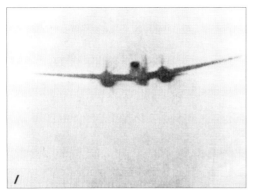

Top sequence: Camera gun film of the Ju88 of KG40 shot down by Joe Singleton and Geoff Haslam over the Bay, 11 June 1943.

Bottom: 201 Squadron in front of 'S' (W6014) l to r seated: F/L Norris, F/L Fairclough, F/L Hewitt, S/L Flint, W/C J C Burnett, S/L Bunting, F/L Sanderson, F/L Harvey, F/L Hayes, F/L D M Gall, Capt Sheldon; middle: F/O Harcourt-Williams, F/O Matthey, F/O Robertson, F/O Lowth, F/O B E H Layne, F/O Gallemaerts, F/O Robinson, F/O Lingard, P/O Mold, F/O Bates, F/O Harrild, F/O Muffitt; rear: F/O Hamer, P/O Jay, P/O Hodgson, F/O Davies, P/O Hewett, F/O Dunn, F/O Walters, F/O Wood, P/O Willert, P/O Alexander, F/O Stevens, P/O Harvey, F/O Dawson.

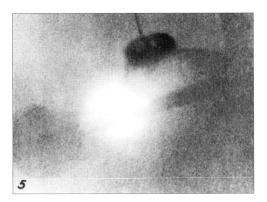

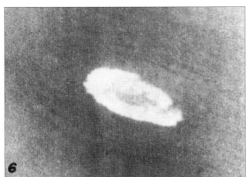

Top right: Sergeant Alex Coumbis of 172 Squadron, sank U-126 on the night of 2/3 July 1943.

Bottom: Liberator II (AL507) 'Dumbo', flown by Peter Cundy and crew, 224 Squadron. Note Mk V ASV radar bulge under aircraft's chin.

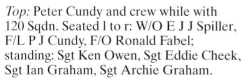

Top: Peter Cundy and crew while with 120 Sqdn. Seated l to r: W/O E J J Spiller, F/L P J Cundy, F/O Ronald Fabel; standing: Sgt Ken Owen, Sgt Eddie Cheek, Sgt Ian Graham, Sgt Archie Graham.

Bottom left: Liberator FL963 'J' of 224 Squadron in which Cundy and crew sank U-628 on July 1943, despite the submarine's fire knocking out one engine

and causing other flak damage. L to r: S/L P Cundy, F/O Perry Allen, Lt-Col Farrant, Sgt Jock Graham, Sgt Ian Graham, Sgt Eddie Cheek, Sgt D Doncaster, Sgt Ken Owen and F/O Ronald King.

Bottom right: Squadron Leader T M Bulloch DSO DFC, 224 Squadron 1943, with Liberator BZ721 in which he and his crew sank U-514 on 8 July, using rockets.

Top left: Liberator BZ721 'R' – Bulloch's special rocket B24. Note rocket installation at base of fuselage beneath the cockpit. L to r: Sgt R McColl DFM, F/L B Hennesay, -?-, S/L Bulloch, F/O F B Lewis, Sgt A G Dyer, F/Sgt N E Lord, F/O D E H Durrant, F/Sgt D Purcell.

Top right: Wellington HF113 'G' of 172 Squadron in September 1943. Note ASV chin bulge.

Middle: Mumford's crew, 172 Sqdn, August 1943. L to r: front – F/Sgt D A Radburn (WOP), P/O Doug Mumford, Sgt Jimmy Wyatt (WOP); rear – F/Sgt R T G 'Bob' Bird (2P), W/O G M 'Lofty' Brydon NZ (Nav), Sgt J T 'Jack' Hunt (WOP).

Left: Sgt A A Turner, 172 Squadron, sole surviver of the crash into U-459 on 24 July.

Top left: Liberator 'G' of 224 Squadron.

Top right: Davey's crew, 502 Squadron. Front –
Johnny Johnson (WOP), 'Army' Armstrong (2P),
Johnny Davey DSO, Jock Finlayson (Nav); rear –
Harold Archer (AG), Bill King (Radar Op),
Harry Barrett (Eng).

Above: Sunderland DV960 'H' 461 Squadron RAAF.
On 17 May F/L J G P Weatherlake had a running
fight with Ju88s in this aircraft but survived despite
severe damage.

Right: Bob Sweeny and crew, August 1943. L to r:
rear: F/O R King, F/L R Sweeny, F/O Perry Allen,
Sgt Ian Graham; front – F/Sgt Ken Owen,
F/Sgt Eddie Cheek, Sgt Archie Graham.

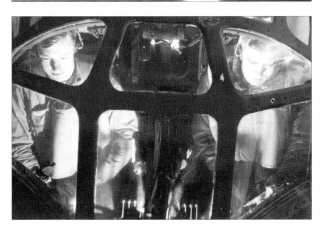

Top: US Navy PB4Y Liberator crossing the Cornish coast, 1943.

Above left: Clouston's attack on U-558, 17 July 1943.

Above: Sergeant Bill Owens, 547 Squadron.

Left: Cockpit of a PB4Y showing the two pilots. On the right, Lt Charles F Willis Jr.

Top: U-218 surfacing on 2 August 1943, photographed by Bill Owens. He and Sgt L Davies of 547 Sqdn inflicted so many casualties with their turret gunfire that she had to abort and return to base.

Bottom: U-106 under attack by F/L Irwin Clarke RAAF, 461 Squadron, and F/O R D Hanbury of 228 Squadron, 2 August 1943.

Top; HMS *Wren*, one of Walker's sloops of the 2nd Escort Group.

Bottom left: Richard Wulff and Franz Alex, U-461.

Bottom right: Wilhelm Höffken, U-461.

Gerhard Korbjuhn, U-461.

Alois Momper, U-461.

Helmut Rochinski, U-461.

Alfred Weidermann, U-461.

our enemy was a vast and widening circle of flotsam, oil and many bodies. As we again ran in over the water, we could see no sign of the other two U-boats. Looking down we could see that many of the men were still alive and swimming. The sun threw a great shadow of our aircraft on the water and as the shadow crossed these swimmers, they paused to shake their fists at us.

'To us, safe above, these men were no longer the hated enemy. We felt sick at the carnage, as with every passing second the numbers in the water decreased, naked bodies slipped into the depths.

'A voice on the intercom, "For God's sake, can't we throw the poor devils a dinghy, skipper?" It spoke for us all, no thought of our own reduced chances of survival in an emergency. All our basic instincts cried out for us to help our fellow creatures who were now a pitiful small group.

'Down we sped again, a mission of mercy now, not destruction. Out went our rear dinghy. We watched as it hit the water near them, watched as the strongest swimmer struck out and reached it, watched breathlessly as he fumbled with the release valve and inflated the dinghy. Seven survivors reached the dinghy and managed to clamber aboard, seven men out of some seventy-odd. The time was now 8.15 am.

'We now climbed higher to regain radio contact and stayed over the dinghy homing a naval rescue force by radio. At 9 am five Ju88s flew in low out of the sun and circled the dinghy. They obviously thought they were RAF survivors because of the dinghy pattern and went on their way, probably feeling smugly satisfied that the U-boats had claimed yet another victim. Had it not been for the dinghy attracting their attention, no doubt they would have seen us high above them, despite Hanbury dodging into some sparse cloud. We may have had to join our vanquished foe. Not a happy thought with one dinghy short.

'Of the seven survivors picked up from our dinghy by the Navy, four were officers, including the captain. Our skipper received the DFC and our front gunner the DFM, richly deserved in each case for great courage. We were all delighted to receive a personal message of thanks from the grateful captain of U-607 safely in a PoW camp. This reward we treasured most of all.'

Hanbury's D/Cs had indeed exploded around them, causing U-607 to break its back. As Hanbury turned he saw the bows of his target blown right off. Jeschonnek was on the bridge of his boat. Also on deck with him had been his first officer, his 3rd officer and coxswain. Manning the guns had been three men on the quad 20 mm, with a supply man. Two men had been on the single 20 mm, each with a supply man, as well as the boat's gunnery officer,

Leutnant zur See Gassaver and a sailor to clear empty cartridges, plus two others to hoist ammunition. There was also the port and starboard lookouts. In the attack some of these men were killed, the others going into the sea. A few escaped from inside the submarine but only a few. None of these were wearing life jackets and quickly drowned. The U-boat went down almost immediately, leaving about 25 men in the water.

As Clutterbuck made a turn, he saw eight men swimming in the sea and a spreading oil patch 200 feet across. On circling again he saw more men in the sea. His attack had been on U-455 which in the event was undamaged. Whether the men they saw in the water were some of the gun's crew swept overboard, or left on the top is unclear, or perhaps he confused the survivors of U-607 with his attack on U-455.

The Commanding Officer of 53 Squadron, Wing Commander H.R.G. Edwards AFC, was on patrol in the Musketry area and had been ordered to home on the U-boats. When he arrived he saw only the dinghy with the survivors in it, floating in a large patch of oil. As they circled, with other aircraft which arrived, and saw too a number of twin-engined, single fin aircraft circling nearby, but they then disappeared. Edwards then saw a U-boat below but this quickly crash-dived. The 2nd Escort Group that had also arrived were making an Asdic search when Edwards reached PLE.

The survivors drifted throughout the day, but were finally rescued early on the 14th by HMS *Wren* of the 2nd Escort Group. They were hailed at first and asked the number of their U-boat. The Germans refused to give it but were then told, 'No number, no rescue!' This speedily decided Jeschonnek to give the number and the whaler from the *Wren* then picked them up. The 2nd Escort Group then returned to Plymouth leaving the Bay clear of Navy surface vessels until the 21st.

Leutnant Wolf Jeschonnek's 24th birthday ended in disaster. He had been with U-607 since her commissioning, as first officer for three patrols, and commander for two. He had previously served in mine-sweepers. He was also superstitious and had had a premonition of disaster. As he later told his captors, the loss of a favourite cap, worn on all his previous engagements which he had regarded as a talisman, blown overboard on the 12th, was the cause of his premonition.

Later, the commander of U-455 reported the loss of U-607. He also criticised the scheme of sailing in groups of more than two on the grounds that delay in transmitting orders constituted a grave danger. Close formation he felt, was too clumsy when air attacks and open formation made it too difficult for the senior officer of the group to judge the most favourable opportunity for diving. For his part, Dönitz was not totally convinced and so the three boat groups were continued.

On the evening of the 13th, Flight Lieutenant Baird of 461 Squadron found a U-boat 80 miles north of the morning's action. This boat – U-603 inbound – had crash-dived on the Sunderland's approach. A good attack failed to damage the submarine, although oil was seen on the surface for over an hour and a number of seagulls circled over the spot for a long time.

> 'Skipper Hanbury was a great character who when not flying usually trundled around Pembroke Dock on his bicycle. He was quite tall and invariably had a sweater draped over his shoulders with the sleeves knotted around his neck. Unfortunately I missed his second U-boat attack by hours, due to my 1,000 hour first tour of ops rest having been reached. Hank Hanbury had flown Empire Flying Boats pre-war and often when we were patrolling down as far as Lisbon (a wonderful spectacle, ablaze with light at night), he would jokingly say if the old girl ('N' 228) packed up, we could ditch on the River Tagus and be interned in Portugal for the rest of the war in comfort.
>
> 'Hank said he had all the right addresses in Lisbon and we would not go short!!! On the serious side, Hank was a born leader and I, amongst many others, am proud to have known and flown with him. This, of course, equally applies to the "N" 228 crew during my time with them.'
>
> *Flight Sergeant G.D. Williames, 228 Squadron.*

After 13th July there were few U-boats crossing the Bay until nearer the end of the month, but most that did were sighted and attacked by air patrols. Three outward and four inbound were attacked while three more inbound submarines were seen only.

Early on the 14th, a Ju88 was encountered by the crew of Flying Officer B.A. Williams of 10 Australian Squadron, flying on a parallel course. It turned to attack the Sunderland, opening fire at 900 yards. The Australian mid-ships gunner returned fire, scoring hits on the 88's wing, but cloud prevented too serious a contest developing.

The next day U-558, commanded by Kapitänleutnant Günther Krech, on her tenth patrol, was spotted and attacked off Cape Rocaby by 179 Squadron. An experienced U-boat man, Krech was 29 years old and had been in the Navy since 1935, having initially trained as a pilot in the Naval Air Arm. He transferred to U-boats when war began. In September 1942 he was awarded the Knight's Cross, after his sinking tonnage reached 130,000 tons (some 20 ships, including a corvette and an armed trawler) .

U-558 had been out since 8th May to the North Atlantic, then south to the Azores. When the Wellington attacked it was met by return fire. Krech was keen on fighting back and trained his gunners accordingly. Although the Wellington was not badly hit, it caused the crew to miss with its D/Cs and then Krech dived below the waves.

No 10 Australian Squadron sighted two U-boats on the 16th – U-43 and U-403, both outbound. Flight Lieutenant R.C.W. Humble was circling in cloud, and then dived. The two U-boats had separated slightly but then came together, meeting the Sunderland with concentrated fire. Circling again, Humble seized another opportunity to attack the nearest boat, his exploding D/Cs blowing several sailors overboard. Then the submarine submerged, undamaged, the other boat also going under.

That evening Flying Officer J.G. Grant of 502 Squadron was attacked by four Ju88s out of the sun off the Spanish coast. Grant jettisoned the anti-submarine bombs as his gunners began defensive fire. The rear gunner fired at one 88 as it closed from 500 to 100 yards when it broke away. Other attacks were pressed home but finally one was hit by the front and rear gunner at point blank range. Smoke came from the fighter and two of the crew were seen to bale out and later only three 88s were seen as they flew off. The Halifax (JD178 'V') was holed in the fuselage but not seriously damaged.

Krech was picked up again on the 17th, his U-558 being seen by 224 Squadron's Commanding Officer, Wing Commander Clouston, out from Gibraltar. At 2.33 the contact came at 18 miles and later the submarine was seen through binoculars despite a rain squall.

Clouston came in to meet heavy flak and the Liberator was hit several times. Keeping a steady run-up, Clouston dropped 24 anti-submarine bombs and two strong concussions were felt. His rear gunner, however, saw nothing positive but strafed the boat as they flew over.

Clouston pulled round to approach U-558 from astern, seeing diesel oil streaming from the left side of the boat which then began a turn to the left. As she turned, U-558 began a roll to the left and started to dive at a sharp angle. Günther Krech believed the Liberator had used all its bombs, hence his decision to dive but Clouston had another stick. As his bomb aimer took aim, part of the U-boat could still be seen and gunners were still firing from the bridge. The bombs were dropped, but twelve hung-up and the first twelve overshot. As the U-boat went under, some of the Liberator crew saw that two German gunners had remained at their guns until too late. Clouston circled, seeing oil and bubbles which continued for seventeen minutes and by the time he flew off the patch was several hundred yards across. However, U-558 was far from dead.

Ju88s were active on the 18th, attacking a Liberator of 224 Squadron mid-morning, flown by Flying Officer J.V. Gibson, right in the middle of the Bay. Three Ju88s came in and worked their way round to get up-sun. The load of anti-submarine bombs were jettisoned, then two more Ju88s arrived. The five 88s now positioned themselves for attack.

Two flew ahead, one flew to each side and one dead astern. Then the two on each quarter began the battle, Gibson weaving the Liberator to and fro, preventing both 88s making a simultaneous pass. The RAF gunners returned fire and the 88s seemed reluctant to come in too close. Some damage was caused to the Liberator, but most of the dozen or so attacks proved ineffective. Only three 88s were now visible and one of these was then hit by the rear and mid-upper gunners – white smoke, possibly glycol, streamed out and when last seen the fighter was going down towards the sea in a controlled dive. Finally only two 88s made a few more attacks, then Gibson reached the safety of some cloud.[5]

A couple of hours later a 53 Squadron Liberator piloted by Flight Lieutenant A.J. Dewhirst, requested a fix while in the Musketry area. While this was being done the aircraft radioed an SOS – then silence. Had the Ju88s at last gained a success? Yes they had. KG40 shot down the Lib (BZ731 'D') claimed by the same pilot who had damaged Gibson's machine.

Just before 8 am on the 19th, a 461 Squadron had a brush with enemy fighters, battling with Me410s. That evening a 59 Squadron Liberator over Seaslug, flown by Flight Lieutenant E.E. Allen found a surfaced U-boat at eight miles. She began to take evasive action and opened fire with her 20 mm cannon. Allen circled, his waist and tail gunners blazing away with their .5 guns, but the Liberator was hit in the port wing. Allen climbed to 3,500 feet and made a stern to bow attack but the attempt overshot. Allen then pretended to fly off, only to fly back at low level to machine-gun the submarine. She too opened fire and one of Allen's gunners was wounded. The last D/C fell 100 feet ahead of the target. Finally Allen flew off; his aircraft had been hit ten times.

The boat had been the inbound U-667 commanded by Heinrich Schröteler, and it showed how the lack of a front gun in some Liberators was proving a problem. HQCC were aware of the problem but resolving it was not proving too speedy a process.

* * *

Meanwhile, Kapitänleutnant Günther Krech in U-558 was still homeward bound, despite a narrow escape to Wing Commander Clouston on the 17th. (On his boat's conning tower was painted a badge depicting the head of a man in profile with a finger laid alongside its nose.) He was almost through the Musketry area – 4510/0940 – but at 12.18 pm he was spotted yet again. This time it was a Liberator crew of the 19th USAAF Squadron that saw him.

The two American squadrons, the 4th and the 19th, had begun operations over the Bay just one week earlier and already, on the 18th, the 4th Squadron had dropped D/Cs on a diving U-boat in two attacks.

Lieutenant Charles F. Gallimeir from Fort Wayne, Indiana, was flying at 2,000 feet when they got a S/E contact on U-558. At 12.15 pm they saw a wake, then the U-boat, on the surface five miles dead ahead. Gallimeir immediately went into an attack approach from the port quarter.

---

[5] Gibson and his crew failed to return from a patrol on 2nd September 1943 after reporting presence of enemy fighters. In the above encounter the Lib was claimed as damaged by 14/KG40.

The attack caught the crew of U-558 by complete surprise. One moment the sky was clear, the next the seemingly huge Liberator was hurtling towards them at 600 feet. They had had no warning on radar or radio. The hands were relaxed, not expecting an attack. On suddenly seeing the aircraft, the officer of the watch yelled the order: 'Hard a'starboard – utmost speed!'

Due to the sudden panic, the rating, instead of obeying this order, stopped both engines completely. The alarm bell then sounded. Efforts were made to use the engines but they failed to function. The boat became a sitting target. Even the gunners did not react until the Liberator was almost passing over them. When they did fire it was from just two light guns aft of the conning tower.

Gallimeir's navigator opened fire with the front guns, scoring hits, followed by top turret and waist gunners. The late fire from the U-boat, however, hit the aircraft in the port inner engine and left waist position, wounding the gunner in one leg. But the stick of seven D/Cs were going down, exploding close along U-558's port side, the seventh splashing by the bow.

More flak came up as the U-boat and the Liberator's rear gunner exchanged fire while Gallimeir circled, intending to make a second attack. But at that moment the damaged port inner engine cut and could not be feathered. At the same moment a RAF Halifax was seen approaching. Looking at the U-boat, the Americans could see it rolling heavily. The boat was down by the stern, only its bows and conning tower visible, and as the Liberator flew by the left waist gunner sprayed what could be seen.

On the submarine, the gunners had made an attempt to man the 20 mm gun on the 'bandstand' and despite the difficult angle, one or two hits were made. Certainly the Germans saw a flash of flame come from it. The 20 mm gun on the lower bandstand also got in some fire as the Liberator began a wide banking turn. They were then depth-charged. It was at that moment that the Halifax came up.

At first the Halifax, flown by Flight Lieutenant G.A. Sawtell of 58 Squadron, merely exchanged gunfire with U-558, as the boat commenced tight circles. Then some of the crew began climbing onto the fore-deck but a number were hit by the Halifax gunners and fell into the sea. By now the submarine was settling in the water and Sawtell flew in to drop eight D/Cs from 50 feet. U-558 keeled over, twelve feet of bow visible through the spray of the D/Cs. Bodies were thrown up into the air. 'We thought they were preparing to man the guns,' said Sawtell later, 'so we raked the deck with our guns, shooting some off the deck and driving the rest for cover. Then when our depth charge plumes had risen, some of my crew saw debris, and bodies rise into the air on the crest of the plumes. Later there was nothing but five or six men in a dinghy with a few others swimming around it.' [6]

---

(6) *Coastal Command Leads the Invasion* op cit.

Moments before Sawtell attacked, the U-boat's guns fell silent as ammunition ran out. No more could be hoisted because water had now got into the boat's batteries, filling the inside of the hull with deadly chlorine gas.

Gallimeir had flown off, jettisoning his final D/Cs, heading for home on three engines, which he reached safely. Sawtell circled as the U-boat went down, leaving 40 to 50 bodies in the water, dead and alive. Six of the survivors got into a dinghy that had been launched, some 30 others all trying to hang on to its side. Then Geoff Sawtell flew back to base.

Left in the now silent sea, most of the German survivors went under or died mostly as a result of their bad gassing. Next morning only eight men remained, and hoping to reach the Spanish coast. On the 23rd, another man died after drinking sea water. Then two more died. An unidentified aircraft dropped them a canister of fresh water on the 24th (probably Squadron Leader Terence Bulloch of 224 Squadron who dropped emergency packs to five men he found in a dinghy). On the 25th the five men were picked up by the Canadian warship *Athabascan*. [7]

They comprised two officers, including Krech who had been wounded in two places, and three ratings. Gallimeir was credited with the kill and was decorated for his action. Geoffrey Sawtell too was rewarded with the DFC. His rear gunner, Sergeant Banks Mitchell and mid-upper Pilot Officer Robert Marshal, received the DFM and DFC respectively.

Before Krech finally gave the order to abandon ship, he had signalled B.d.U. informing them of his plight. Dönitz sent surface and air escorts out while U-193 and U-195, returning from the Cape and in the vicinity were asked to go to her assistance. They had, however, been sighted themselves by three aircraft and their attentions kept them below. Ju88s were delayed by bad weather and when two torpedo boats finally reached the area, there was no sign of U-558.

* * *

During this week in July and following the arrival of USAAF squadrons, Bomber Command's No 10 OTU ceased their attachment to Coastal Command's control. They had begun the attachment in August 1942 and until 9th July 1943, the crews had flown 16,455 operational flying hours from St Eval.

Ostensibly they were, of course, a training unit so their crews, almost ready to join an operational bomber squadron, only flew a few operations prior to this posting. Thus they did not gain experience in A/U activities. Nevertheless they had a good record. They had made 89 U-boat sightings, attacked 55, sunk two and damaged three. The cost was 50 aircraft, many lost due to flying hazard and temperamental engines on their Whitley aircraft.

---

[7] The *Athabascan*, *Iroquois* and *Orkan* comprised Force W. They had been on their way home to Plymouth when they picked up U-558's survivors.

* * *

On 22nd July, a fair but hazy day in the Bay, three Beaufighters of 248 Squadron took off at 6.13 am. One crew had to return with engine trouble but the other two carried on. An hour and a half later the two crews, Flight Lieutenant J.C. Newbury/Flying Officer D. Allcock and Flying Officer F.S. Lacy/Warrant Officer G.G.Harker spotted not aircraft, but a U-boat.

As the two pilots altered course and climbed to 100 feet, the U-boat opened fire from an aft gun. Lacy made a shallow dive and fired at the conning tower, the submarine altering course to port still firing from the aft gun. Newbury did not attack as he was uncertain of their exact position. He knew there was a British submarine in the vicinity and decided not to go in. Lacy formated on his leader and they continued on their patrol. In fact they had found and attacked U-664, outbound, and while some damage may have been inflicted, it did not prevent her from continuing her patrol, from which she later failed to return.

That afternoon a Canadian Sunderland of 423 Squadron (DD680) piloted by Flight Lieutenant J. Musgrave, met a FW200.[8] 423 had a detachment at Pembroke Dock, flying Seaslug patrols. At 2.05 pm his rear gunner saw the four-engined Focke Wulf behind them. It opened fire, damaging the flying boat's hydraulics. The Canadian gunner's turret was then out of action and he was slightly injured in the face, while the second pilot was wounded in the arm. The front gunner too was hit and wounded in the right knee.

Musgrave's trim controls were shot away, the port carburettor cock and port jettison control damaged while two D/Cs were hit by ricochets. Musgrave finally managed to pull up into cloud and escape. With damage to the flying boat's hull below the water line. Musgrave had to land close to the slipway and taxi to it very quickly. 'All was well,' the squadron diary recorded. 'Perfect handling in the true Musgrave style.' Johnny Musgrave received the DFC later that autumn.

> *Flight Sergeant D. Kneale, 228 Squadron:*
> It was certainly a very hectic and eventful time and it required an all-out effort on the part of both aircrew and ground staff to keep the ball rolling. During this period my heart used to go out to the ground staff, the fitters, the riggers, armourers, and all the various other tradesmen who worked round the clock to keep us flying – and I do mean round the clock. There was one occasion I recall when two Sunderlands had been so damaged in combat they appeared only fit for the scrapyard. But one was damaged to the fore and the other to the rear – and somebody's brains began to tick and work overtime. Yes you've got it, they split them in half, joined them together and made one serviceable aircraft. And that is how "Half and Half" came in to being and went back on ops.

---

[8] John Musgrave had shared the sinking of U-456 on 13th May 1943 while defending an Atlantic convoy.

'In the midst of all the pressures all round there was, however, always something to create a laugh and help ease the tension. One can think of dozens of such incidents but in my view the off the cuff or unconscious humour incident beats the lot. If I were asked to recall what gave me my biggest laugh during that hectic period I would quote the following incident.

'A new sergeant navigator was posted to the squadron and he proved particularly unpopular. There was no give and take with him; he behaved in a rather superior manner. In next to no time at all he applied for a commission and was accepted (God knows why), and off he went to Officers' Training Unit. The bloke hadn't been in the RAF five minutes! In due course back he came in all his new sprog regalia, snootier and more aloof than ever.

'The event I now recall happened before my very eyes and I can vouch for it being genuine. It was lunch time and the ground staff were literally crawling their way from the hangars, workshops and slipways. They had been working flat out round the clock for weeks and were absolutely shattered, just slouching along. One in particular seemed to be walking in his sleep, eyes down and oblivious to anyone or anything about him. I don't think he even realised he was passing Squadron HQ. In retrospect I think it is now generally accepted that under the pressures we were in those days, bull and red tape went out the window. Getting on with the job was what really mattered.

'But to get back to our lonely seemingly insignificant little erk! As he passed HQ, our new Pilot Officer appeared from round the corner and was approaching the airman. The poor little fellow didn't see him, his eyes, if open, were on the ground. That is to say until our new sprog officer began to rollick him for not saluting.

"You must always recognise and acknowledge the King's commission at all times in the manner in which you have been trained. So that you don't forget in future you will stand there and salute me ten times."

'My heart went out to that poor little chap, standing there in all his grime and grease, pumping his right arm up and down to satisfy this pimp of an officer.

'But unbeknown to any of us this strange state of affairs was being observed through his upstairs window by the Commanding Officer. He opened the window and asked, "What on earth is going on down there?"

"Oh, it's this airman sir, he passed me without saluting. To teach him a lesson I have ordered him to salute me ten times." "Is that so!" replied the Commanding Officer. "Well, when you have been an officer a little bit longer you may come to realise that it is always the done thing for an officer to return a salute. Will you kindly do so now?"

'One could see the faint smile on his face as he said this, the smile becoming even wider as he stood at his window watching the two of them standing there facing each other, their arms pumping up and down like mad. There was considerably more bounce in that airman's step as he walked away. The story obviously went round the officers' mess as it did throughout the whole base, and it came as no surprise when within a very short time our sprog was posted away from the squadron. And good riddance too!'

CHAPTER EIGHT

GO IN AND SINK THEM

Coastal Command, still very much on the crest of a wave in the Bay, was nevertheless aware that there had been a number of occasions when groups of U-boats had been located but escaped. This was due either through delays in getting other aircraft to the scene, or to failure in co-ordinating the actions of those that did arrive.

R/T performance left much to be desired and some navigation so poor that positions of sightings, rather than helping HQ planners, actually confused them. These problems were tackled by the appropriate branches at squadron level, but this took time, and time Slessor felt sure, was not on his side. Dönitz must surely see the error in his tactics soon. So, in the short term, Slessor issued an immediate signal on 22nd July to his three air groups. He cancelled the previous instructions which required a sighting aircraft to shadow two or more U-boats and begin a homing routine, until more aircraft arrived. Instead, a sighting aircraft must henceforth attack at once, using to the full his front guns to smother the flak. This was fine in theory but as we have already seen, not all anti-submarine aircraft 'bristled' with front guns, and certainly not heavy guns when duelling with 20 mm cannon and 37 mm guns.

Experience, however, had shown that U-boat groups seldom remained on the surface while being shadowed. Fighting it out when attacked was one thing. Waiting around for the attackers to multiply, was quite another.

So, from the 22nd, it was to be a question of attack first, home in other aircraft afterwards, by which time some damage might have been already inflicted. But to whom, must have been a thought going through the minds of many aircrew – the U-boat or the aircraft! There was a school of thought that flak from three U-boats was no more formidable than from one. This statement too might have been questioned by aircrew at the sharp end!

Following an initial attack, when homing procedure commenced, Group HQ would also ensure the area was saturated for the rest of the day and the night, even at the expense of other parts of Seaslug and Musketry areas. Except on these occasions, not more than six Leigh Light aircraft would be assigned during the hours of darkness, the other Leigh Light aircraft flying in support of daylight aircraft.

* * *

During the period 21-27th July, there were never more than two or three singleton U-boats crossing the air patrol areas. Also on the 21st, the cruiser HMS *Glasgow* entered the Bay areas as additional support. The Navy had Escort Group B5 in the area at this time, now including the escort carrier *Archer*, sailing on the western edge of Musketry North. She carried Swordfish and Martlet (Wildcat) aircraft, that carried out patrols until the 26th but they failed to make any sightings.

The aircraft of KG40 were active, several Ju88s being seen and one FW200 was attacked by Martlets but it reached cloud safely. The Navy also had Force W in the Bay area, to the south-east of Musketry between 20th and 24th July, but all they saw was one FW200.

On the 24th, one of only three U-boats in the Musketry area was spotted by a Wellington of 172 Squadron. The account of what happened was related afterwards by the sole survivor of the Wellington, Sergeant A.A. Turner.

Turner was the aircraft's rear gunner, his pilot being Flying Officer W.H.T. Jennings, out on a day, rather than night patrol. They were at the bottom of their patrol leg and about to turn on the short westerly course leg when the 10 cm radar picked up a contact, six miles to starboard. Jennings was in cloud at 1,000 feet, letting down to come out five miles away. Dead ahead was a surfaced U-boat.

The boat was U-459, a Type XIV tanker submarine of 1,688 tons, commanded by Korvettenkapitän Georg von Wilamowitz-Möllendorf. She had sailed from Bordeaux at 9.30 am on the 21st on her sixth war cruise, to the Atlantic. She remained at the mouth of the Gironde the next day where she was joined by U-117 (Korvettenkapitän Hans Neumann). U-461, another tanker, commanded by Korvettenkapitän Wolf Stiebler also arrived but had to put back to Bordeaux when his boat developed a leak.

In order to get this supply boat, which was urgently required in the Atlantic to re-supply existing wolf-packs, Dönitz had ordered a destroyer escort for U-459 and U-117, as far as 46°N/10°W, nearly 200 miles north-west of Ortegal. The escort had only left these two boats that same morning. She was now in position 4553/1038 – the time 5.50 pm.

She carried a heavy defensive armament. One 37 mm gun, one quadruple 20 mm and two single 20 mm cannon; and twin Type 81 heavy machine guns. On her previous cruise U-459 had shot down an attacking 10 OTU Whitley.

As Jennings headed into the attack he remarked to his crew that it looked as if the submarine was going to stay and fight but told them he was still going in. Dropping to 100 feet, the U-boat began to put up a veritable barrage of gunfire. Unknown to Jennings, he had almost caught U-459 by complete surprise and despite the heavy fire, the gunners did not have time to get their 20 mm quad gun going. Ratings were still trying to get ammunition up through the conning tower when there was a tremendous explosion.

In his rear turret, facing aft, Sergeant Turner noticed pieces of the Wellington's fuselage being shot away by the U-boat's fire, the pieces passing by his position. In those moments Jennings was either killed or wounded. Then the Wellington went straight into the submarine's conning tower. Whether Jennings, mortally hit, had done this deliberately will never be known, but the next thing Turner remembers was that he was under the water, struggling to get to the surface.

On the U-boat, the Wellington smashed into the bandstand on the starboard side, carrying away one of the single 20 mm guns, then it slewed round into the quad gun, tearing it from its mounting.

Then the wreckage slithered away into the sea, but left on the deck some bits and pieces of wreckage and three depth charges. All the ratings abaft the bridge were killed in the impact, but others carefully rolled these D/Cs over the side but the slow speed of the boat failed to take her away from the resultant danger and as the D/Cs exploded, the boat was badly damaged aft. U-459 was left incapable of diving and out of control. The chief engineer quickly informed von Wilamowitz that the boat was finished and impossible to get underway.

Von Wilamowitz was reluctant to abandon ship, hoping the damage could be repaired. But his hopes were dashed when another aircraft came into view.

Turner came spluttering to the surface and kicked off his flying boots. There was an aircraft dinghy floating a short way off, beyond two burning oil fires. He swam to it and also saw a body which he believed was the second pilot. He climbed on top of the dinghy, which was upside-down. Looking round he saw the U-boat seemingly dead in the water, its crew on deck. As he watched he realized it was circling slowly, smoke pouring from its stern. Turner took off his Mae West and tried to attract their attention but he then realised the submarine was out of control. Certainly it came no nearer to him, which was perhaps just as well as things turned out. Turner righted the dinghy although he lost his coat and Mae West in the process. He then heard aero engines.

Flying Officer J. Whyte in his 547 Squadron Wellington spotted the damaged U-boat just on 6 pm. She was eight miles off, circling slowly, amid a widening patch of oil. Whyte went into the attack, his front gunner opening fire as they closed. Some desultory and ineffectual return fire came from the submarine. Seven D/Cs went down, one landing to starboard, the others to port. As the Wellington swooped over 50 feet above, the rear gunner raked the decks. As the D/Cs exploded, the stern of the U-boat lifted, then she rolled to starboard. The crew began pouring out of the conning tower and jumping into the sea as the boat went down. Twenty to thirty seconds later there was a violent explosion below the surface and several of the sailors in the water were blown into the air. When last seen there was about twenty to thirty men in the sea, joining up their dinghies to form a raft. As Whyte circled, they saw a section of wing from an RAF aeroplane and about 1$^1/_2$ miles off, a man in a dinghy – Sergeant Turner. They dropped some supplies but were not certain if they were recovered. They circled the area for over two hours, then had to return to base. After nine hours in his dinghy, Turner was picked up by a Polish destroyer ORP *Orken*[1] whose crew heard his shouts at 2.30 am on the 25th. The German survivors were also picked up by *Orken*.

They comprised five officers including the surgeon and 32 ratings. Von Wilamowitz was not among them. He had been the oldest surviving U-boat commander on active duty. Born in November 1893, he was 49 years old and had served in submarines during World War One. With U-459 he had supplied 75 times in his five cruises. The survivors told their rescuers that their commander had set demolition charges after they had abandoned ship. This was the explosion Whyte and his crew had seen. Von Wilamowitz had, however, gone down with his command.

'The incident regarding Flying Officer Jennings is very clear in my mind, as I could have been a member of same – but for a change of crews. Wellington "Q"'s crew was a scratch crew made up of three of Pilot Officer J.L. Tweddle's crew (Tweddle had just completed his tour) of which I was a member. Buxton (navigator) and Les Harrop (W/OP) needed only a few hours to complete their first tour and volunteered along with A.A. Turner. I had joined Pilot Officer Mumford's crew as first W/Op a few days previous, Mumford having returned from OTU with a green crew. I had known Mumford in Iceland with 612 Squadron and was pleased to complete my last 100 hours with him. "Ches" Turner had a lucky escape, finishing up in the turret under water, he started kicking and the bottom dropped out (lucky for him). On surfacing he found a single dinghy upside down (his day?) and scrambled inside. His next job was to make a distance between himself and the Germans abandoning the U-boat. Turner played for Charlton Athletic in the Cup Final after the war – quite remarkable.'

Flight Sergeant D.A. Radburn, 172 Squadron.

Pilot Officer D.L. Mumford of 172 Squadron was out over the Bay on the

---

[1] *Orken*, with the other two ships of Force W, had just rescued survivors of U-558 when they turned back to pick up Turner and U459's men.

24th, with Flight Sergeant Duncan Radburn in his crew. They picked up an S/E contact but it turned out to be six enemy aircraft. As they turned away one unidentified aircraft was seen astern but luckily they lost it in poor visibility.

With Force W having finally returned to Plymouth, Captain Walker's 2nd Escort Group returned to the Bay on the 25th. On this Sunday morning four Mosquitos of 264 Squadron were on patrol and came upon a twin-engined aircraft. As they identified it as a Wellington, they saw it drop its bombs, or D/Cs, and head away rapidly. Later a Wellington crew reported seeing four Ju88s, but the 3,000 rounds fired by the rear gunner had forced them away!

However, they were *real* Ju88s that found an American Liberator at noon on the 26th. Lieutenant Grider of the 19th US Squadron took evasive action into cloud, hotly pursued by nine Junkers. It took eleven minutes to reach the cloud during which time several attacks were made, but there was no damage. In all probability Ju88s also found a 304 Squadron Wellington flown by Flight Lieutenant S.J.Rolinski. They had flown out on patrol at 5.57 am and failed to return. The Wellington was claimed by KG40.

The following afternoon four Ju88s engaged Flying Officer Humble of 461 Squadron. They came in from all angles firing cannon and machine-guns. In one pass, Humble was hit and wounded but kept flying and achieved some fine evasive manoeuvres. One engine was also hit but when the fight ended, Humble's gunners claimed hits on three of the 88s, two being seen to trail smoke.

* * *

Wednesday, 28th July began five (of six) climactic days in the Bay, yet it did not start well. At 3 am Flight Lieutenant G.A. Davey of 53 Squadron took off on an early Musketry patrol. Thirty minutes later the Liberator crashed near Tisbury, Wiltshire. All the depth charges went off, and every member of the crew died instantly.

In the Bay on the 28th, were four outward and one inward-bound U-boats. At 11.37 am one of the outward boats, U-404, on her seventh patrol, under Oberleutnant Adolf Schönberg, was spotted by Major S.D. McElroy of the 4th US Squadron. She had sailed from St Nazaire on the 24th, this being Schönberg's first patrol as commander. McElroy brought his Liberator into the attack but his D/Cs hung-up. The American remained in the area, his patience being rewarded at 3.17 in the afternoon at which time the boat surfaced again. The U-boat's gunners opened fire on the antagonist, one 20 mm shell exploding inside the cockpit but miraculously no one was hurt. The shell passed through the co-pilot's fuse box, exploded behind the armoured plating and damaged the radio. The American gunners replied, seeing three men knocked off the bridge, but the boat was now diving. As it did so she commenced a turn to starboard, the right waist and rear gunners firing at the conning tower. McElroy approached from directly ahead and released eight D/Cs. The resulting explosions enveloped the swirl left by the diving boat. Oil began to stain the surface and it looked as if the boat had at least been damaged. McElroy found the oil pressure in No.3 engine falling and he suspected it had been damaged. Because of the damage to the fuse box, instruments for the No's 2 and 3 engines were useless. He returned safely to base, however.

Whether damaged or not from McElroy's attack, U-404 was found again at 5.45 pm by another 4th Squadron Liberator flown by First Lieutenant Arthur J. Hammer. Hammer had picked up a message about McElroy's attack at 4 o'clock and flew to the vicinity to investigate. Intercepting messages that indicated the U-boat had gone down, Hammer turned for home but at 5.52, flying at 4,000 feet, saw a surfaced U-boat, five miles away. He altered course in order to attack from out of the sun, from U-404's port beam. Eight D/Cs straddled the boat and as he turned to the left, so the U-boat also turned to the left. Hammer came round in a wide circle, commencing a second run from $2^1/_2$ miles. As he neared, so the U-boat's gunners began firing, with two guns aft of the conning tower. It was heavy but they failed to hit the Liberator. As they came within range the American front and top gunners began firing, hits being seen along the deck and two men fell overboard. On the second run, the front turret gun jammed and then the aircraft was hit in the port outer engine and it had to be feathered. Hits were also scored on the tail and fuselage. Then another Liberator came into view, Hammer turning for home.

The crew of Flying Officer Bob Sweeny's 224 Squadron Liberator had received word of a submarine and commenced a square search at 2.30 pm. They found nothing so continued on their original patrol line. Just past 6 pm, Sweeny saw exploding D/C plumes some 24 miles dead ahead and flew to investigate. The sea was calm, visibility was fairly good with only 1/10 cloud. The ASV Mark 5 was on but there was no radar contact until after the sighting. As Sweeny headed in, more D/C plumes were seen, now eleven miles ahead. Then he picked out the submarine and Hammer's Liberator circling at around 6-700 feet. As Sweeny got to within 1,000 yards, the U-boat's gunners opened fire.

'Flying Officer Bob Sweeny and crew were briefed to operate Liberator W/224 on a patrol in the Bay of Biscay. After sighting a 740 ton U-boat Bob made a direct attack, releasing 7 x 250 lb Torpex D/Cs. During the run-up we were under heavy and sustained fire from the U-boat, the starboard outer engine was hit and seized. We were just able to see that our attack had been successful, but our immediate concern was our own predicament. At this time we were flying at about 15 to 20 feet, apparently unable to gain height and Bob ordered me to commence the radio distress procedure. I was able to make immediate W/T contact with HQ 19 Group at Plymouth, giving them details of our situation and position. I now had a nasty suspicion that my planned 21st birthday party (July 29th) instead of a riotous party with the "boys" would, at best, comprise a few Horlicks tablets in a heaving rubber dinghy.'

Flight Sergeant E.S. Cheek, 224 Squadron.

As Sweeny struggled by U-404, the mid-upper gunner saw their D/C straddle perfectly and just forward of the conning tower, the No 3 splash being very close to the starboard side, No 4 close to the port side.

Sweeny pulled round to the left, the mid-upper watching the target and the explosions. The boat had disappeared but then immediately re-appeared on an even keel as if she had been forced to the surface by the explosions. Almost at once the U-boat went down again, still on an even keel, but not in a normal diving attitude. When the water had settled down there was a good deal of floating debris and about ten bodies in life belts. 224 Squadron had finished off U-404, but Sweeny's troubles were not over:

'Things had become fairly frantic, as attempts were made to lighten the aircraft. Guns, belts of ammunition and all loose impedimenta (sadly including the flight engineer's prized toolbox) were consigned to the deep via the open bomb doors and beam hatches. Having spent many hundreds of hours being mesmerised by the revolving time base of the ASV Mark V, I very generously offered to disconnect the main heavy units and deep six them; sadly my generous offer was declined by Bob – no doubt it would serve as a useful navigation aid when (if) we returned to the coast. After about 15 minutes of fearful uncertainty, our flight engineer (Ken Owen) returned to the flight deck, where he was able to rectify omissions on the part of our "drivers" and normal flight was resumed, albeit on three engines. We were instructed to land at the neighbouring airfield at St Mawgan, which offered a very long runway, no doubt deemed more appropriate for a relatively inexperienced pilot making a 3-engined landing.

'It was a fairly common practice in the squadron to cast envious eyes on the possessions of other aviators and ask, "Can I have that when you get the chop?" (it was always "when" and never "if"). Having spent some six months in the States during 1942 many of my effects were unavailable in wartime UK, and I was subject to many such requests. After landing at St Mawgan, we drove over to St Eval for debriefing and a meal. I then went to the hotel in which we were accommodated only to find that many of my prized possessions had disappeared, it seemed that everybody had heard my SOS. It took me some time to reclaim my possessions from the very embarrassed, temporary custodians, who all assured me that they were delighted that I was safe – but did they really mean it? Bob Sweeny was soon awarded the DFC, and left the squadron in November 1943, when our co-pilot, Perry Allan, assumed the captaincy.'

Flight Sergeant E. Cheek, 224 Squadron.

Eddie Cheek recalls Bob Sweeny:

'Robert Sweeny was an American by birth, the grandson of a mining magnate. He was educated at Oxford and was a fine amateur golfer, becoming the UK Amateur Golf Champion in 1937. He lived in England and rnay be said to be an Anglo-American. Together with his brother Charles he formed the Eagle Squadron of American pilots who flew with Fighter Command. Bob was a grand chap, not at all ostentatious, in spite of the lofty circles in which he moved. I was told, but cannot confirm, that he was known to the Royal Family by his christian name. However, I do recall an occasion when Bob took the crew to dinner in the Dorchester; at a nearby table I noticed a very senior naval officer with reams of gold lace on his sleeve. I asked Bob if he could identify this distinguished naval officer, and he said, "Oh, that's Mountbatten." Very shortly Mountbatten walked over to our table and said, "Hello Bob, what's this, a crew party?" Bob replied, addressing him as Dickie, we were most impressed. Bob died, aged 72, in 1983.

'Perhaps my most hair raising experience occurred during a period when my crew were non-effective, (probably due to sickness) and I volunteered to fill-in on other crews. On 9th September 1943 I was flying with Pilot Officer E.T. Batchelor in A/224 on an anti-submarine patrol. We were engaged by six Ju88s for about 25 minutes, when Batch managed to insinuate the aircraft into a small cumulus cloud, and did his very best to remain within it. We could have stayed there all day! However, after about 20 minutes out we popped, only to find that our friends had hung around, this was not our lucky day. After 15 minutes of attacks by the Ju88s, I could see, from the tail turret, that five of our assailants were in orbit astern, and we assumed that we had destroyed one of them, which in fact was later confirmed. My abiding memories of this sortie are:

(a) how lonely and remote it was for the tail gunner, and I can now appreciate the German psychological approach of keeping all crew members in one compartment.

(b) when the engagement commenced my first thought, irrelevant though it was, was the fact that I had been let down, here I was, a member of the strongest air force in the world, and they had allowed such an unequal contest to occur.

(c) I distinctly heard the engine noise of a Ju88 as it flashed over the tail, after a head-on attack. This may seem unlikely, so let me assure you it is not a figment of inaccurate senile nostalgia.

'On another occasion our crew, under the captaincy of Bob Sweeny had come to the top of the stand by list, and we were called into the Operations Rooms.

'The briefing map display showed a patrol area very close to the French coast, obviously a task for the fighter boys. The briefing started and we were more than surprised to find that we had been looking at our patrol. Of course nothing was said, but the concern, or was it fear, was palpable. It seemed to us that the patrol area was within German radar coverage and our intrusion there could only be a sacrificial offering. No time had been ordered for take off, and our very subdued crew just hung around the Operations Room. For myself, I had a very strong desire to meet the "clown" at Coastal Command HQ who had ordered such a Kamikaze sortie.

'After some time, the senior operations officer called us together to tell us that Wing Commander Clouston had ordered another crew to carry out this sortie, as he considered that our crew lacked the experience. Our delight was soon followed by a feeling of outrage; we were as good, if not better, than any other crew in the squadron, or even the command. We insisted that as we were the prime standby crew this sortie was ours, and ours alone. While we were pressing our point, a signal arrived from HQ Coastal Command cancelling the operation.

'In retrospect it demonstrates the fragility of courage, the slur cast on our professional ability was enough to change us from the apprehensive to the "gung ho". My God, how stupid we were.'

Flight Sergeant E. Cheek, 224 Squadron.

Two other outward-bound U-boats were sighted by a US Navy Catalina of VP63 Squadron. Lieutenant Parker saw both boats at 3.50 pm but they submerged. Beginning homing procedures, two RAF Sunderlands joined him but little could be seen. At 4.10, Parker dropped his 30 x 35lb contact bombs in a pattern, but without results. They had seen but not damaged U-760 and U-262.

VP63 Squadron was a recent American reinforcement for the Bay battle. It was equipped with MAD (Magnetic Anomoly Detection) which could detect a submarine down to 400 feet below the aircraft. When released on receipt of a positive magnetic indication, the 'retro-bombs' could be propelled backwards so they would fall vertically from the aircraft in a salvo pattern with no forward momentum travel – hence 'retro-bombs'.

* * *

German fighters always seemed motivated by losses in the submarine arm of the Navy. The following day, Thursday the 29th, a FW200 was seen by a 502 Squadron Halifax, flown by Flying Officer John Grant DFC. Grant was no stranger to enemy aircraft – his fight against Ju88s was still fresh in his mind from the 16th. They were north-west of Cape Finisterre at 7.30 am when they saw it, Grant turning his aircraft to engage. His gunners fired four bursts from 800 to 100 yards, before the Focke Wulf escaped in mist and was lost.

As this action was happening the Commanding Officer of 172 Squadron, Wing Commander R. G. Musson, was heading his Wellington towards Bishop's Rock and the Bay. Rowland Musson was a pre-war pilot, and had been boss of 172 Squadron since March 1943.

At around 10.45, while at 1,200 feet in cloud, his radar operator picked up a contact on his centimetric set. It was on a bearing of 45°, six and a half miles in position 4642/1103 – 275 miles north-west of Cape Ortegal. From its appearance on the radar screen, it was thought probable the submarine – if that's what it was – was surfacing.

Musson made a turn but remained in cloud until just three-quarters of a mile from the contact. It was almost like their more usual night attacks. When finally Musson broke cloud, there ahead was a fully surfaced U-boat on a course of 260°, travelling at 10 knots. In accordance with instructions, the front gunner immediately opened fire on the submarine, although there was no sign of anyone on the bridge. Musson brought his Wellington over the boat in a gentle glide, releasing six D/Cs from 50 feet at an angle of 135° to the boat's track. The rear gunner watched them explode, forming a perfect straddle, four to one side, two the other, Nos 4 and 5 exploding in close. The rear gunner fired into the explosions as Musson began a turn to the right. As they came back over the spot the U-boat had gone. All there was was a turbulent patch of water, then several men could be seen swimming about in the sea, wearing yellow life-jackets and some with yellow skull caps. Most were either waving – or shaking their fists! Musson circled for fifteen minutes then resumed patrol. It had been a perfect surprise attack, unhindered by defensive gunfire or a crash-dive. Unhappily Musson and three of his crew had less than a month to live.

Their victim had been U-614 – Kapitänleutnant Wolfgang Sträter. They had sailed from St Nazaire on the 25th for a patrol in the Atlantic. It had been U-614's third war patrol.

* * *

During the first hour after noon, Beaufighters of 248 Squadron were down in the area where 502 Squadron had met the FW200 earlier that day. The patrol was led by Flying Officer P.A.S. Payne/Flying Officer A.M. McNichol, with Flying Officer J.K. Thompson/Sergeant G.F. Barnes, Flying Offficer Lacy/Warrant Officer Harker, and Lieutenant Newman/Flying Officer Cochrane. At 12.19 pm they saw a FW200 in position 4530/0906, 120 miles north-west of Ortegal. Payne immediately turned and followed by the other three, attacked. Payne hammered a long burst of cannon from 300 yards from the Focke Wulf's port quarter, scoring hits on its port wing root and cockpit. As he then curved in behind the enemy 'plane he fired a long burst from 150 yards and both port engines caught fire.

As Payne broke away, Flying Officer Johnny Thompson attacked, firing bursts into the big aeroplane but because of the volume of smoke pouring back from the port engines could not see results. Just as Lacy was about to fire Lieutenant Newman cut ahead of him. The FW200 was now gliding gently towards the sea, Newman opening fire, scoring hits on the starboard inner engine. The Kondor was now skimming along the surface of the sea, then pancaked onto the water. Eight men were seen swimming around the aeroplane that had stopped burning and was still floating when the Mosquitos flew off.

Just over half an hour after this bit of excitement Payne sighted another aircraft, identified as a Ju88. The four RAF fighters turned towards it, a white five-star cartridge being fired by the German, as the 88 began a climb towards some cloud. Johnny Thompson, however, cut it off and making a steep climbing turn, attacked the 88 from below. A long burst smashed the German's port engine which burst into flames. The Junkers went into a steep diving turn to the left, pieces falling away from the doomed fighter. The flames spread and within seconds the whole machine was a blazing mass. Then it hit the sea and disappeared, leaving only a burning patch of oil on the sea.

Return fire from the 88 had hit Thompson's Mosquito in the port engine which commenced to vibrate so badly that the whole aircraft began juddering. He tried to feather the propeller but without success, so closing down the engine he started for home, the propeller windmilling. To add to his problems, flames began to issue from the engine, but they were extinguished, using the graviner switch. No sooner was this sorted out than his starboard engine began to splutter and cut out, but Thompson succeeded in coaxing his Mosquito along for over three hours, just managing to clear the cliffs at base, to crash-land in an adjoining field.

Thompson sustained a cut forehead and concussion, Sergeant Barnes also had a small laceration to his forehead. Thompson needed hospital treatment but received an Immediate DFC.

At 8 pm the following evening, HMS *Woodpecker* of the 2nd Escort Group, picked up the downed crew of the FW200, some being wounded.

The Luftwaffe exacted revenge on a 224 Squadron Liberator in the Musketry area. Flight Sergeant W.E. Smith had flown out from England at 4.05 pm and simply failed to return. With the number of Ju88s active over the Bay it seemed fairly certain that Bill Smith fell foul of a patrol of them. However, there is no record of a KG40 claim.

A 304 Squadron Wellington crashed on this day soon after take-off from Davidstow Moor. Flight Lieutenant Z. Janicki and his co-pilot were killed but the rest of the crew survived.

CHAPTER NINE

DESTRUCTION OF A WHOLE GROUP

Eleven U-boats put to sea during the last four days of July. Dönitz was particularly anxious to get one important group of three boats through and out into the Atlantic, as two were supply boats. He had a number of submarines needing urgent supplies out in the grey waters of the North Atlantic. Losses and damage already inflicted on his supply boats made these two boats, U-461 and U-462, doubly important.

The submarine U-461, it will be recalled, was due to sail on 22nd July in company with U-459 and U-117 from the mouth of the Gironde. A leak in her No 6 diving tank made this impossible and she had to put back into Bordeaux. Repaired, U-461 with Korvettenkapitän Wolf Stiebler on the bridge, sailed at noon on the 28th. U-462, commanded by Oberleutnant zur See de Reserve Bruno Vöwe, was with her, plus another supply boat, but this boat developed a faulty clutch control and put back into Bordeaux. Her place was taken by U-504 under Kapitänleutnant Wilhelm Luis, outbound for another destination, who would act as escort. Vöwe's U-462 was headed for the Atlantic to refuel the submarine group (wolf-pack) *Monsum*, urgently requiring replenishment, 300 miles east of St Paul's Rock.

The initial escort for all three U-boats was provided by three Narvik Class destroyers, one Sperrbrecher, six minesweepers and air cover of six Ju88s. These stayed with them until 11 pm on the 29th. The three U-boats stayed together that night, U-461 being designated the leader boat.

On the morning of the 30th, they were all on course 230° travelling on the surface at ten knots. They were quickly spotted. At around 9.30 a Sunderland was seen which kept out of AA range some 3,000 yards away, but the U-boats' radio men could hear it signalling for other aircraft. A Liberator (53 Squadron) then appeared, followed by what the Germans thought was either another Liberator or a Halifax. Finally five RAF aircraft were circling nearby.

* * *

According to Coastal Command, it was the Liberator of 53 Squadron that first sighted the U-boats. Flying Officer W.J. Irving (BZ730), who had begun his Musketry patrol at 4.26 am, sent the signal: 'Am over three enemy submarines in position KHJE/0024, on surface course 230°.' Unfortunately the given position (translated into 4510N x 1030W) was 80 miles in error to the south. This led to the diversion of several aircraft in the belief that there were two U-boat groups. However, it was a 228 Squadron Sunderland, that finally picked them up 20 minutes later. Flying Officer S. White (JM679) had been on patrol since 2.21 am when he saw the three U-boats. Initially the boats opened fire on him until he withdrew out of range. White radioed in the position (the correct one but as far as HQ 19 Group were concerned, a second group position) and began homing procedure. At 10.47 a Ju88 was seen by White's crew, forcing him to take evasive action and to jettison his D/Cs as he raced for cloud cover.

Shortly afterwards, a Catalina of 210 Squadron, co-operating with the 2nd Escort Group, and flying a routine square search, also spotted the U-boats. After calling in his sighting report to 19 Group, the Catalina pilot headed back to the Escort Group to give them a visual message of the submarines' position. Stiebler reported to base HQ that the group was being threatened by a number of aircraft and requested air cover. Nine Ju88s already on patrol were ordered to help but they had insufficient fuel to reach the scene of action. The RAF's sighting of the three boats had started considerable W/T activity between air and surface forces, all picked up by the Germans. Due to this, orders were sent to the group to dissolve and proceed independently. If the group ever received this message it was already too late.

The next aircraft the German look-outs saw was not a hoped for German however, but an American Liberator of the 19th Squadron. It had intercepted 228's signal. This was at 11.15 am, which coincided with Flying Officer White's return to the scene having shaken off the Ju88. There were now three aircraft circling, 53's Liberator, 228's Sunderland and the American Liberator, each making vain efforts to get into R/T touch with each other in order to co-ordinate tactics. Ten minutes later they were joined by a Halifax of 502 Squadron, piloted by Flying Officer W.S. Biggar. They had made a radar contact at 20 miles, and later picked up visually the Escort Group with its attendant 210 Squadron Catalina. Heading on they then found the U-boats and their circling antagonists. Biggar tried to make contact with the other aircraft but this failed so he decided upon independent action. At 11.48 he selected one U-boat which was slightly separated from the others, and attacked. He was met by a barrage of gunfire and his three 600lb bombs which were dropped from 1,000 feet, overshot by 70-100 yards. The Halifax was holed in the starboard elevator but his gunners returned the fire as they flew over.

Another 502 Squadron Halifax was also on its way in, flown by a Dutch pilot, Flying Officer A. van Rossum who had also homed in on 228's signal.

They themselves had picked up the radar contact at 36 miles, finding first the Escort Group sloops (code-named 'Fisher') steaming full speed towards the position of the submarines, still twenty miles further on, confirmed by signal from the destroyers. August van Rossum arrived just before Biggar attacked. Meanwhile, a 461 Squadron Sunderland had arrived, captained by Dudley Marrows.

Flight Lieutenant D. Marrows, 461 Squadron:
  'The fight took place on a normal anti-submarine patrol, though in those very critical times when shipping losses had been critical for some time, when anti-submarine action was just beginning to gain some ascendency and different U-boat tactics were being used – U-boats not submerging, but being more heavily armed and staying on the surface "fighting back" and being given fighter cover. We were well south on patrol, when we received a signal to divert to a position some considerable distance away where a U-boat had been sighted.
  'It was a relatively cloudless day with some of the usual haze and we were flying at a height whereby we thought we had maximum U-boat sighting range – some 2,000 feet. The feeling at that time was that we would be very near our maximum range when we reached the position and that most likely the U-boat would have submerged before we arrived.
  'From wireless traffic it started to become more interesting and positive; obviously other aircraft had already arrived there and were reporting sightings of three submarines! Pilot Officer Jimmy Leigh sighted the submarines first by binoculars whilst some distance off – there were three in tight "V" formation on the surface. We thought that they were destroyers. Then soon we were part of what has been called the greatest single U-boat action of the war. Apart from the U-boats and our RAAF Sunderland, eventually engaged were RAF Liberators, Sunderlands, a Catalina, Halifaxes and a US Liberator and the famous Captain Walker's squadron of five anti-submarine sloops. There was much to see! I forgot the Ju88. The main responsibility up to this stage had been with the navigator, Jock Rolland and the First WOP/AG Peter Jensen. Jock had a rather frightening responsibility – we were really at the end of our outward endurance. He knew his navigation had to be most accurate if we were to stay long, do much and get home without running out of fuel.' [In this instance he was not helped by base giving him an inaccurate location of the subs. Ed.]

Pilot Officer P.T. Jensen, 461 Squadron:
  'An early morning take-off on a T3 patrol – that is, pick-up the

Scillies then in a straight line to the Spanish coast south of Cape Finisterre, a coast crawl to Finisterre, then straight back to the Scillies.

'It was a beautiful day; just outside the three mile limit of Spain we could see people on the beaches, the water was sparkling and blue, how we envied them, even in the aircraft it was warm – I had my jacket off and sleeves rolled up, (we kept strictly outside the limit because one day when we strayed in a bit the Spaniards had a shot at us with a coastal gun – boy it was close!).

'On our way back, just after leaving Finisterre I was on the set and intercepted a sighting report from another aircraft. It was near us (grid co-ordinates FKJE/1010 – funny how things stick in one's memory) so we changed course and came upon three U-boats on the surface, with three other aircraft circling – a British Liberator, an American Liberator and a Halifax.

'As we came on the scene the British Liberator attacked and the U-boats opened up – each boat had two or three batteries each of 4x20mm with self-destroying shells timed for (I estimate) 1,000 yards – what a barrage!! It looked like a brick wall – the Liberator broke off the engagement and continued circling.

'I thought "well that precludes us" – ours was an early Mark III kite with a single pan-fed Vickers gas operated gun in the nose turret – (later versions had two Brownings in the turret plus four fixed Brownings). We certainly weren't equipped for a head-on attack. I reckoned our role would be to home in the sloops I knew were nearby. Much to my dismay the klaxon went to run the depth charges out!!'

Sergeant G.M. Watson, 461 Squadron:
'I did not get a grandstand view of all that went on during that never-to-be forgotten day, as I was at the engineer's desk, facing aft. I was like the engineer in a battleship, hearing the fight but not in it.

'We took off from Pembroke Dock at 02.48 hours. At 10.17 hours we were coming home from the coast of Spain when we heard a signal from Liberator "O" of 53 Squadron of a U-boat sighting. Then, a message came from 19 Group directing us to 45 degrees, forty-two minutes north, eleven degrees west. I remember the radar operator picking up the "blip" of the U-boats at 90 miles' range, which was surprising to me!

'At 11.48 three U-boats were sighted, estimated tonnage 740 each and sailing west at ten knots, quite close together with a Halifax and a USA Liberator circling. Then commenced a nerve-racking anti-clockwise circling of the U-boat pack, with more and more Sunderlands and Liberators joining the circus. I kept thinking about

Ju88s and felt they should be arriving at any moment to attack us.

'I heard Dudley say, after an attack to get close to the pack, "Hell, look at that flak. We cannot make it through that." Looking over my shoulder I could see many white puffs of smoke, like little grey balloons, ahead of us, which were deadly 20 mm cannon shells exploding. Meanwhile the Halifax had gone in and dropped bombs, which appeared to hit one of the U-boats, as smoke was seen coming from it. Flying Officer van Rossum now elected independent action, deciding to select and drop single 600 lb anti-submarine bombs. At 11.58 he headed towards the port U-boat at 3,000 feet. The first bomb landed close to the stern, spray covering the aft part of the boat, then smoke was seen coming from the conning tower and the sub began to circle slowly. Van Rossum pulled round, lost some height and came in again, despite an intense flak barrage. "We saw the German putting up a protective core of greyish-white and red tracer fire," said van Rossum afterwards. "It was good shooting, but we pressed through and dropped another bomb. We didn't see the explosion, but when the spray cleared smoke continued to stream from the U-boat and it came to a standstill."' [1]

His target had been Vöwe's U-462, and the second bomb went down to explode about 250 feet astern.

This action seemed to break the spell among the earlier aircraft. Flying Officer Irving took the opportunity of this diversion to attack U-461 which was on the starboard side. At the same time the American Liberator came in and so too did Marrows' Sunderland.

Pilot Officer P.T. Jensen, 461 Squadron:
'The voice of the skipper, Dudley Marrows, came on the intercom to Jimmy Leigh the first pilot: "We'll take the port one Jimmy." – then Jimmy came on: "OK skip – (pause) why not go diagonally across and get the lot in one go." I thought, "my God, we haven't got one maniac on board, we've got two." Then Dudley came on: "One at a time Jim – (pause). Get ready to take over if I'm hit."

'Then we were into it, violent evasive action, shrapnel rattling on the hull like hail with incessant loud bangs as pieces of shrapnel were picked up by the props and flung against the hull. It was too thick even for Dudley; he broke off to port and as he did so saw that the Liberator had taken advantage and had attacked again.

Flight Lieutenant D. Marrows, 461 Squadron:
'When we got within attack range, aircraft were circling. The

---

[1] *Coastal Command Leads the Invasion* op cit.

U-boats were manoeuvring in formation, keeping bows on to the
aircraft and putting up a very formidable barrage of fire – cannon and
machine gun. From our height of some 1,000 feet the Royal Navy
sloops were not visible. Together with other aircraft we joined in the
circuit (circus!) First thought was of recommended tactics – avoid
submarines' maximum fire power, avoid having to fly over the other
two when attacking the outer subs, could we contact the other
aircraft. Soon found that the subs could out-turn us, their turning
circle was small, ours large. Could not get effective contact with
other aircraft. Eating up fuel, time running out. Could feel the support
of the crew. All the time the other aircraft were circling too,
"feinting" attacks when they thought they were in position. When we
did this, the fire power we ran into was extremely heavy. The
shrapnel could actually be heard hitting the fuselage somewhat like
hail. We just could not get in a position whereby we could do
anything else but have the three subs broadside on by the time we
would be on the final run in.'

Flying Officer Irving's Liberator was hit repeatedly on the run-in, and his
D/Cs undershot. So damaged was his aircraft (BZ730 'O', in which Flying
Officer Merrifield had won his DFC on 1st July when engaged by Ju88s)
that Irving knew he'd not fly it home. He headed south towards Portugal.
    Hoping to profit by the distraction of Irving's attack, Marrows turned
towards the U-boats.

Flight Lieutenant D. Marrows, 461 Squadron:
    'Watching I think only one attack from rather high level by another
    aircraft. I decided the only thing to do was to go in as low as I
    possibly could, hoping that there would be some trouble when the
    subs were broadside onto the swell, for them to adequately depress
    their guns at all times. Whilst they rolled with the swell, some fire
    being blanketed by the sub being attacked – the outer sub. At that
    time another aircraft, a Liberator, made another high level attack and
    appeared to have been hit and his bombs missed.
    'We then went in, violently jinking as we lost height to sea level.
    As expected by this time the subs were broadside on and the sight of
    all the guns and cannons firing was impressive indeed. I forget what
    the actual fire power was – it would need checking. My memory is
    that there were something in the vicinity of ten cannon/machine guns
    on each sub making 30 in all rising at us.
    'Here is where the crew come in again. Pierre Bamber in the front
    turret and Bubbles Pearce (who incidentally was a noted competitive
    rifle shooter pre-war) came into their own. I can but know that they
    did a marvellous job, otherwise we would not be here. I was

concentrating on my alignment and distance to drop the depth charges – there were no sights used – it all had to be the judgement of the pilot – and can only remember (even minutes after the attack) upturned faces, figures. Others saw German gunners falling and throwing themselves about. They were to concentrate on the gunners and this they obviously did.

'We carried eight depth charges and the plan then was to drop seven in a stick, keeping one for reserve. I had to endeavour to straddle the sub with a stick – a line of charges.

'I remember being as low as possible, just skimming the swell tops – submarines sit low in the water and I had to pull up as I dropped the depth charges, to clear the sub.

'All this time, I was worrying about what was going to happen when I passed over the outer sub, the one we were attacking, and come upon the other two.

'I believe my idea of coming in very low was the saver. I believe that at some stage the other two subs could not fire at us because the sub being attacked was in the way.

'At any rate, there is a big factor of luck – very, very big – one inch the other way can make a vital difference.'

Pilot Officer P.T. Jensen, 461 Squadron:

'By this time the Halifax had bombed another U-boat from about 4,000 feet – out of range of their 20 mm's and it (the boat) was going around in circles blowing smoke with the crew jumping into the water each with a one-man dinghy inflating around him. (It looked like a mass of flowers bursting into bloom).

'Dudley continued the turn and bored in behind the Liberator – the Liberator was hit and turned away smoking badly but by now we were in to about 600 yards and all the guns turned on us. "Bubbles" Pearce was in the nose – he only had 100 rounds – and held his fire to 400 yards then opened up and swept the decks of "our" U-boat. We just cleared the conning tower and straddled it with seven D/Cs. It must have been blown apart. We turned around again and flew over to verify the kill. There were about 25-30 men struggling in the water so we dropped them one of our dinghies and took photos'.

Sergeant G.M. Watson, 461 Squadron:

'Then the Liberator "O" Flying Officer W. Irving of 53 Squadron, and followed closely by the American Liberator, led a charge towards the pack. Dudley realised this was his best chance to get at them, while their fire was on the bombers – with throttles flat open, we dived down, weaving from side to side as if he was flying a Tiger Moth! I heard the nose gunner ("Bubbles" Pearce) open up. Dudley shouted: "Bloody good shooting Bubbles," as he cleared the U-boat's decks of gunners. Seven depth charges were dropped as Dudley cleared the conning tower of U-461 at 50 feet.

'I heard the tail gunner open up with his four Browning machine guns, as we passed over, then he shouted over the intercom, "We have split him in half, skipper." Dudley was too busy climbing and weaving away from the flak from the other U-boats to listen! Having gained height and distance from the scene of action, we could see a bright orange pool of scum, oil and wreckage below us. About thirty men were down there. He decided to drop them one of our three dinghies. Meanwhile, the Halifax, captained by a Dutchman had "another go" and fighting his way through the flak, dropped more bombs, which dropped close to U-462 and crippled her. Soon they were to scuttle her and took to their life-rafts. Dudley then turned his attack to the one remaining U-boat U-504, but flak was all around us and the midships gunner called: "Five ships on starboard beam, they are firing." He abandoned his attack, with relief, to Captain Walker who were now firing their heavy guns at the lone U-boat, which was soon to dive. After some time, it was reported that oil and wreckage coming to the surface was sufficient to confirm a final "kill".'

Pilot Officer P.T. Jensen, 461 Squadron:
'We turned to the last U-boat and as we bored in Dudley was surprised to see splashes all around it. He looked around and saw the sloops had arrived. He decided he'd leave it to them so he pulled out and we took stock, we had collected a couple of shells but no real damage. The only problem was fuel, all the combat had been done in rich mixture and we had barely enough to get home, so we set course for home.'

It is a noteworthy coincidence of fate that Marrows' Sunderland (W6077) was aircraft 'U' of 461 Squadron, and that his victim had been U-461.

Her commander, Wolf Stiebler, had been unable to turn to starboard when he saw the Sunderland boring in due to the short distance between his boat and the damaged U-462. Machine-gun fire from the Sunderland was very heavy and one or two of his officers were severely wounded and two men on the 20 mm quad were cut down, which reduced the effectiveness of their main defense at a crucial moment. One German gunlayer on the port 20 mm gun also said later his ammunition ran out when the Sunderland was 60 yards away. Two of the D/Cs fell along one side and two close to the other. It was the two that fell forward of the conning tower (starboard side) that had done the damage, as the boat travelled over them. U-461 went down like a stone. She carried a complement of 59 officers and men, but only 15 survived, including the 35-year-old Stiebler, and 39-year-old Oberleutnant zur See Herbert Ludewig, his first officer, who had been wounded. Only one of the survivors came from within the U-boat. He managed to pull himself up through the conning tower despite water pouring in. He had been preceded by a propaganda company's camera man, but he later disappeared.

The American Liberator made another attack, also from low level and was hit by gunfire from U-504. This smashed the Liberator's release gear, causing the D/Cs to hang-up. Van Rossum then dropped his third bomb on U-462, but his first bomb had caused enough damage already and she had begun to sink. About 40 of her crew were taking to dinghies or diving into the water. The American pilot made another run but even when they used the jettison mechanism, the D/Cs failed to release. Van Rossum recorded:

'We were right over it as it began to go down slowly. As it sank lower and lower more and more men came running along the deck and jumped into the water. When only the conning tower was left above water we saw shell splashes off to one side. The Navy had arrived and the sloops were shelling our sinking U-boat. They were too late for this, though, and all the men had jumped overboard.' [2]

By this time, Captain Walker's ships were fast approaching – just five miles off. Seeing these on the horizon, U-504 crash-dived, ending the air action which had lasted just eighteen minutes from van Rossum's first bomb.

The Escort Group radioed van Rossum, asking what was happening. He replied that two U-boats had been sunk and that the third had dived, on a westerly heading. The hunt was started for U-504 and at 12.34 am an asdic contact was made. However, asdic conditions were not good and D/C attacks were not made until 1.49. These lasted for some time until, in the mid-afternoon, oil, wreckage and human remains came to the surface, confirming the death of U-504. The Bay's air and surface forces had destroyed completely, a whole U-boat group.

With the last kill confirmed, Walker's ships returned to the area of U-461 and 462's sinkings to pick up the survivors, HMS *Woodpecker* taking Stiebler and his men on board. It had been the German boat's sixth patrol and he had supplied U-boats 80 times, in the previous eighteen months since her commissioning.

(See appendix V for the recollections of some of U-461's survivors.)

* * *

Following this successful attack, the crew of the Australian Sunderland turned for home.

---

[2] *Coastal Command Leads the Invasion* op cit.

Flight Lieutenant D. Marrows, 461 Squadron:

'At this time Jock Rolland knew that our fuel was dangerously low so there was nothing we could do but go. We signalled the Navy as we left that there were survivors in the water.

'We set a bee line for home, but the day was not over yet. Much to our surprise we came upon another sub on the surface. Knowing of our fuel position, I went straight in to attack. Then, somehow or other, as I set the remaining depth charge, I must have knocked the auto pilot lever on. When I went to level out I could not lift the nose and had to call on Jimmy Leigh to help me overcome the auto pilot. The sub had elected to stay on the surface and fight and was firing at us and our nose gunner effectively returned the fire causing some casualties on the sub. Somewhere on the way we were hit by a cannon shell which went through our depth charge carriage under the port side mainplane and exploded against the main spar. It prevented the remaining depth charge from dropping, so we were only able to effect machine gun damage as we flew over. There was an electrical fire that the crew put out. We could not be effective, the sub was submerging and we were almost certain then that we had insufficient fuel to get home.'

Pilot Officer P.T. Jensen, 461 Squadron:

'Half an hour later – another U-boat. Dudley went straight in with our last D/C hoping to catch it unawares but they were waiting for us; again the mad evasive action, the shrapnel, then we were hit, on fire, and the kite filled with smoke, but what I didn't know at the time, the controls had locked and we were heading straight for the U-boat. Dudley yelled to Jimmy and together they pulled on the wheel and just managed to clear the conning tower, the D/C was jettisoned and we prepared to ditch. While this was going on Paddy Watson, the engineer, had put the fire out with an extinguisher (the fire was in the bomb release gear), then Dudley found he had accidentally pushed the lever to put in auto-pilot, he flicked it out and the kite responded again. Again we assessed damage, again the kite appeared OK but fuel very low.'

Sergeant G.M. Watson, 461 Squadron:

'We turned for home. Checking the tanks, which I had drained from the outer, small tanks to the larger inner tanks, I could assess that we would never make Pembroke Dock! We set our sights on the Scillies and I asked Dudley to reduce speed to 115 knots and maintain 2,000 feet for maximum economical range flying.

'Amazingly, no Ju88s had appeared and we set off happily for the Scillies. One of the memories I have was the sight of three U-boats, swinging together, to present their full broadside fire, whenever we came in to attack. The commander of the pack, Wolf Stiebler, was a very cool and experienced man, who had a lifetime of seafaring behind him.

'I moved to the nose gun position and "Bubbles" took over the engineer's panel. Just one hour after the battle, coming home, we had a lot of excited chatter, with reaction from the tension setting in, when I suddenly spotted a U-boat on the starboard bow and reported it to Dudley. "One and a half miles and 40 degrees starboard, skipper." At first he could not see it, nor could our co-pilot, Jimmy Leigh. I had a reputation for reporting non-existent Ju88s on the horizon, coming home tired and jumpy in blue skies, after a long patrol – they just did not believe me! But this time I was not seeing spots!

'We went down in a steep dive and the U-boat took no action to dive or fire back, so it appeared we had surprised him. The official report said that the U-boat opened up with 20 mm cannon when we were at 1,000 yards' range. I had a Vickers Gas Operated machine gun, which had a "pan" of 100 rounds of .303 bullets. This would empty in a few seconds; – choice – open up on them early and "keep their heads down" or wait till I saw the "blue of their eyes." I decided on the "keep heads down trick," but of course, as we closed in my ammunition ran out and I had no time to put on a new "pan" before we were over and away from the U-boat.

'This was the only time I fired a gun at the "enemy" with intent to kill. The official report said, "I scored several hits on the conning tower!" I do not think I killed anyone! I must say, even now, I can remember feeling very vulnerable in that nose turret and wondering what it would be like to receive a bullet in my guts.

'As we passed over the U-boat's conning tower at a ridiculously low height, for a moment I thought we were going to crash into it, all hell broke loose on the intercom. "Bunny" Sydney called up, "Skipper, we are on fire back here." In fact, we had been hit by a cannon shell just beside the release control of our one remaining depth charge, which did not drop. Soon fire extinguishers put out the blaze. It was only later that I realised how close we had been to piling in on top of the U-boat. Dudley, in selecting the depth charge release button had knocked in "George", the auto-pilot, which kept us flying down. Dudley could not pull her out of the dive and he is a very big and strong man, even today, so he called on Jimmy Leigh to help. Together with a superhuman effort, they managed to overcome the hydraulics and clear the U-boat – by feet! I can still remember seeing a gunner in the conning tower, crouching, in fright!

'When the cause of our troubles was discovered, we went on our way, feeling sick at the thought of not getting another crack at the enemy with our last depth charge, which had now to be jettisoned, or it might blow us up on landing. A bit of work with the boat hook, through the galley hatch soon removed it. Again we relaxed and the chatter over the intercom was full of released tensions and cheer. The Aussies are fantastic in the face of adversity. The problem now was to get home.'

Paddy Watson continues:

'I really was worried now about our fuel situation and kept reporting "estimated range" to Dudley. However, at 15.15 hours we "made it" to St Mary's, Scillies, with a few gallons left. I think we "might" have had 15 minutes flying time left. A close call!'

Pilot Officer P.T. Jensen, 461 Squadron:

'We headed for home again throwing out all surplus gear in order to lighten the old kite, and made it to the Scillies with about a pint of fuel left in the tanks. There were no refuelling facilities there so we refuelled by bringing four gallon drums to the aircraft by launch, passing them through the wardroom and galley, up the stairs to the top deck, out the astro-hatch on to the wing and pouring the fuel into the tanks.

'When we got back to the squadron, poor old "U" went straight up the slip for inspection, they found a large lump of mainspar had gone (if the shell had been a couple of inches higher, it would have gone into a tank) so our faithful old kite was pensioned off and we were issued with "E".

'Despite the notable achievement of destroying a complete group of U-boats, this had been accomplished by chance sightings rather than a planned sequence. Although the basic patrol set-up was sound enough, analysis of the actual events of this day made by the Operations Room at Coastal Command HQ, revealed a number of faults of the overall scheme.

'Deficiencies in signal communications, navigation, R/T failure and homing efficiency had all played a part in a particularly unco-ordinated effort at a moment when experience should have enabled a successful co-ordinated attack.

'Command HQ ordered a renewed drive by the Coastal Command Communications and Navigational branches to intensify training in these fields. Action and signal procedures were amended and a revised order issued, covering all aspects of co-operation between air and surface forces. Known as *Operation Packhorse*; it was begun on 1st August.'

* * *

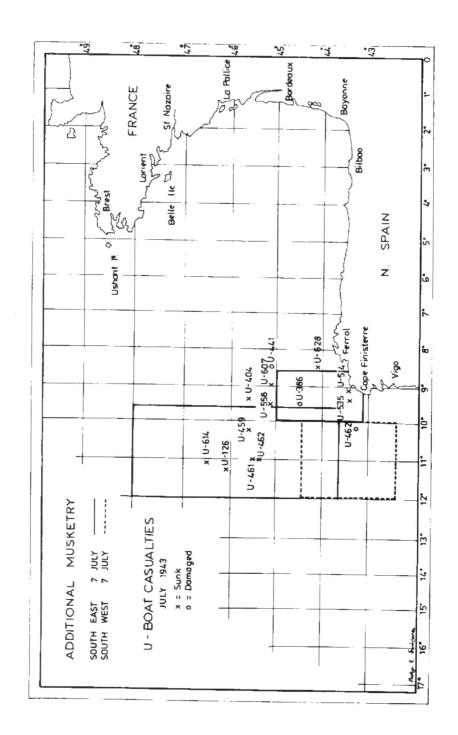

July 1943 had been a very active month in the Bay. John Brooks of 224 Squadron had also been kept busy as evidenced by his diary and log book:

> 3rd July Flight Lieutenant Cundy and crew in an attack. Got shot up and returned on 3 engines.
>
> 6th July Anti-submarine Musketry patrol. Bay of Biscay. FL960. Kept on our toes by aircraft sighting reports but made no contacts.
>
> 14th July Anti-submarine and shipping patrol, Bay of Biscay. BZ 766. Took photographs of all ships for intelligence. Landed Gibraltar.
>
> 17th July Just made the take-off on Gibraltar's short runway and no wind with full load. BZ 766. Anti-submarine and shipping patrol on way home. Photographs taken – no U-boat sightings.
>
> 25th July Anti-submarine patrol. Bay of Biscay. Not a cloud in the sky and very much on our toes. FL 960.
>
> 28th July Robert Sweeny, Junior (A Yank in the RAF) got a confirmed kill but shot up by flak and returned on 3 engines.
>
> 29th July Willie Smith, Briggs, Pilot Officer Drew and the rest of the crew of A Apple failed to return.
>
> 30th July Anti-submarine patrol. Bay of Biscay. Visual sighting by beam gunner at extreme range. Turned in to attack what turned out to be a whale. Lucky timing again returning through the fighter belt in the dark. FL 960.
>
> *Flight Lieutenant J.H. Brooks, 224 Squadron.*

CHAPTER TEN

THE BEGINNING OF THE END

Following the tremendous events and results of 30th July, there were still eight U-boats in the Bay, all on outbound courses.

One of these, U-107, was spotted by Flying Officer Davey of 502 Squadron. A little earlier, on their way to the patrol area, they had an encounter with a Ju88:

> 'A lone Junkers 88 got us on this trip, but the encounter taught us a lesson. We had been flying just above miles and miles of flat cloud, our slipstream making four long sausage shapes as it whipped up the cloud top which looked beautiful in the dawn's yellow and orange "hues". "Army" was in command, Johnny having gone back to relieve nature's call, when suddenly a Ju88 emerged from cloud right behind us and opened fire. Our rear gunner yelled out and "Army" nosed down into cloud followed by a stream of tracer. Archer in the tail turret found that he had not turned his guns to "fire" and, in the initial panic, put his elbow through a Perspex panel.
>
> 'We continued the patrol but the weather clamped down and it was soon apparent that we should have to return early. Jock insisted we check the weather's base, so with me in the bomb aimer's position, we slowly lowered the Halifax down. The idea was that as soon as I found a break, I would yell out; but when we finally emerged from cloud at about 50 feet above the grey sea, right ahead sat a surfaced U-boat! In that first moment I saw a head in the conning tower, light reflecting on a peaked cap. Following my rapid report of what I had seen, I was thrown bodily out of the way by Jock and by the time I had scrambled to my position and plugged in my head set, we were about to let go a depth charge. Immediately we did so we had to lift up into cloud again and after turning we could not locate the exact spot of our attack.
>
> 'Finally landing back at base, we found a line of bullet holes in one of the wings, a souvenir of the Ju88; while later the ground crew extracted an incendiary bullet from one of the petrol tanks. As the

tank had been only half full when the attack came, we were more than fortunate that the bullet had failed to ignite in the fume-filled tank. We also reported being fired on by the U-boat – thus explaining the "damage" to the rear turret.'

Flight Sergeant H.E.R. Barrett, 502 Squadron.

Although this attack only forced U-107 to dive and shake up her crew, the next two days was to see the climax of air operations in the Bay.

On Sunday 1st August, a further six U-boats sailed in three groups from Lorient and St Nazaire but none of these reached Coastal's patrol areas during the next two crucial days. To the west within Musketry, a Wellington of 304 Squadron (Flight Lieutenant Bialecki) sighted either U-454 or 706 in position 4550/0940 – they were sailing in company and a further sighting of both these submarines was made at 2.40 pm by a Catalina of 210 Squadron, attached to the 2nd Escort Group. Walker headed his ships towards the sighting and shortly afterwards a 10 Australian Squadron Sunderland arrived to join in the hunt. Flight Lieutenant K.G. Fry had lifted off from Mount Batten at 10 am, heading for Musketry and to co-operate with Walker's ships.When he saw the U-boat it was in a rough sea and only six miles from the Escort Group's ships, which were themselves about 165 miles north west of Ortegal. As the submarine (it was U-454) was on its own, Fry immediately turned onto an attacking course in order to come in on the U-boat's starboard side. To do this he at first flew across in front of it, then pulled the flying boat round into a tight left hand turn. As he lined up for the final run-in, the Australian crew met heavy defensive fire. Kapitänleutnant Burkhard Hacklander had elected to stay up and fight.

Hacklander was 28 years old and this was U-454's tenth war patrol, five while with the Arctic Flotilla. On those Arctic patrols he had sunk two Allied ships, a British destroyer and a Russian minesweeper. He had originally sailed from La Pallice on the 23rd with U-706. At the Gironde U-454 had her compass go u/s so both boats had returned to La Pallice. They then had sailed from La Pallice at 10.00 am on 29th July, escorted by a Sperrbrecher and a minesweeper. On the night of the 31st, he had remained submerged as usual and surfaced at 8.30 am the next morning. However, he had been forced down almost immediately owing to the presence of hostile aircraft. At 11 o'clock he resurfaced in order to recharge U-454 batteries, but again aircraft on the horizon forced him below. At 2 pm he tried again, but was diving again five minutes later. His situation was fast becoming serious. The boat's batteries were almost exhausted and the air inside the hull becoming increasingly foul.

At 2.40 pm he came up yet again, the radar immediately picking up an aircraft bearing 65°, two miles away. U-454 was seen and the aircraft fired two red star-shells to attract nearby surface vessels. Moments later the aircraft turned onto a final attack run. Fry was coming in low and fast.

The boat opened up with its 20 mm guns and almost at once scored a hit while about $^1/_4$ mile off. The Sunderland shuddered, being hit repeatedly. The starboard inner engine caught a cannon shell while the starboard main fuel tank was damaged. The co-pilot, Flying Officer H.R.Budd, had been badly wounded and the flight deck was a shambles and flooded with petrol.

Fry continued to attack, his machine surrounded by flak and tracer shells. Over the boat he released six DCs, three falling just ahead of the U-boat, the other three exploding right next to the wardroom, CPO's and PO's mess, and starboard bow. The shattered boat went under and down in less than a minute and only fourteen of the crew escaped. Among them was Hacklander, his second officer, Leutnant zur See Gerhard Braun, who had been officer of the watch, the boat's quartermaster and two other sailors from the bridge. Most of the others who escaped had been ammunition supply men who had been near the conning tower hatch.

Once over the U-boat, the Sunderland, severely hit and damaged, became unmanageable. Fry struggled to keep it in the air but his efforts were to no avail. The flying boat ditched onto the sea about six miles away from the nearby ships. It did so into a 15-20 foot swell and crashed. Six of the Australian crew survived and were later rescued by HMS *Wren*, while HMS *Kite* fished the fourteen Germans from the water.

The ships then moved to the north where a 59 Squadron Liberator flown by Flight Lieutenant Charlton, despite return fire, had made an unsuccessful attack on U-106 at 9.50 pm, but made no contact.

* * *

An hour after Fry's very gallant and courageous attack on U-454 (he died just nine days short of his 30th birthday), an American Catalina of VP63 Squadron, USN, 380 miles or so from the north-west corner of Spain, spotted three Ju88s (4700/1200). Lieutenant Tanner hauled his aircraft into some cloud but cover proved insufficient to conceal them. As he flew out, there were about ten 88s waiting for him. At first the 88s attacked singly and the Catalina's gunners claimed hits on two of them. However, concerted attacks followed that really shredded the flying boat, killing or wounding seven of the crew. An aileron and rudder were shot away and then the Catalina caught fire. The only message they got off had been a coded signal: "Am being attacked .." at 3.55 pm, and five minutes later they were in the sea. Tanner ditched his blazing machine which only floated for a short time. Ensign Bedell secured a dinghy and got Tanner and Paterson, who was badly wounded, into it. Twenty hours later HMS *Bideford* picked up three survivors.

The PBY had been shot down by four Ju88s of KG40, although the Americans had hit one fighter which was forced to ditch before reaching land. However, its crew were later rescued by a seaplane of Nr.1 Seenotstaffel.

As evening came on that first August day, there was more action not far from where Lieutenant Tanner had been shot down. At 8.02 pm, in position 4724/1040, a 228 Squadron Sunderland sighted a fully surfaced U-boat on the port beam. The pilot was Flight Lieutenant Stanley White, who had found U-461, 462 and 504 on 30th July; the U-boat was U-383, who in company with U-218 was heading out into the Atlantic.

These two submarines had left Brest on the 29th, U-383, under Horst Kremser, heading for an Atlantic patrol, on her fourth cruise, U-218, a Type VIID, sailing to lay mines off Trinidad, her fifth war patrol.

White's first attack approach was met by a hail of flak, several hits slamming into the Sunderland, forcing violent evasive action. The starboard float was shot away together with the aileron, the hull was holed as was the port wing. The flying boat's gunners blazed away at the U-boat scoring hits over the conning tower.

Despite this, White circled behind the boat as she began a left turn away from its 180° course. Coming in again from U-383's starboard rear quarter, the German gunners kept up a steady rate of fire but this time White went over the boat and released several DCs in a perfect straddle. The U-boat was enveloped in spray, and when this subsided the boat was listing heavily to port. Then men were seen jumping over the side – they were abandoning ship.

Because of the damage to the Sunderland – it was almost impossible to turn because of the smashed aileron – White had to fly off at once, but he reached base to land safely. He later received the DFC. The crew probably thought they had made a certain kill but U-383 had not sunk – yet.

Kremser signalled B.d.U., reporting his boat seriously damaged. U-218 was ordered to stand by to help her, while instructing U-706 and 454 (B.d.U. had not yet been made aware that U-454 had already been sunk that afternoon) to go to her assistance. Air escort was promised at first light the next day while three "T"-class torpedo boats were sent out to her. However, U-383 foundered during the night, going down before being able to inform B.d.U.

* * *

The next day was August Bank Holiday Monday, but the men of 19 Group had no day of rest – it was business as usual. War business.

The first occurrence was the sighting of Kapitänleutnant Alexander von Zitzweitz's U-706, which had sailed from La Pallice on 29th July in company with U-454. She was sighted by Squadron Leader C.G. Ruttan flying a Hampden of 415 RCAF Squadron on a Musketry patrol at 9.03 am. She was in position 4615/1125. Ruttan turned to attack but defensive fire from the submarine forced him away. He tried again, this time flying from the starboard quarter. His front gunner opened fire but his single .303 gun jammed after just 10 rounds. Ruttan flew over the boat, dropping six D/Cs from 100 feet. Results could not be determined but the U-boat seemed to be a little lower in the water, and her speed had been reduced to three knots. [3]

A Liberator of the 4th US Squadron then came onto the scene, piloted by Lieutenant J.L. Hamilton. Its crew had picked up a radar contact at twenty miles and at ten miles saw the Hampden circling and then saw the submarine. Lieutenant Hamilton went straight into the attack, curving round into a left hand diving turn in order to put the sun behind him. He approached from the U-boat's starboard side, but despite the sun, the submarine's gunners, when they opened fire, scored hits on the Liberator. Twelve D/Cs splashed down across U-706 from 50 feet. As the explosions subsided, the boat was going down by the stern. At least fifteen men were seen swimming in the sea, amidst oil and wreckage. The Americans flew back over the spot, dropping a dinghy into which some men began to clamber.

A 210 Squadron Catalina arrived, which was co-operating with the 40th Escort Group – that had joined the 2nd Escort Group on the 31st July. It sent a message to the surface vessels who began to close the position and then a 10 Australian Squadron Sunderland arrived. Later HMS *Waveney* arrived too, picking up the survivors.*

Further west on the 2nd August, a Wellington of 407 RCAF Squadron, relocated U-106 at 9.28 am. Wing Commander J.C.Archer, squadron commander, saw it dead ahead, ten to twelve miles. Archer climbed into cloud, then turned to starboard in order to fly ahead of the U-boat. When seven to eight miles ahead, Archer looked at his target through field glasses identifying a definite German boat. At two miles Archer began to lose height and made straight for it. Four minutes after the first sighting, six D/Cs went down from 50 feet but the U-boat was turning. The front gunner blasted the conning tower, and the German gunners also opened fire. This was taken up by the rear gunner who also saw the D/Cs splash by the starboard bow. U-106 began circling seemingly unmoved by the explosions and remained on the surface. Archer circled for nearly an hour, signalling his sighting report, until forced to fly home.

However, U-106 had been damaged and after Archer left, she turned towards France. The boat's crew effected repairs and limited diving capacity was restored. The commander, Oberleutnant Wolfdietrich Damerow, signalled B.d.U. for assistance. Dönitz detailed Ju88s to fly air cover and then instructed the three torpedo boats already vainly searching for U-383, to extend their sweep in order to pick up U-106 at 8 pm that evening and escort her home. Both the 2nd and 40th Escort Groups were not far off, the 2nd already closing in following Wing Commander Archer's sighting report.

---

[3] Ruttan was promoted to Wing Commander this same day and took command of No.415 Squadron. The following spring he received the DSO.

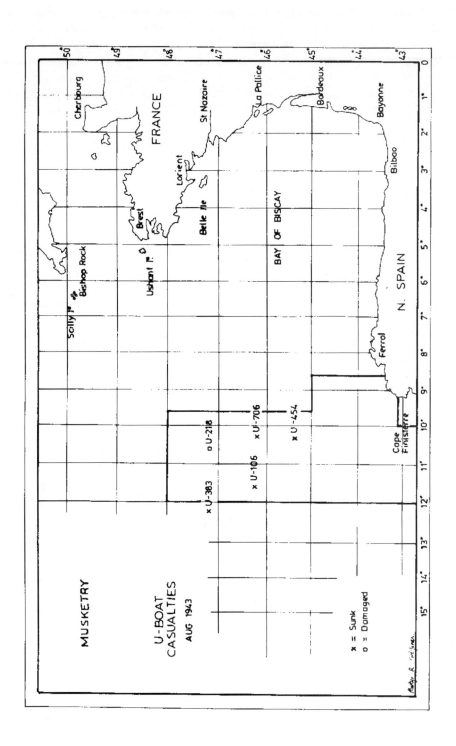

Meanwhile German air activity was apparent. At 10.45, 248 Squadron had a four-aircraft patrol out, led by Flight Lieutenant J.C. Newbury. They were 160 odd miles to the east of the attack on U-706 and had been patrolling for 3¹/₂ hours prior to Flying Officer J.F.Green/Pilot Officer G.B. Forrest DFM, seeing a FW200 at 1,000 yards off to port, at 50 feet.

Green warned the others, then pulled round after the Kondor,which had already started a climb for some clouds. Green closed to 700 yards, firing short bursts of cannon. A dark red glow rapidly turned to a blaze of flame that seemed to emanate from somewhere below the cockpit. As he edged nearer, Green's Beaufighter caught return fire from the German, shattering his windscreen. He was temporarily blinded by dust and glass splinters. The Beaufighter overshot the FW, only to be hit by the German front gunner who scored hits on the fighter's tailplane and port propeller. Pilot Officer Forrest fired back with his rear machine gun, as Green instinctively broke away.

The FW200 was now well alight and shedding bits and pieces. Pilot Officer V.R. Scheer (Canadian)/Flying Officer R.W. Twallin, who had followed Green's attack, now fired a long burst of cannon from dead astern and slightly below. Following a second burst from 400 yards,the rear half of the enemy's ventral gondola seemed to tear away, causing Scheer to break away quickly to avoid being hit by the falling debris. Flying Officer P.J. McGarvey (another Canadian)/Flying Officer A.M. Barnard, now attacked from 300 yards. The enemy 'plane was blazing furiously now, and went into a steep dive towards the sea. Hitting the water it carried on and could be seen below the surface for several seconds, its tailplane sticking vertically above the waves. Burning oil was soon all that remained on the surface.

* * *

The Canadians of 415 Squadron were very active on this Monday. Flight Sergeant D.R. McNeill-Watson came upon the scene of U-706's sinking just after 11 am, a Sunderland and a Catalina still circling nearby. He could see an oil patch on the sea and also a dinghy with some men in it.

Some time later Pilot Officer W.R.R. Savage of 415 Squadron also came upon the scene. A Sunderland was still present and below naval ships were near some burning smoke markers. Savage resumed his patrol, but at 2.26 pm had some unwelcome visitors. Five Ju88s appeared. With visibility good and cloud cover quite the reverse, Savage needed to take violent evasive action as the fighters attacked from all directions. He kept corkscrewing his Hampden, making for small patches of cloud whenever he could, while his gunners blazed away at the attackers. They later claimed hits on all five. After twenty minutes of high action, ammunition was running low and the rear gunner was having trouble with his weapons. The Hampden had been hit and damaged but finally the 88s broke off and Savage flew back to St Eval. None of the crews had been injured but the aircraft was in a sorry state. Its hydraulics had been shot away, petrol tank punctured and the perspex to the pilot's cockpit blown out.

These same Ju88s were encountered by the crew of 224 Squadron's Flying Officer J.B. Marsh, in whose crew was rear gunner, Sergeant John McMahon. They had flown into the area, spotted the Escort Group and an empty raft. Then they saw the Ju88s about three miles off. Flying Officer Marsh hauled his Liberator towards some cloud as the 88s began to peel off as they began their attack, but Marsh got to the cloud way ahead of them.

*

At 3.20 pm, U-218 was still looking for the damaged U-383 which had foundered twelve hours or so earlier. She was sighted by a Wellington 'B' of 547 Squadron, flown by Pilot Officer J.W Hermiston RCAF, who had recently received a commission. Bill Owens was still a member of his crew.

> 'On 2nd August 1943 we attacked U-218. It was a dull overcast day and we were on the homeward leg of our patrol. I was in the front gun turret again (Coastal Command Wellingtons carried three WOP/AGs and we usually changed positions every two hours, i.e. front turret, wireless set, rear turret). I liked being in the front turret, especially when low flying, there was a great sensation of speed and visibility was excellent. Davies was in the rear turret and Horwood was at the wireless set.
>
> 'I spotted the U-boat about a mile distance on our port quarter. It appeared to be low in the water and moving slowly in the heavy swell. It seemed to pop-up from nowhere and I think it had just surfaced, otherwise I would have spotted it much further away. There was no planning about this attack as we thought the U-boat was about to submerge. Hermiston swung to port and I opened fire as soon as I had the U-boat in my gun sight. I remember seeing a huge white dragon painted on the conning tower and could see the gun crew on the deck. I sprayed the deck and conning tower as we came in. We dropped our depth charges and climbed away. As we banked round we could see we had overshot and although very close, the U-boat appeared undamaged. We made two or three machine gun attacks before the U-boat submerged. I am surprised to hear this U-boat had to return to Brest following this attack. Both Davies and myself gave it a good going over with machine-gun fire but certainly our depth charges did not appear close enough to cause any damage.'
>
> *Sergeant W. Owens, 547 Squadron.*

'We were returning home, at about 3,000 feet. I informed my friend Hermiston that far ahead I could see the wake of a U-boat and was instructed to take photos to confirm our impending attack. We dropped a bomb from 2,000 feet whereupon the U-boats formed a protective circle, engaging us with considerable flak.

'The next approach was made from 50 feet to drop our D/Cs, which missed. Bill Owens in the front turret fired continuously at the U-boat gunners. A further attack of 50 feet was made with machine-gun fire, after which the U-boat submerged. It transpired that the U-boat was engaged on mine laying operations when our Wellington appeared on the scene.'

Flight Sergeant F.G. Duff, 547 Squadron.

In the event U-218 was not damaged, but Owens' and Davies' fire had caused so many casualties – six seriously wounded – that she had to abort her patrol and return to Brest, where she arrived on the 6th. Upon their return, Bill Owens and the rest of the crew had their day in London.

'The highlight of any U-boat attack was the visit to Northwood, North London for debriefing. Many crews spent months on Biscay operations without seeing anything and here we were at Northwood, twice within two months. Northwood appeared to be staffed by group captains and above. We had never seen so many senior officers under one roof. They were all very nice and polite and treated us well. The debriefing took about two hours and then we were let loose on London for 24 hours before returning to Cornwall.

Jim Hermiston and Loyd Speyer did not survive the war. In October 1943, 547 Squadron converted from Wellington to Liberators and the crew was split up. The former stayed with 547 and Davies, Horwood and self went off to a whole new ball game flying in Warwicks with an airborne lifeboat slung underneath.'

Sergeant W. Owens, 547 Squadron.

* * *

At 4.20 pm, a 228 Squadron Sunderland sighted what at first looked like three U-boats, but upon closer inspection, turned out to be the three German torpedo boats (T.22, T.24 and T.25) heading for their rendezvous with U-106. These opened fire on the flying boat which flew into cloud, but reporting to HQ that they had seen three Z-class destroyers. Homing procedure brought two aircraft to the scene: Flying Officer Reader Hanbury of 228 Squadron and Flight Lieutenant I.A.F.Clarke of 461. These began shadowing the three torpedo boats while sending frequent position reports. (They still believed the vessels were destroyers.) These brought a Halifax of 58 Squadron to the spot, which had been with the 40th Escort Group. This broke cloud directly over the three boats and was immediately damaged by their AA fire and compelled to fly home.

The 40th Escort Group was now about 65 miles away from the three torpedo boats. Forty minutes after the damaged Halifax flew off, the first Sunderland was compelled to leave when PLE was reached. Its place was taken by a 502 Squadron Halifax, which also reported them as destroyers. A few minutes later a fourth aircraft joined in, a Liberator of 224 Squadron, which had been diverted by base to fly to the sighting position.

At four minutes past 6 pm, Hanbury sighted the 40th Escort Group's ships and began to fly to and from the destroyers giving them bearings by visual signals. An hour later the group was within fifteen miles of the German ships, HMS *Bideford* seeing them momentarily.

Then the Liberator had to go home, leaving the Halifax and Sunderland still circling the torpedo boats. Quite suddenly, the Australian Sunderland crew spotted something else on the sea – a U-boat. It was about three miles south-east of the torpedo boats, steering a course of 050°. It was in fact the damaged U-106.

Ten minutes later Hanbury who had also seen the submarine, moved in to begin a gun duel with the German gunners. The U-boat began to make a turn to starboard as both aircraft captains decided almost simultaneously to make an attack.

The crew of U-106 had heard by hydrophone the approach of the torpedo boats from the east. But then the hydrophone bearing started to draw away to the north. Damerow, anxious not to lose his escort, surfaced and tried to follow. Damerow later recorded:

'...7.52 pm: Sunderland approaching from ahead, range 800 metres, medium height. I open fire on her at once and she sheers off to starboard, circling us outside gun range. In order to deny her the opportunity of attacking, I am forced to keep her ahead, so that I gain little on the torpedo boats. Two minutes later a second Sunderland dives out of the clouds and commences to circle us. On reaching favourable positions, they attack from each bow, blazing with their guns. The one to the starboard is engaged by the quadruple 2 cm; the one to the port by the single 2 cm and machine guns. The former turns off a little and drops at least six bombs, which detonate about 50 metres astern and cause severe concussion to the boat. The latter, whose fire has knocked out the layer, trainer and two loading number of the quadruple, dropped her bombs almost simultaneously on the port quarter. The port engine-room switchboard is torn from its securings and catches fire. The starboard diesel stops. Thick smoke fills the boat, which lists to port with a bad leak.

'Five minutes later the aircraft return to the attack. We engage them as before [but] the single 2 cm [gun] is shot out of action. The bombs fall very close and cause further damage. The port diesel also stops. Both electric motors are out of action. The boat is out of control and settles appreciably by the stern because of the inrush of water.

Chlorine gas is coming from the batteries. At 8.08 pm a third attack is made and since casualties among the guns' crews have been replaced by non-gunnery ratings, our fire is less accurate. The aircraft, engaging with all her guns, drops four bombs which detonate about 10 metres away.'

'Chic' Clarke came in first as Hanbury turned towards the U-boat off to starboard, the sun almost dead astern of him. Clarke straddled his D/Cs aft of the conning tower and 30 seconds later, Hanbury spaced his D/Cs across it from the rear starboard quarter.

Damerow continued:

'The boat continues to settle and the Senior Engineer reports that she can no longer be kept afloat. "Abandon ship!" Rafts are manned and inflated. The crew spring overboard with them, except five men manning the AA armament.'

The U-boat stopped, many of her crew being seen coming onto the deck. Some began jumping overboard while others attempted to re-open gunfire but were shot down by machine-gun fire from both aircraft. At 8.40 the U-boat blew up, leaving a sea littered with debris and four dinghies full of survivors. It had been their tenth war patrol. Damerow's report continued.

'08.15 pm: Fourth attack. Aircraft repeatedly attacks with gunfire, wounding several men in the water and shooting up a number of rafts. My guns have run out of ammunition, and I jump overboard with the last five men. Shortly afterwards there is a heavy explosion in the boat and she sinks rapidly, stern first, to the cheers of the swimming crew.

'The aircraft flies over us several times without shooting and then drops two smoke-floats. I and 35 of the crew, clinging to lifebuoys and a rubber dinghy, are picked up at dusk.'

Following this attack and some confusion over the exact position of the torpedo boats, the latter finally escaped. They were still regarded as destroyers and Plymouth had sent out two additional Royal Navy destroyers to re-inforce the Groups in the Bay. The 502 Squadron Halifax finally made a bombing attack on the torpedo boats before he had to leave, but his three A/S bombs missed by 100 yards. Shortly afterwards, the ships found the survivors of U-106, rescuing 36 men, including the submarine commander. Having lost the torpedo boats, the ships turned for home. Another 502 Squadron Halifax found the three boats later but when night came they finally got away.

* * *

While the action with U-106 had been going on, 100 miles to the south-east, an Instep patrol consisting of three Mosquitos of 307 Polish Squadron and one of 264 Squadron, lost one of their number. At 7.45 pm, Flight Lieutenant J. Bienkowski/Pilot Officer C. Borzenski reported their petrol pump was causing problems and he was returning to base. They were later plotted over the Channel Islands but failed to return.

CHAPTER ELEVEN

ANTI-CLIMAX

In four days Dönitz had lost U-454, 383, 706 and 106, and U-218 had been forced to abort her patrol. With the three lost on 30th July and three lost earlier – the 28th and 29th – this made nine boats lost to Coastal Command controlled aircraft in six days. It was too much for him. He issued immediate orders. He recalled the six boats which had recently sailed from Lorient and St Nazaire, then cancelled all further group sailings. Incoming U-boats were told to enter the Bay via Cape Finisterre and proceed independently along the Spanish coast, ignoring the nicety of territorial waters.

At a conference with Hitler, Dönitz had to report that the Allied blockade of the Bay had forced the cancellation of group sailings and seriously disrupted his U-boat campaign. In addition, the loss of a number of urgently needed supply U-boats had compelled boats already out in the Atlantic to cut short their patrols in order to return home to re-arm and refuel.

* * *

The period 1st July to 2nd August, saw the climax of operations in the Bay. During that period a total of 9,689 flying hours had been flown on Musketry and Seaslug patrols, together with operations around Cape Finisterre down to latitude 40°N. There had been 25 anti-U-boat squadrons working these areas, with a total strength of 368 aircraft.

These had made over 90 sightings and 63 attacks in a period in which 86 U-boats were crossing the areas, either inbound or outbound in groups or singly. The air patrols attacked or sighted 55 of these 86 boats and sank 16 (a 17th was sunk by the 2nd Escort Group) and forced six more to turn back to harbour. In addition the Finisterre patrols sank three U-boats and damaged another out to the west.

Air losses (according to 19 Group) had been four anti-U-boat aircraft shot down by U-boat flak, six by German fighting and four lost to unknown causes. RAF fighters lost two Beaufighters in air combat, but destroyed two FW200s and two Ju88s.

Following Dönitz's conference with Hitler, the Grand-Admiral reviewed his Bay operation. Co-operation, he knew, between Allied aircraft and surface vessels had increased, and he believed that the recent losses were due in part to this co-operation. He also was forced to admit that his tactics over recent weeks had failed. While his group sailing idea had some sound basis for success, ie. greater continued defensive fire power, an increase in look-out coverage, shared radar watch on several wave bands, the possibility of mutual assistance if in trouble together with the psychological effect of crews in company – it had failed. It had failed because Coastal Command had adapted to these tactics. Increased defensive fire was nullified by not attacking until a number of aircraft could divide the fire. Also, the mere act of staying on the surface, gave the attacking aircraft a far better target than one that had just crash-dived. The major error, however, was that the sinking of a U-boat for the possible cost of an aircraft, was far better arithmetic for the Allies. Aircraft and even a crew could be replaced far more easily at this stage of the war than a U-boat and its crew.

Other factors that hindered the Germans were not so easily seen by them until the tactic was used. Passage in company was something new to U-boat crews and they had not trained for it. In point of fact it needed a large part of the crew's attention. It was far easier for a singleton boat commander to take advantage of a favourable chance to dive, than for a group leader. Once a group boat was hit and damaged, practical help while still under attack was simply not possible by the other boats.

The Germans knew too that the presence of surface vessels that could also be homed to their position was a problem. If they stayed on the surface too long, they might soon see destroyers bearing down upon them over the horizon. Asdic searching and depth charge attacks, perhaps lasting for hours, would be sure to follow. Strangely too, this also gave the U-boat crews a psychological shot in the arm, for if they did abandon their damaged boat there was a fair chance they would be rescued by the enemy destroyers. This same destroyer presence gave similar encouragement to RAF crews, knowing that if they were brought down, at least British ships were nearby, even though they might be flying several hundred miles away from the English coast.

A major factor in the U-boats' defeat in the Bay in 1943 had been the radar battle. The Germans finally established that their Metox search receiver produced sufficient radiation of its own to enable RAF operators to detect a U-boat without having to use its own airborne search radar at all. While this was true to a point, the real reason the boats were being located was a combination of Enigma intercepts and centimetric radar. Bletchley Park where the Enigma codes were being broken were able to tell the Admiralty approximately where U-boats were, which made Coastal's work in finding them much easier. Coastal had still to 'protect' the intelligence by scouring various area of the ocean, but at least it knew that if a boat surfaced in a certain location, at least one aircraft would pick it up on radar.

Meanwhile, on 31st July the German Group West Experimental branch working with Fliegerführer Atlantik's aircraft, set up Metox radar search receivers on shore. It was found and reported that Metox radiations could be detected by aircraft from between 23 to 50 kilometres when they flew at heights between 500 to 2,000 metres.

Dönitz immediately issued a precautionary order that Metox should be switched off when sailing in good visibility and tuned continuously through the whole wave-band 120 – 250 cm in poor visibility. If hostile radar transmissions were in turn detected, the Metox had to be switched off and the U-boat must dive at once. Until positive proof could be found, the uncertainty made it necessary to cancel all sailings until boats were fitted with a Luftwaffe Hohenweil radar set. This had to be used instead of the Metox when proceeding on the surface. A new search receiver was also built by the Hagenuk Company – the W. Anz G.I, which was virtually free of radiation. These would shortly be issued to all U-boats.

Incoming U-boats were instructed to stay close to the Spanish coast which should give them some protection when their plot would be lost in the echos from the land.

The German Air Force had failed to stop or even curtail Coastal Command aircraft from operating over the Bay and there seemed no likelihood that they would ever do so. Me410s that had been allocated to operations over the Bay had been recalled for home defence after only one sortie in July.

The U-boats' situation would be improved greatly when the promised Schnorkel submarines began arriving. Their apparatus for diesel engine air intake and exhaust would allow U-boats to traverse the Bay without surfacing but that was still some months away. But even that would not be the panacea hoped for. But by then the conduct of the war was changing.

* * *

As a result of the recent successes in the Bay, Dönitz had been bludgeoned back into using a relatively safe, though protected, passage procedure. In spite of increased flying hours during the following months the Bay offensive was never again to reach the killing efficiency of this summer. From the period 1st May to 2nd August 1943, 25 U-boats had been sunk in the Bay and at least another 16 damaged. On all fronts the Germans and Italians lost 118 submarines from May to mid-August. Seventy eight to aircraft, six shared between aircraft and Naval ships and 34 to ships only.

With Dönitz convinced he now knew why his Bay losses had occurred and Hitler too being sympathetic, the commander of the U-boat arm was pleased that losses had suddenly stopped in the Bay. In the first sixteen days following his order to switch off the Metox receivers, not one boat had been lost. However, this was due as much as anything to the fact that far fewer boats were operating in the Bay. Also that U-boats were only surfacing at night and only then when close to the radar clutter of the Spanish coast.

By 16th August the first five inbound boats to use the coast route had arrived safely without loss. Then eight boats had cleared to the Atlantic by the same route by the 22nd. On this latter date he sent two boats from Brest across the middle of the Bay, independent of each other, diving by day and only surfacing by night long enough to recharge batteries. He followed these with eleven more across the Bay, plus four via coastal routes. More inward and outbound boats followed so by 1st September, U-boat traffic had increased, though not on the scale of the summer. In any event, Dönitz now had only 139 U-boats operational in the Atlantic Command as compared to 206 in May.

As luck would have it, the frequent requests by Dönitz to Hitler for increased air support in the Bay, finally bore fruit in August. Too late to help in the recent offensive, but it surprised the still victorious Coastal crews. Quite suddenly U-boat kills dropped, air combats increased and losses escalated.

* * *

The losses began on Tuesday, 3rd August. Flight Sergeant W.H.Smitham of 612 Squadron had taken off at 11.50 pm on the 2nd only to return at 00.48 am with engine trouble to MP654 'J'. Changing aircraft, he took off again at 1.48 am (in HP 128 'P') but this time failed to return. Then after a quiet day Flying Offficer B.A.Williams of 10 Australian Squadron met seven Ju88s at 6.37 pm.

Basil Williams' Sunderland was hemmed in by three 88s on each side while the seventh dived from cloud to make head-on attacks. His aircraft (DD 852 'J') was carrying four fixed forward-firing guns, a new modification just fitted to 10 Squadron's flying boats for U-boat attacks. These were fired in addition to the front gun, but the 88 was on target and although it was hit, its fire killed the Sunderland's front gunner, Flight Sergeant H.A. Bird. One section of three 88s then attacked from both quarters. Flying Officer Reg Gross, the navigator, co-ordinated the defensive fire until he was wounded. Cannon shells severed the hydraulics and knocked out the R/T, so Gross, despite his wounds, had to pass orders to Williams by hand. Three more of the crew were wounded and the Sunderland hit repeatedly but one 88 was probably destroyed and others hit. Williams finally managed to secure cloud cover after an hour long battle. He and Gross were awarded DFCs while Sergeants William Moser and Rhys Owen received DFMs.

An event in the North Transit Area showed that U-boats still fought it out despite Dönitz's change of tactics. U-489, a 1,600 ton supply boat, was attacked by Flying Officer A.A. Bishop. His attack sank her but his Sunderland (DD 859 'G') was shot down with the loss of five aircrew, and the others wounded. A destroyer rescued them plus survivors from the U-boat. Bishop received an Immediate DFC.

Late on the 6th, Pilot Officer P.W. Phillips took off for a night patrol in his 172 Squadron Wellington. At 1.42 am the starboard engine cut out. An SOS went out, the DCs jettisoned and a ditching made. As Phillips brought it down, the port wing dug into the high seas and the aircraft crashed. It filled with water and went under. All the crew got out, except Peter Phillips who went down with the Wellington. Two others drowned before they could reach the dinghy, but the others were rescued by HMS *Landguard* three hours later.

> 'Peter Phillips was a personal friend. His father had been bodyguard to the Duke of Gloucester at Barnwell Manor, Peterborough during the war. He was a very charming young man and only recently married when he was killed.
>
> 'I shall always remember the morning when (7th August, 1943) I returned from a gunnery course at Talbenny, Wales and was informed that Peter had gone into the drink. I think it was the first time I cried as an adult.
>
> 'Information from the crew revealed that he had received a broken neck when ditching.'
>
> *Flight Sergeant D.H. Hobden, 172 Squadron.*

The three survivors had been located by a 53 Squadron Liberator flown by Flight Lieutenant R.T. Merrifield DFC on patrol over Musketry. They were told to home in surface vessels, and later Terence Bulloch of 224 Squadron also found the dinghy (BZ 721).

During this rescue operation, Beaufighters of 248 Squadron on patrol gave air cover above the dinghy and aircraft for an hour. On their return to Predannack, Flying Officer McNicol (navigator to Flight Lieutenant Schofield) spotted four FW190s. All the Beaufighters made for cloud at 3,000 feet having been flying at 50 feet. The 190s came in from astern, one chasing Schofield's machine. Three more chased Squadron Leader R.D. Winnicott/Flying Officer A.E. Stoker. Then his Beaufighter was seen to be on fire. Flying Officer J.F. Green/Pilot Officer Forrest were also being attacked, but Green evaded into cloud. Turning sharply, they emerged a few moments later, only to be attacked by another 190, the Beaufighter being hit in two places. Forrest got in a quick non-deflection burst from 150 yards and scored hits on the 190's engine, and it broke away. Meanwhile, Lieutenant Newman (FFAF)/Flying Officer O.C. Cochrane, saw Winnicott go down in flames and crash into the sea. The 190s were from the 8th Staffel of JG2.

The 88s of KG/40 were out the next day, shooting down an American Liberator 'Q' of the 4th US Squadron flown by Captain R.L Thomas Jr, then attacking another of the 19th US Squadron – Captain Owen – but he managed to evade them. Thomas and crew did, however, manage to shoot down one of their attackers. Flight Lieutenant N.C.Gerrard of 10 Australian Squadron was also attacked by Ju88s but escaped with only slight damage.

There were few sightings of U-boats. Slessor and Geoffrey Bromet guessed the Germans had again altered their tactics. What they feared had at last happened. Dönitz, realising his error in ordering his U-boats to stay on the surface and fight back, had finally caused so many casualties he had reversed his earlier decision. Coastal Command stepped up its night Leigh Light flights again from 11th August. But during the next eleven days there were no sightings. The only three brief sightings at the beginning of August had all been close to the north-west corner of Spain and on 22nd August Slessor informed all Groups that he believed now [Ultra Intelligence?] that U-boats were entering and leaving the Bay close to the Spanish coast between Finisterre and Ortegal. The Admiralty agreed to move two escort groups to this area. Musketry and Seaslug were ended and their place taken by a system of patrols called Percussion.

Percussion A – Daylight patrols by No 19 Group in an area from 4800N x 0930W to 4600N x 0930W to Cape Ortegal, along the Spanish coast to latitude 4300N, then westward to longitude 1100W, up this longitude to 4400N, thence to 4500N x 1200W and due north to latitude 4800N.

Percussion B – Daylight patrols by No 15 Group, after satisfaction of convoy commitments, in an area between 48° and 43°N from longitude 13°W to the westward boundary of Percussion A.

Percussion C – Night Leigh Light Catalina and Wellington patrols in an area between latitudes 4500N and 4245N from longitudes 11° to 9°W.

Percussion D – Night patrols by ordinary aircraft in an area between latitudes 45° and 44°N and longitudes 0800 and 0945W. These aircraft were to be supplied from Nos 304 and 547 Wellington Squadrons to act as scare-crows with flares to illuminate all ASV contacts but were not to carry depth charges or bombs.

Percussion E – Day and night patrols in an area between latitudes 42° and 43°N from longitude 11°W to the Spanish coast. The AOC Gibraltar was requested to put in the maximum possible effort including US aircraft by arrangement with the American commander of the Moroccan Sea Frontier. It was emphasised that the night effort was of the utmost importance.

Coastal Command, especially 19 Group and the American squadrons under Coastal Command control, continued to search for the elusive enemy, but the only enemies they found were in the air.

On the 11th August, Terence Bulloch, still flying his BZ 721 with 224 Squadron, edged into the coast of Spain, only to be fired on by AA guns at Cape Prior as a warning not to come too close. At 2.10 that afternoon, Flight Lieutenant Norman C. Gerrard of 10 Australian Squadron who had had a lucky escape from 88s just three days earlier, reported his position as

4356/0948 – just 30 miles off the Spanish coast – but that was the last that was heard of him and his crew (DP177 'F'). KG40 got them this time.

The next day Squadron Leader E.J. Billy Wicht of 224 Squadron saw six Ju88s on his patrol but fortunately they did not see his Liberator.

'In the Bay in 1943 there is little doubt that look-outs on anti-submarine aircraft raised their eyes to the sky, not in deference to the Lord, but in defence of themselves against the wretched Hun. When the enemy pitched fast, heavily armed, fighter aircraft against the lumbering sub-hunters we soon realised that the rules of the game had changed, and the change was certainly not in our favour. The only comfort we sometimes enjoyed was to skulk just below the cloud base, prepared to seek haven, if our stately progress was threatened. However, on fine cloudless days we felt about as secure as Martin Luther King at a Ku Klux Klan rally.

'Intelligence on the GAF was disseminated, among other ways, by the display of silhouettes on the walls of the Operation Room. One day, at St Eval, we saw a fresh poster which depicted a large,ungainly German flying boat, with the designation Blohm & Voss 222, without any evidence of defensive armament. There was general agreement that our morale would be considerably raised by an encounter with this sitting duck. Here was the possibility of a quick conversion from prey to predator.

'With the passage of time we noticed that the Intelligence Officer was making hand amendments to the silhouette, here a turret, there a turret, and so on. There followed a swift reappraisal, and gone were thoughts of predation. Some time later one of our flight commanders on 224 Squadron, Squadron Leader Wicht, a Swiss national, was operating over the Bay in a Liberator. He had been in cloud for some time, and emerged into bright sunlight. He made a quick visual scan, and to his amazement saw that another aircraft had also just emerged from cloud, a few hundred yards on his port, and the aircraft was identified at a Bv222. His reactions were predictable; he applied full power and reefed his aircraft round to starboard. Less predictable were the actions of the captain of the Bv222; he was seen to increase speed and reef his aircraft round to port. Short of a rapid circumnavigation of the globe, an engagement seemed unlikely, much to the relief of both crews, I suspect.'

Flight Sergeant E.S. Cheek, 224 Squadron.

On the night of the 12th Sergeant E.R.H. Widdows of 172 Squadron flew a Leigh Light patrol. Returning to Chivenor at 4.30 am on the morning of the Friday the 13th, he flew a circuit in poor visibility and crashed about two miles inland from Clovelly. The Wellington caught fire and the DCs exploded. All six crewmen were killed. Flying Officer W.J. Dowling of 461 Squadron failed to return on the afternoon of the 13th. His crew on this patrol was that of Flight Lieutenant C.B. Walker DSO, who had been with him during the epic Ju88 battle on 2nd June, including Galt, Simpson, Fuller and Goode who had all been decorated for that battle. Indeed, Dowling himself had been Walker's second pilot on that epic occasion. A message from them at 2.49 recorded they were being attacked by Ju88s – but this time they were not as lucky. They had been flying DV968 'M' in which Chic Clarke had sunk U-106 eleven days earlier. Also on this day an American Liberator flown by Lieutenant McKinnon got into a fight with a FW200 and succeeded in shooting it down; his own B24D (42-40104) was undamaged.

Three more aircraft were lost on the 15th. Pilot Officer K.Harrison on an early patrol over Musketry failed to bring his 612 Squadron Wellington home. Flying Officer J. Whyte of 547 Squadron took his Wellington off just before midday and headed to Musketry and was not heard of again. The same Squadron lost Sgt D.P. Stephen and crew that afternoon. Then at 3.48 pm Flight Sergeant I.S. Dunbar of 58 Squadron got off a brief message, 'Am being attacked by five enemy aircraft' – then silence. Lieutenant Pardue of the 19th US Squadron was luckier and escaped the clutches of sixteen Ju88s that he encountered.

Flight Lieutenant P.R. Davenport's Sunderland (JM685 'X') of 461 Squadron was also caught by 88s just after quarter past three that afternoon. Davenport headed for cloud but his aircraft was hit and damaged before he reached them. Flight Sergeant R.V.Woolhouse in the midships turret was killed in one pass, Wireless Operator Warrant Officer I. Jones being wounded.

Number 58 Squadron lost another Liberator to KG40 the next day, Flying Officer M.H. Jenkins failing to return. Two American crews of the 19th US Squadron got away from Ju88s, Lieutenant Barnell surviving a fight with a Ju88, and Lieutenant Gallimeir (who had sunk U-558 on 20th July) evading eight Ju88s. Captain Maxwell of the 480th Group (which comprised the 1st and 2nd US Squadrons[1]) ran into two FW200s on the 17th and although his B24D was so badly damaged he had to put it onto the sea, his gunners did destroy one of the big Focke Wulfs.

There were more losses on the 18th. Flying Officer R. Armstrong of 415 Squadron lost an engine of his Hampden following a bad vibration. They jettisoned their DCs, but later the whole engine just fell off. Armstrong ditched five miles from the Scilly Isles, being picked up 45 minutes later by a launch. 547 Squadron lost a Wellington flown by Flight Sergeant J. Clark that just disappeared during the afternoon.

At least HQ knew about Flight Lieutenant H.W. Skinner of 10 Australian Squadron. At 6.45 pm they received an SOS from him – but nothing else.

---

[1] The 4th and 19th US Squadrons formed the 479th A/S Group.

Ju88s had got them too. They also got the Liberator flown by Lieutenants S M Grider and C H Moore of the 19th US Squadron, but they and all but four of the crew were rescued from the sea by a Royal Navy sloop on the 23rd after five days in a dinghy. At 6.25 another 19th Liberator flown by Lieutenant A.L.Leal was damaged by seven Ju88s, but he escaped without casualties.

At 4.55 am on the 21st, John Brooks' crew had a few anxious moments at St Eval; he was now flying with Pilot Officer Wilson.

> '21st August. Operations took off at 04.55, just cleared end of runway when petrol started pouring out of No.1 tank, frightening the beam gunner to death. He just finished reporting it when we had a fire in No.2 engine. Engine cut back and feathered and fire went out. Had great difficulty climbing clear on three engines with full load. Had a very busy time for a few minutes. Tried to jettison depth charges over the sea but the bomb doors refused to open, so we landed way over landing weight after four hours of low flying over the sea. BZ767.'
>
> *Flight Lieutenant J.H. Brooks, 224 Squadron.*

Flying Officer Eric Hartley of 58 Squadron was to have a few 'exciting' moments in mid-August, beginning on the 21st. About a quarter of an hour after sighting two French tunnymen, his Halifax was attacked by seven Ju88s. There was quite a battle for half an hour before cloud cover saved them. His gunners claimed hits on two of the German fighters. Another 58 Squadron crew were also in trouble.

Squadron Leader H.E. Brock sent out an SOS at 4.35 pm, reporting engine trouble. He was forced to ditch but that night they were located by a Leigh Light Wellington.

This had been the second 58 Squadron Liberator lost in two days, for on the 20th, Flying Officer T.H. Minta arrived back at base at 9.55 pm. When 20 miles from St Ives the aircraft sent the message: 'Where may I land?' and was told to land at base. At 11.25 the aircraft crashed at Bowerchalk. Two of the crew were killed and five put in hospital. Flight Sergeant P. Cherry of 547 Squadron flying a Musketry patrol saw three Ju88s at 5.34 pm, three miles off. Cherry headed for cloud and once in its white protection saw a Ju88 just above him. The rear gunner later said he thought there was as many as eight Junkers. After some skirmishes in these clouds, Cherry finally evaded them.

No. 311 Czech Squadron became operational on the 21st August, having converted to Liberators from Wellingtons. The Commanding Officer flew the unit's first Liberator patrol (in BZ780) but Wing Commander Jundrich Brietcetl DFC and crew failed to get home. His last known position at 6.19 pm was 4900/0716 – 80 miles south-west of the Scillies, on their homeward run. They had been intercepted and shot down by a Me110 from II/ZG1 operating from Brest.

A Polish aeroplane was lost on the 22nd, a Mosquito of 307 Squadron. Squadron Leader M. Lewandowski led with his navigator, Flight Lieutenant C. Krawiecki (DZ761) on an Instep patrol. At position 4994-0650, flying at 100 feet, the Poles spotted four FW190s in pairs, heading NNE and slightly above. The four Mosquitos turned away but the 190s had seen them and gave chase. Squadron Leader Lewandowski evaded one pass, but it left Flight Sergeant T. Eckart/Flying Officer K. Maluszak in an outside position. Two FWs, dropping their long range tanks, went down on Eckart. His tailplane disintegrated under their fire and the Mosquito (DZ655) fell into the sea.

At 11.24 Squadron Leader K.T.P. Terry DFC of 547 Squadron was part of three aircraft to help rescue Squadron Leader H.E. Brock's crew from the previous day's ditching. He and two Liberators circled the two dinghies until surface ships arrived. Terry could see five men in the dinghy and even dropped supplies but the packs disintegrated as they hit the water.

It was the Luftwaffe that certainly had the last word in August. Lieutenant K.H.Dustin of the 4th US Squadron was attacked by nine Ju88s on the 23rd. They shot up his B24D, but his gunners claimed three of the 88s, either shot down or certainly damaged. [KG40 lost one fighter.] Three of the Americans were wounded. Two days later Flying Officer B.F. Gaston DFC of 86 Squadron, an Australian, escaped two Ju88s that tried to attack him.

However, the Luftwaffe were more successful against six Beaufighter XIs of 143 Squadron during an Instep patrol. 143 had sent a detachment down to St Eval on 17th August to help give escort air cover to anti-submarine aircraft. As it turned out they were intercepted by six long range FW190. Four of the Beaufighters were shot down, including the detachment leader, Squadron Leader R.A. Ullman. They fell victim to aircraft of 1/128.

'I recall the arrival at St Eval of 143 Squadron, equipped with Beaufighters, and we naturally felt that help was at hand. I was being briefed in the Operations Room, at the same time as six of the 143 crews, making their first sortie into the Bay. Because of the German radar cover from the Brest Peninsula, we always entered and returned from the Bay via what was known as the Datum, a point well to the south-west of the Scilly Islands. The Beaufighters were recommended to take the same route, but with the confidence or arrogance (depending on your point of view) of fighter boys said that they would proceed directly from St Eval to their patrol line. In the event the six Beaufighters, flying at low level, were bounced by German fighters, and only two returned to base. Our offer of Liberators to escort the Beaufighters, was received as well as the presentation of a portrait of the Pope to the Kremlin.'

Flight Sergeant E.S. Cheek, 224 Squadron.

On the 24th Flight Lieutenant G A Sawtell of 53 Squadron was attacked by 14 Ju88s of KG40 and shot down into the Bay with no survivors from his Halifax crew. Geoff Sawtell had won the DFC for his actions back in July against U-558.

On the evening of the 24th, Wing Commander Musson, who only a month earlier had sunk U-614, took off on a Leigh Light patrol at 11.35 pm. They crashed two miles inland from Clovelly at 11.48. The Wellington caught fire and the D/Cs exploded. He and three of his original successful crew all died with two others.

Lieutenant McKinnon of the 480th US Group failed to return on the 27th, following a call that his B24D was under attack. 15/KG40 claimed one Liberator. It was not only the enemy that caused losses among Coastal aircraft. Flying accidents were always a danger to aircraft whether over the sea or land. Weather over the south-west of England can be treacherous even in high summer. Mist, clouds, high cliffs – all were potential and lethal flying hazards.

On 30th August, 311 (Czech) Squadron had its second casualty since converting to Liberators. Pilot Officer Josef Stach DFC was attacked by Ju88s over the Bay, beginning a fifteen minute battle. One Ju88 was shot down in flames and crashed into the sea, but Sergeant Andrej Simek, one of the beam gunners, was killed. On this same day 461 Squadron lost a Sunderland. Flying Officer C.R. Croft was off at 3.03 am, but at 9.53 base picked up a call that they were under attack by three Ju88s. After an anxious 27 minutes came the message that they were safe. Forty-five minutes later, however, the drama re-opened with the receipt of another message that three enemy aircraft had found them again. This time there was no 'safe' call, the Sunderland going into the sea in position 4621/1135 at 11.06 am.

September began with two losses on the 2nd, both from 224 Squadron. Flying Officer J.V. Gibson took off at dawn and failed to get home; Ju88 presence over the Bay was suspected. Ju88s did in fact cause both losses. Flying Officer G.H. Wharram flew a later patrol and was attacked by 88s, killing Wharram and Sergeant E.A.Moloney. Sergeant R.J. Foss took over the controls, but with one engine knocked out, a second on fire and the remaining two both cutting out, he had no choice but to ditch. The crew got into their dinghy without further mishap, but their ordeal had only just begun. They were spotted by a German U-boat which surfaced near them but when they discovered the survivors were British, they left them and went down again.

They were next seen on the 6th by a Sunderland and that night two Catalinas flew around and overhead looking for them with Leigh Lights but failed to pick them up in their beams. The next day Flying Offficer J.C. Miller – a Canadian – died. A Sunderland found them on the 8th and dropped supplies but the men were too weak to haul them into their rubber craft. Finally on the 9th – a week after being shot down – a Catalina directed

HMS *Wild Goose* to them. Unhappily it was too late for Pilot Officer W.R. Collins and Sergeant D.H. Bareham, the flight engineer, who both died on *Wild Goose* before reaching Liverpool.

* * *

One of the few U-boat sightings came on the night of the 24th. 179 Squadron at Gibraltar also had a detachment at Predannack, adding some of their Leigh Light Wellingtons to the Bay operations. Flying Officer D.F. McRae took off on the evening of the 24th and around 11.15 pm, while south-west of Ortegal, they picked up a radar contact at five miles. Closing in, they illuminated at $1/2$ mile, picking up a stationary U-boat on the surface which made no move to evade. Switching off the Light, McRae flew a circuit, came in again, and as the Light was switched on again, the Wellington ran into gunfire. His front gunner replied as they dropped to 100 feet, letting go six DCs from the U-boat's starboard quarter. The German gunners continued firing for just seconds after the attack, then the flak eased, then ceased. McRae circled again but the boat was gone.

However, success attended them. They had found U-134 in this outer Bay area, commanded by Oberleutnant Hans Günther Brosin and sent it to the bottom. There were no survivors. U-134 had been spotted earlier that evening by a Catalina of 202 Squadron but had been unable to attack due to the appearance of a FW200.

Brosin's boat had in fact been attacked by a US Navy Blimp (airship) on 18th July off the Florida coast, but the unfortunate Americans found themselves an easy target for a U-boat that didn't dive and stayed to blast the airship from the sky. 179 Squadron more than evened the score, even though at that moment McRae flew back to Gibraltar without knowing he and his crew had made a kill.[2]

This last sinking was not strictly in the Bay battle of 1943, but it gave heart to Coastal Command that U-boats could still be found. Certainly everyone knew that German tactics had changed – and for Coastal they had not changed for the better.

According to 19 Group's reports the following U-boat sightings and attacks had been made within the Bay area (although they are not in strict accordance with known losses today):

---

[2] Donald McRae DFC, a Canadian, sank two U-boats and was credited with a third 'probable', U-134 on 24th August, and U-211 on 18th November. On 6th September he so badly damaged U-760 its commander had to put into a Spanish port where it and the crew were interned.

	Sightings	Attacks	Sunk	Damaged
March	49	28	1	2
April	57	32	1	3
May	88	72	8*	6
June	67	22	2	6 +
July	45	27	11	3
August	13	7	4	1
	319	188	27	21

* including 1 by 15 Group
+ including two by 15 Group

After the harvest of May, June and July and the first two days of August, sightings and attacks fell away. The next U-boat successfully attacked in the Bay came on 7th September, again by a Leigh Light Wellington, this time by 407 RCAF Squadron. Only four more were sunk by 19 Group before the end of 1943.

One of these was U-221, destroyed by Flying Officer Eric Hartley of 58 Squadron. It was his 27th anti-submarine patrol and flying with him on this occasion was Holmsley South's Station Commander, Group Captain R.C. Mead AFC. At 9.40 pm another Halifax – of 502 Squadron – intercepted an SOS but the call was very faint. Hartley had found a surfaced U-boat at 5.10 pm, attacked and made a good straddle. However, return fire from the U-boat holed the Halifax (HR982 'B'), the starboard fuel tank was set ablaze, and its controls were damaged. Despite this, Hartley succeeded in ditching but only six of the crew survived to get into a dinghy. They were adrift for eleven days before being rescued by the destroyer HMS *Mahrata*, including Group Captain Roger Mead.

Hartley received an Immediate DFC, while one of his gunners, Flight Sergeant Kenneth E. Ladds (mid-upper), who had been on his 47th sortie, received the DFM.

* * *

While U-boat sightings in August had been few, enemy aircraft had been plentiful. Coastal Command recorded the loss of seventeen anti-U-boat aircraft and six fighters. In addition to these casualties, Coastal Command lost one to engine trouble and two to flying accidents. German losses had been five Ju88s destroyed plus one FW190.

It was not surprising. The numbers of Ju88 fighters having increased, the combats increased too:

GAF strength in Bay Area

Month	Fighter	Bomber/ Recce	Combats	Coastal losses A/S a/c	Ftrs	German Losses Ftrs	Recce
May	49	64	8	6	nil	5	nil
June	42	73	16	5	8	7.	2
July	60	120	20	5	2	2	1
Aug	80	132	34	17	6	6	1
Sep	111	104	25	7	1	6	nil

According to 19 Group, its crews reported seeing no less than 269 German aircraft during August, 232 being Ju88s, 20 FW200s, three Me 110s (sic) and 14 FW190s. They believed the 190s around Brest were starting to be a good deal more active.

* * *

The Battle of the Bay was over for 1943. Coastal Command's 19 Group with support from 15 Group and AHQ Gibraltar, had made the most of Dönitz's tactical errors. They had inflicted grievous losses on the U-boat arm which, added to the overall losses that summer, was a severe blow to Germany's submarine war.

In 1944 the Biscay area would see more U-boat kills, but the tactics had changed again then, because of the Allied invasion of Normandy and the capture of the Cherbourg peninsula. Until then, Coastal Command had to be satisfied with the victory it had achieved. Its aircrew had performed magnificently, facing the challenge, grasping the opportunities and overcoming the dangers. They had met the ever dangerous Luftwaffe aircraft and slugged it out with the U-boats. What they achieved in 1943 was a resounding victory and a positive contribution to the eventual defeat of Germany.

APPENDIX I

MAIN SQUADRONS INVOLVED IN THE BATTLE OF THE BAY, MAY TO AUGUST 1943

Sqdn	Aircraft	Bases	Commanding Officers
10 RAAF	Sunderland I & III	Mount Batten	W/C G.C. Hartnell
53	Liberator V	Thorney Island – Det: St Eval	W/C H.R.A. Edwards AFC
58	Halifax II	Holmsley South – Det: St Eval	W/C W.E. Oulton DSO DFC
59	Liberator V	Thorney Island & Aldergrove Det: St Eval	W/C G.C.C. Bartlett AFC W/C P.A. Gilchrist DFC
172	Wellington VIII & XII	Chivenor	W/C R.G. Mussen W/C E.G. Palmer
179	Wellington VIII	Gibraltar Det: St Eval	W/C A.N. Combe AFC W/C J.H. Gresswell DSO DFC
201	Sunderland III	Lough Erne	W/C R.E.C. Van der Kiste DSO
206	Fortress II	Benbecula – Det: St Eval	W/C R.B. Thomson DSO
210	Catalina III	Hamworthy – Det: Gibraltar	W/C C.H. Brandon
220	Fortress II	Benbecula – Det: St Eval	W/C P.E. Hadow
224	Liberator V	St Eval	W/C A.E. Clouston DFC AFC
228	Sunderland III	Pembroke Dock	W/C N.F. Eagleton DFC
304 Polish	Wellington X	Davidstow Moor	W/C M. Pronaszko
311 Czech	Liberator V	Beaulieu	W/C J. Breitcetl DFC
407 RCAF	Wellington XII	Chivenor	W/C J.C. Archer
415 RCAF	Hampden I	Thorney Island – Det: Predannack	W/C G.H.D. Evans
423 RCAF	Sunderland III	Castle Archdale – Det: Pembroke Dock	W/C F.J. Rump W/C L.G.C.J. Archembault
461 RAAF	Sunderland III	Pembroke Dock	W/C D.L.G. Douglas DFC
502	Halifax IIA	St Eval	W/C J.C. Halley
547	Wellington XI	Chivenor – Det: Davidstow Moor	W/C R.M. McKern
612	Whitley VII Wellington XII	Chivenor – Det: Davidstow Moor	W/C J.S. Kendrick W/C J.B. Russell
10 OTU	Whitley V	St Eval	

American Squadrons:
1st, 2nd, 4th and 19th USAAF Squadron flying Liberator B24Ds, USN Liberators (PB4-Y) of VB103 and the VP 63 Squadron USN, flying PBY-5 Catalinas.

Fighters:

25	Mosquito NF11	Church Fenton - Det: Predannack Jun/43	W/C S.N.L. Maude DFC
143 RCAF	Beaufighter XIC	North Coates - Det: St Eval Aug/43	W/C R.N. Lambert
151	Mosquito XII	Colerne- Det: Predannack Jun/43	W/C S.P. Richards AFC
235	Beaufighter VIC	Leuchars – Det: Predannack May/43 Det: St Eval Jun/43	W/C G.H.B. Hutchinson
236	Beaufighter VIC	North Coates Det. Predannack May/43	W/C H.N.C. Wheeler DFC
248	Beaufighter VIC	Predannack	W/C F.E. Burton DFC
264	Mosquito II	Predannack	W/C W.J. Allington DFC AFC
307 Polish	Mosquito I	Fairwood Common – Det: Predannack	W/C J. Orzechowski
410 RCAF	Mosquito II & VI	Coleby Grange – Det: Predannack Jun/43	W/C G.H. Elms
456 RAAF	Mosquito IIF	Middle Wallop Det: Predannack Jun/43	W/C M.H. Dwyer

APPENDIX II

U-BOAT LOSSES IN THE BAY, MAY TO AUGUST 1943

Date	U-Boat	Commander	Patrol	Psn/Time	Aircraft, Sqn & Crew
2 May	U-465 VIIC	Kptltn Heinz Wolf	5th Sailed St Nazaire 29 April, outward to Nth Atlantic	4448/0858 19.15 pm	Sunderland DV 968 'M' 461 Sqn F/Lt E.C. Smith pilot P/O C.J. Dawson P/O Grainger F/L F.B. Gascoigne Sgt L.W. Cox Sgt R.V. Stewart F/Sgt H. Smedley F/Sgt J. Gamble Sgt J. Barrow Sgt R. Macdonald P/O E.R. Critcher
7 May	U-663 VIIC	Kptltn Heinrich Schmid	5th From Brest 5 May, to Atlantic	4706/1058 12.28 pm	Sunderland W3993 'W' 10 RAAF Sqn F/L G.G.Rossiter F/O M.H. Jones 2nd pilot F/O J.P. Roberts nav F/O W.C. Felgenhaur Sgt A.F. Leggett Sgt K.L. Dowling Sgt W.C. Moser

Date	U-Boat	Commander	Patrol	Psn/Time	Aircraft, Sqn & Crew
11 May	U-528 IXC/40	Oblt zS Georg von Rabenau	1st From Kiel, 15 April, inbound from Nth Atlantic	4655/1444 09.31 am	Halifax HR742 'D' 58 Sqn P/O J B Stark pilot P/O H.W. Burroughs W/O G.A. Roy P/O G.P. Ruickbie Sgt J.P. Young Sgt J.E. Abbey F/Sgt K. Hopper F/Sgt E.D. Jones
15 May	U-266 VIIC	Kptltn Ralf von Jesson	2nd From St Nazaire 14 April, to the Atlantic	4528/1020 18.10 pm	Halifax HR746 'M' 58 Sqn W/C W.E. Oulton pilot P/O N.A. Lyes P/O R.W. Mee Sgt R.A. Burniston Sgt H.A.C. Cooke Sgt B.D. Wyatt Sgt L. Brewis Cpl J.P. Lusina

Sgt E.C. O'Brien
Sgt F.K. Cowled
Sgt G.C.E. Hore
F/Sgt R.F. Mattner
F/O A.L. Coomes

Date	U-Boat	Commander	Patrol	Psn/Time	Aircraft, Sqn & Crew
16 May	U-463 XIV tanker	KvtKpt Leo Wolfbauer	5th Left Verdon-sur-Mer, 10 May, for the Nth Atlantic	4557/1140 20.03 pm	Halifax HR774 'R' 58 Sqn F/O A.J.W. Birch pilot P/O R.H. Collishaw 2nd pilot F/Sgt W. Hale nav Sgt J.R. Shaw eng F/Sgt W. Cawthorne sig Sgt J.D. Rice AG F/Sgt T.H. Linton AG
31 May	U-440 VIIC	Oblt zur See Werner Schwaff	5th From St Nazaire 26 May, outward Atlantic	4538/1304 17.15 pm	4538/1304 Sunderland DD835 'R' 201 Sqn F/L D.M. Gall pilot F/O S.C. Roberts F/O J.C. Hamer P/O H. Martin S/L N.L. Smith F/Sgt D.M. Briden Sgt T. Lansdale Sgt E. Thompson Sgt W.G. Turner Sgt T.G. Grosvenor Sgt W. McKonkey
31 May	U-563 VIIC	Oblt zS Gustav Borchardt	8th Sailed from Brest 29 May, outward Atlantic	4635/1040 17.35 pm	Halifax HR 774 'R' 58 Sqn W/C W.E. Oulton pilot Sgt R.S. Crick F/O R.M. Cooper

Date	U-Boat	Commander	Patrol	Psn/Time	Aircraft, Sqn & Crew
					Sgt G.J. Stoddart
					Sgt J.H. Oliver
					Sgt D. Jackson
					Sgt J. MacKinley
					Sunderland DD838 'X' 228 Sqn
					F/O W.M. French pilot
					F/O A.S. Pedley
					F/O R.W. Fox
					Sgt D. Skinner
					Sgt C. Black
					Sgt P. Brown
					Sgt D. Norman
					Sgt T. Kilsby
					Sgt J. Armstrong
					Sgt S. Baker
					F/Sgt W.J. DeBois
					Sunderland DV965 'E' 10 Sqn RAAF
					F/L M.S. Mainprize pilot
					Sgt C.C. Clark 1st pilot
					F/O T.M. Ryan 2nd pilot
					Sgt A.W. Reeves eng
					F/O C.N. Austin nav
					Sgt M.R. Delaney WOM
					Sgt A.C. Carrett WOP/AG

Date	U-Boat	Commander	Patrol	Psn/Time	Aircraft, Sqn & Crew
1 Jun	U-418 VIIC	Leutnant zS Gerhard Lange	1st From Kiel, 24 April, inbound from Nth Atlantic	4705/0855 11.05 am	Beaufighter T5258 'B' 236 Sqn F/O M.C. Bateman pilot F/Sgt C.W.G. Easterbrook nav Lt Cdr F.J. Brookes obs
14 Jun	U-564 VIIC	Oblt zS Hans Fiedler	10th From Bordeaux 9 June, outward to Atlantic	4417/1025 16.45 pm	Whitley BD220 'G' 10 OTU Sgt A.J. Benson pilot P/O T.J.J. Lee nav Sgt R.L. Rennick 2nd pilot Sgt G.T. Graves WOP/AG F/O A. Kingsley AG
3 Jul	U-126 IXC	Oblt zS Siegfried Kietz	6th From Lorient 20 March, inbound from West Africa	4602/1123 02.43 am	Wellington 'R' 172 Sqn F/Sgt A. Coumbis pilot F/O C.S. Rowland F/O D.J. Ashworth Sgt G.W. Yung Sgt J.F. Wilmer Sgt H. Hever

Sgt I.V. Speirs fitter
Sgt L.J. Lang arm
Cpl B.C Leech fitter u/t
Sgt F.C. Callander AG
LAC B.E. Steer fitter

Date	U-Boat	Commander	Patrol	Psn/Time	Aircraft, Sqn & Crew
3 Jul	U-628 VIIC	Kptltn Heinrich Hasenschar	4th Sailed from Brest 1 July, outward to Atlantic	4411/0845 14.02 pm	Liberator FL963 'J' 224 Sqn S/L P.J. Cundy pilot F/O R.W. King nav P/O E. Allen 2nd pilot F/Sgt I.A. Graham WOP/AG F/Sgt E.S. Cheek WOP/AG Sgt A.H. Graham AG Sgt D. Doncaster AG
5 Jul	U535 IXC	Kptltn Helmut Ellmenreich	1st Sailed from Kiel 25 May, inbound from the Azores	4338/0913 17.04 pm	Liberator BZ751 'G' 53 Sqn F/Sgt W. Anderson pilot Sgt G.B. Tomlinson W/O I.C. Brayshaw Sgt R.N. Lord F/Sgt G.H. Sheeran Sgt C. Coley Sgt W.R. Robinson
8 Jul	U-514 IXC	Kptltn Hans-Jürgen Auffermann	4th From Lorient 3 July, outward to Sth Africa	4337/0859 13.20 pm	Liberator BZ721 'R' 224 Sqn S/L T.M. Bulloch pilot F/Sgt N.E. Lord 2nd pilot F/O D.E H. Durrant nav Sgt A.G. Dyer WOP/AG F/Sgt D. Purcell WOP/AG Sgt R. McColl eng F/O F.B. Lewis WOP/A(G F/Sgt L. Larkin AG F/Lt C.V.T. Campbell

Date	U-Boat	Commander	Patrol	Psn/Time	Aircraft, Sqn & Crew
13 Jul	U-607 VIIC mining	Oblt zS Wolf Jeschonnek	5th From St Nazaire 10 July, outward to Jamaica	4502/0914 07.50 am	Sunderland JM708 'N' 228 Sqn F/O R.D. Hanbury pilot P/O T. Pearson P/O W.K. Knights F/Sgt A. Beal F/Sgt G.A. Williames F/Sgt B. Lacey F/Sgt E. House F/Sgt N. Wilson Sgt A. McFarlane Sgt F. Akers
20 Jul	U-558 VIIC	Kptltn Günther Krech	10th From Brest 8 May, inbound from the Azores	4510/0942 12.18 pm	Liberator 'F' 19th Sqn USAAF Lt C.F. Gallimeir pilot Lt Rosoff nav and crew Halifax DT642 'E' 58 Sqn F/L G.A. Sawtell pilot P/O J.M. Clark F/Sgt T.R. Urquhart Sgt B. Hilldon P/O R.W. Marshall AG Sgt W.A Tennant Sgt B.E. Mitchell AG Sgt L.C. Matthews

Date	U-Boat	Commander	Patrol	Psn/Time	Aircraft, Sqn & Crew
24 Jul	U-459 XIV tanker	Kovtkpt Georg von Wilamowitz -Möllendorf	6th From Bordeaux 22 July, outward to Nth Atlantic	4553/1038 17.50 pm	Wellington 'Q' 172 Sqn F/O W.H.T.Jennings pilot F/O J.G. McCormack 2nd pilot F/Sgt J.W Buxton nav F/O J. Johnston WOP/AG F/Sgt L. Harrop WOP/AG Sgt A.A. Turner AG
28 Jul	U-404 VIIC	Oblt zS Adolf Schönberg	7th From St Nazaire 24 July, outward to Nth Atlantic	4553/0925 18.07 pm	Liberator 'W' 224 Sqn F/O R.V. Sweeny pilot F/O R.W. King nav P/O E. Allen 2nd pilot F/Sgt I.A. Graham WOP/AG Sgt C. Owen eng F/Sgt E.S. Cheek WOP/AG Sgt A.H. Graham AG Sgt D. Doncaster AG Liberator 'N' 4th Sqn USAAF Lt A.J. Hammer pilot and crew
29 Jul	U-614 VIIC	Kptltn Wolfgang Sträter	3rd From St Nazaire 25 July, outward to Atlantic	4642/1103 10.50 am	Wellington 'G' 172 Sqn W/C R.G. Musson pilot W/O R. Reynolds F/Lt E. Carr F/Lt L.H. Burden Sgt B. Todd Sgt G.R. Manley-Tucker

Date	U-Boat	Commander	Patrol	Psn/Time	Aircraft, Sqn & Crew
30 Jul	U-461 IV Supply	Kovtkpt Wolf-Harro Stiebler	6th From Bordeaux 27 July, outward to Atlantic	4542/1100 11.55am	Sunderland W6077 'U' 461 Sqn RAAF F/L D. Marrows pilot P/O P.C. Leigh 1st pilot F/Sgt P.E. Taplin 2nd pilot F/O J.S. Rolland nav Sgt G.M. Watson eng Sgt A. N. Pierce fitter F/O P.T. Jenson 1st WOP F/Sgt H.H. Morgan 2nd WOP Sgt D.C. Sidney AG Sgt R.L. Webster 3rd WOP Sgt F. Bamber rigger F/Sgt J. Tainer u/t
30 Jul	U-462 XIV supply	Oblt Bruno Vöwe	5th From Bordeaux 27 July, outward to Atlantic	4508/1057 12.10 pm	Halifax 'S' 502 Sqn F/O A. van Rossum pilot F/Sgt C.D. Aidney F/Lt A.W. Martin F/O G.W Leadson P/O J.A. Riddock F/Sgt R.E. Wiggall F/Sgt F.S. Fraser Sgt A. Sills

Date	U-Boat	Commander	Patrol	Psn/Time	Aircraft, Sqn & Crew
1 Aug	U-454 VIIC	Kptltn Burkhard Häcklander	5th From La Pallice 29 July, outward to Atlantic	4536/1023 14.42 pm	Sunderland W4020 'B' 10 Sqn RAAF F/L K.G. Fry pilot F/O H.R. Budd 1st pilot F/O J.M. Curtis 2nd pilot F/O J.H. Portus nav P/O A.M. Welch nav u/t Sgt H.B. Lydeamore eng Sgt F.O. Pettersson fitter F/Sgt P.E. Cook WOP/AG F/Sgt R.G. Welfare WOP/AG Sgt J.E. Fryer fitter Sgt J. Haslam arm Sgt D.I. Conacher AG
1 Aug	U-383 VIIC	Kptltn Horst Kremser	5th From Brest 29 July, outward to Atlantic	4724/1210 20.14 pm	Sunderland 'V' 228 Sqn F/L S. White pilot F/O A. Neville-Stack 2nd pilot F/O K.A. Mooring nav P/O F. Jackson F/Sgt E. Kampton Sgt F. Baker Sgt B. Hodgman F/Sgt T. Robney Sgt W. Campion Sgt R. Glazier Sgt W. Carteen

Date	U-Boat	Commander	Patrol	Psn/Time	Aircraft, Sqn & Crew
2 Aug	U-706 VIIC	Kptltn Alexander von Zitzewitz	5th From La Pallice 29 July, outward to Atlantic	4615/1025 09.20 am	Liberator 'T' 4th Sqn USAAF Lt J.L. Hamilton pilot and crew
2 Aug	U-106 IXB	Oblt zS Wolfdietrich Damerow	10th From Lorient 29 July, outward to Atlantic	4635/1155 20.40 pm	Sunderland JM708 'N' 228 Sqn F/O R.D.Hanbury pilot F/O D. Pearson pilot F/Sgt A. Beal F/Sgt B. Lacey F/Sgt T. Kilsby F/Sgt E. House F/Sgt N.T.H. Wilson F/Sgt R. Webster Sgt W. Harris Sgt D. Norman Sgt R. Morrison Sunderland DV968 'M' 461 Sqn RAAF F/L I.A.F. Clarke pilot F/O J.C. Amiss Sgt D.M. Jorgenson F/Sgt P. Pfeiffer F/Sgt L. White Sgt R. Jeffries W/O R. Hattam F/Sgt J.H. Royle F/Sgt L.G. Studman F/O E.R. Critcher F/Sgt J.H. Poulton

APPENDIX III

U-BOATS DAMAGED IN THE BAY, MAY TO AUGUST 1943

Date	U-Boat	Commander	Patrol	Psn/Time	Aircraft, Squadron and Crew
1 May	U-613 VIIC	Kptltn Helmut Köppe	3rd From La Pallice 23 March, inbound from Atlantic	4445/1157 00.07 am	Wellington 'N' 172 Squadron Sgt P.W. Phillips pilot Sgt N.J. Harris 2nd pilot Sgt A.A. Turner WOP/AG Sgt W.H. Ware WOP/AG F/Sgt G.W. Duncan WOP/AG
1 May	U-415	Kptltn Kurt Neide	2nd From Bergen 7 March, to Nth Atlantic, inbound to Brest	4438/1150 08.20 am	Halifax 'C' 502 Squadron F/O R. Houston pilot P/O W. McDowell Sgt A.N. Excell Sgt E.S. Bruton Sgt L.S. Collins Sgt J.S. Pope Sgt J. Kershaw
				11.40 am	Sunderland DV968 'M' 461 Sqn F/Lt E.C. Smith captain F/O C.J. Dawson 1st pilot P/O D.A. Sinclair 2nd pilot F/L F.B. Gascoigne nav Sgt L.W. Cox eng

Date	U-Boat	Commander	Patrol	Psn/Time	Aircraft, Squadron and Crew
					Sgt R.V. Stewart fitter F/Sgt H. Smedley WOM F/Sgt J. Gamble WOP/AG Sgt J. Barrow WOP/AG Sgt R. MacDonald fitter P/O E.R. Critcher AG
				15.25 pm	Whitley 'E' 612 Squadron F/Sgt N. Earnshaw pilot Sgt M.G. Millard 2nd pilot P/O L.R. Green nav Sgt L.J. McQuiston WOP/AG Sgt L. Shaw WOP/AG Sgt B. Dennehey WOP/AG
6 May	U-214 VIID minelayer	Kptltn Rupprecht Stock	5th From Brest 5 May, outward to Atlantic	4722/0905 18.05 pm	Whitley BD189 'K' 10 OTU Sgt S.J. Barnett pilot Sgt T.H. Pike Sgt G.O. Sharpe Sgt L. Whitworth P/O E.A. Price Sgt H.A. Weber
15 May	U-591 VIIC	Kptltn Hans-Jürgen Zetzsche	3rd From St Nazaire 12 May, outward	4615/1150 12.36 pm	Whitley LA882 'M' 10 OTU F/Sgt G.W. Brookes pilot F/Sgt J. H. Walton

Date	U-Boat	Commander	Patrol	Psn/Time	Aircraft, Squadron and Crew
			to Atlantic		Sgt S. Fontley P/O J.T. Saunders Sgt K.G. Sewell F/Sgt H.G. Reid
24 May	U-523 IXC/40	Kpttn Werner Pietszch	2nd From Lorient 22 May, outward to Atlantic	4626/0925 11.22 am	Whitley BD414 'J' 10 OTU Sgt C.S. Chatton pilot Sgt C. Langford Sgt L.R.G. Armitage Sgt W.A. Reffin Sgt W. Archibald Sgt L.V.J. Smith
24 May	U-441 VIIC	Kpttn Götz von Hartmann	5th Sailed from Brest 22 May, flak ship/ aircraft trap	pm	Sunderland EJ139 'L' 228 Sqn F/O H.J. Debnam pilot F/O C.L. Houedard F/O A.H. Pelham-Clinton F/O W.C. Haylock F/Sgt F. Capes nav F/Sgt R. Cooper F/Sgt B. Crossland Sgt L. Whatley Sgt E. French Sgt W. Easson Sgt A. Sales

Date	U-Boat	Commander	Patrol	Psn/Time	Aircraft, Squadron and Crew
31 May	U-621 VIIC	Oblt zS Max Kruschka	4th From Brest 22 April, inbound from Azores	4724/1059 18.48 pm	Liberator 'Q' 224 Squadron F/O R.V. Sweeny pilot F/O R.W. King nav P/O E. Allen 2nd pilot F/Sgt I.A. Graham WOP/AG F/Sgt E.S. Cheek WOP/AG F/Sgt C. Owen eng Sgt A. Graham AG
13 Jun	U-564 VIIC	Oblt zS Hans Fiedler	10th From Bordeaux 9 June, outward to Atlantic	4430/1500 20.00 pm	Sunderland DV967 'U' 228 Sqn F/O L.B. Lee pilot F/O D.F. Hill P/O G. Lough F/O A.K. McDougal F/O R.J. Agur Sgt V. Goldstone Sgt R. Shaw Sgt R. Smith Sgt J. Fraser Sgt A. Carmichael Sgt D. Davies
14 Jun	U-155 IXC	Oblt zS Johannes R. Altmeier	5th From Lorient 12 June, outward to Atlantic	4450/0800 09.30 am	Mosquito HJ648 'B' 307 Sqn S/L S. Szablowski pilot Sgt M. Gajewski nav

Date	U-Boat	Commander	Patrol	Psn/Time	Aircraft, Squadron and Crew
14 Jun	U-68 IXC	Oblt zS Albert Lauzemis	7th From Lorient 7 June, outward to Atlantic	4450/0800 09.30 am	
17 Jun	U-338 VIIC	Kptltn Manfred Kinzel	2nd From Bordeaux 15 June, outward to Atlantic	4342/0937 19.30 pm	Fortress FL457 'F' 206 Sqn F/O L.G. Clark pilot P/O G. Niven P/O J.D. Ackerman F/Sgt F.W. Allison W/O A. Garnham F/Sgt G.J. Jones Sgt W.E. Pollard Sgt K. Jarvis
21 Jun	U-462 XIV Supply	Oblt zS Bruno Vöwe	5th From Bordeaux 19 June, outward to Atlantic	4535/0815 12.13 pm	Mosquito HJ655 'V' 151 Sqn S/L B.D. Bodien pilot F/O R.W. Sampson nav Mosquito 'W' 151 Sqn P/O J.D. Humphries pilot P/O H.J. Lumb nav Mosquito 'X' 151 Sqn F/O A.D. Boyle pilot Sgt H.M. Friesner nav Mosquito DZ299 'D' 456 Sqn W/O G.F. Gatenby pilot F/Sgt J.M. Fraser nav

Date	U-Boat	Commander	Patrol	Psn/Time	Aircraft, Squadron and Crew
27 Jun	U-518 IXC/40	Kptltn Freidrich-Wilhelm Wissmann	3rd From Lorient 24 June, outward to Atlantic	4332/1320 12.35 pm	Sunderland W6005 'P' 201 Sqn F/O B.E.H. Layne pilot F/O L.W.H. Stevens Sgt M. Glicker F/Sgt J. Sweet F/Sgt C. Churm Sgt D. Ball Sgt J. Williams Sgt B. Campbell Sgt K.W. Smithies Sgt J. Greenwood Sgt J. Watkins
2 Jul	U-462 XIV Supply	Oblt sZ Bruno Vöwe	6th From Bordeaux 19 June, outward to Atlantic	4337/1005 15.45 pm	Liberator 'J' 224 Squadron W/O E.J.I. Spiller pilot F/Sgt R.H.Humphrey nav Sgt R. Pierce 2nd pilot P/O E. Bentley eng Sgt F.T. Holland WOP/AG Sgt J.R.L. Thompson WOP/AG F/Sgt J. Mackin, WOP/AG F/Sgt R.A. Denny WOP/AG
3 Jul	U-386 VIIC	Oblt zS Fritz Albrecht	2nd From St Nazaire 29 June, outward to Atlantic	4450/0950 14.36 pm	Liberator BZ731 'D' 53 Sqn W/O L.L. Esler pilot F/Sgt J.L. Knight F/Sgt W.R. Kinsman

Date	U-Boat	Commander	Patrol	Psn/Time	Aircraft, Squadron and Crew
					F/Sgt A. Campbell
					F/Sgt A.H. Nopper
					Sgt A.W.G. Brown
					Sgt R.C. Laver
12 Jul	U-441 VIIC	Kptltn Götz von Hartmann	6th From Brest 8 Jul, Flak boat/ aircraft trap	4506/0854 14.05 pm	Beaufighter 'B' 248 Sqn FL C.R.B. Schofield pilot Sgt J.A. Mallinson nav Beaufighter 'V' 248 Sqn Lt G.C. Newman pilot F/O O.C. Cochrane nav Beaufighter 'A' 248 Sqn F/O P.A.S. Payne pilot F/O A.M. McNichol nav
2 Aug	U-218 VIID Minelayer	Kptltn Richard Becker	5th From Brest 29 July, outward to Trinidad	4712/1054 15.19 pm	Wellington 'B' 547 Sqn P/O J.W. Hermiston pilot F/Sgt F.G.Duff 2nd pilot P/O L.G. Speyer nav Sgt W. Owens WOP/AG Sgt J.W. Horwood WOP/AG Sgt L. Davies WOP/AG

APPENDIX IV

COASTAL COMMAND CASUALTIES OVER THE BAY, MAY TO AUGUST 1943

Date	Sqdn	Aircraft			Result	Cause	Crew	
5 May	612	Whitley	EB328	'B'	Lost	Accident	F/O C.H. Norton pilot	KIA
							Sgt J.E. Edge 2nd pilot	Baled out- safe
							P/O D.J. Webb	KIA
							Sgt C.W. Waterer	KIA
							Sgt J. Steele	KIA
							Sgt R.H. Frost	KIA
5 May	58	Halifax	HR745	'S'	Damaged	U-Boat attack	W/C W.E. Oulton & crew unhurt	
6 May	58	Halifax	BB256	'A'	Lost		Sgt N.F. Robertson pilot	KIA
							Sgt R. Brickles 2nd pilot	KIA
							Sgt L.A. Fisher nav	KIA
							Sgt J. Randall eng	KIA
							Sgt R.G. Bridge WOP/AG	KIA
							Sgt W. Mapley WOP/AG	KIA
							Sgt L.T. Brett WOP/AG	KIA
7 May	59	Liberator	FL971	'J'	Lost	Bad weather	S/L W.W. Cave DFC pilot	KIA
							P/O H.J. Summers	KIA
							F/O P.R. Galbraith nav	KIA
							Sgt G. Tisitselis	KIA
							Sgt B. Sainthouse	KIA

Date	Sqdn	Aircraft		Cause	Result	Crew	
						Sgt B.G. Bolkinghorne 2P	KIA
						Sgt J.H.S.Joanette	KIA
9 May	10 OTU	Whitley	BD278 'C'	U-Boat attack	Damaged	Sgt A.J Savage & crew	safe
9 May	58	Halifax	HR743 'N'	U-Boat attack	Lost	F/Sgt J.A. Hoather DFM pilot	KIA
						Sgt T.E . Hamley	KIA
						F/L L.R. Ott	KIA
						Sgt J. Summerville	KIA
						Sgt E. Ramjohn	KIA
						Sgt A. Simpson	KIA
						Sgt H.S. Butler	KIA
						Sgt R.Y. Herd	KIA
13 May	224	Liberator	FL947 'R'	Ju88s	Lost	P/O G.B. Willerton pilot	safe
						F/Sgt J.D. White	KIA
						Sgt K. Hodd	KIA
						F/L T. Luke	KIA
						P/O R.G. Barham WOP/AG	DOW
						F/Sgt H. Bell	KIA
						Sgt P. Gardner	KIA
						P/O J.R. McCall	KIA
						Lt B. Church RNVR	KIA
13 May	224	Liberator	FL946 'L'	Ju88s	Damaged	W/O E.J.J.Spiller & crew	safe

Date	Sqdn	Aircraft	Cause	Result	Crew	
14 May	461 RAAF	Sunderland DV968 'M'	Ju88s	Damaged	F/L E.C.Smith & crew	safe
					Sgt J. Barrow	WIA
15 May	228	Sunderland DD837 'V'	Ju88s	Lost	F/L G.A. Church pilot	KIA
					F/O T.A. Newberry	KIA
					F/O A.J. Hibbard	KIA
					F/O W.L. Leeman	KIA
					Sgt R. Deacon	KIA
					F/Sgt D. Smart	KIA
					F/Sgt J. Rolfe	KIA
					Sgt W.A. Jones	KIA
					F/Sgt E. Maycock	KIA
					Sgt A. Morgan	KIA
					Sgt C. Sheppard	KIA
17 May	10 RAAF	Sunderland W4004 'Z'	Ju88s	Lost	F/L M.K. Kenzie captain	KIA
					F/O K.L. Ridings 1st pilot	KIA
					P/O N.J. McLeod 2nd pilot	KIA
					F/O R.G. Bowley DFC nav	KIA
					F/O V.J. Corless nav u/t	KIA
					F/L T.W. Patrick arm	KIA
					F/Sgt J.E.Jackson WOP/AG	KIA
					Sgt J.A. Pearce WOM	KIA
					Sgt J.H . Hogg eng	KIA
					Sgt T.H. Doran fitter	KIA
					F/Sgt J.C. Kelly AG	KIA
					LAC J. Murdoch fitter	KIA

Date	Sqdn	Aircraft		Cause	Result	Crew	
17 May	10 OTU	Whitley	BD260 'P'	Ju88s	Lost	Sgt S.J. Barnett pilot	safe
						Sgt J.H. Pike	safe
						Sgt G.O. Sharpe	safe
						Sgt L. Whitworth	safe
						Sgt E.A. Price	safe
						Sgt H.A. Weber	safe
17 May	10 OTU	Whitley	Z9438 'J'	U-boat attack	Lost	Sgt J.H. Casstles pilot	KIA
						Sgt R.K. Tewfik 2nd pilot	KIA
						Sgt G.D. Evans nav	KIA
						Sgt J.L. Hamilton WOP/AG	KIA
						Sgt R.E.L. Johnson W/AG	KIA
						Sgt D. Seigal WOP/AG	KIA
17 May	461 RAAF	Sunderland	DV960 'H'	Ju88s	Damaged	F/O J.G.P.Weatherlake and crew	safe
20 May	10 RAAF	Sunderland	W8986 'U'	Accident	Lost	F/L D. Saunders captain	KIA
						F/O V.J. Patston 1st pilot	KIA
						F/O G.L.T. Smith 2nd pilot	KIA
						F/O W.R. Cleland nav	KIA
						Sgt P. McCombie eng	KIA
						Sgt R.W. Dowell fitter	KIA
						Sgt G.M. Walker WOM	KIA

Date	Sqdn	Aircraft	Cause	Result	Crew	
24 May	228	Sunderland EJ139 'L'	U-Boat attack	Lost	Sgt R.S. Moore fitter	KIA
					Sgt M.D. Pollock WTO/AG	KIA
					Sgt I. Hunter AG	KIA
					F/O H.J.Debnam captain	KIA
					F/O C.L. Houedard 1st pilot	KIA
					F/O A.H. Pelham-Clinton 2P	KIA
					F/O W. C. Haylock AG	KIA
					F/Sgt F.W. Capes nav	KIA
					F/Sgt J.L.R. Cooper W/AG	KIA
					F/Sgt D.E.T. Crossland AG	KIA
					Sgt L.R. Whatley eng	KIA
					Sgt E.A. French AG	KIA
					Sgt W. Easson WOP/AG	KIA
27 May	10 OTU	Whitley BD282 'P'	Engine trouble	Lost	P/O W P Hugh pilot	safe
					F/O T.M. Hilton	safe
					Sgt W.R.K. Boles	safe
					Sgt D.G. Rodwell	safe
					Sgt W. Hutchinson	safe
27 May	224	Liberator 'T'	U-Boat attack	Damaged	F/Sgt J.S. Edwards pilot and crew	safe
28 May	461 RAAF	Sunderland JM675 'O'	Rescue landing	Lost	F/Lt W. Dods captain	KIA
					F/O R. deV. Gipps 1st pilot	inj
					P/O D.A. Sinclair	safe

Date	Sqdn	Aircraft		Cause	Result	Crew	
						F/O V. H. Dyason	safe
						Sgt A.J. Taylor	safe
						F/Sgt T.J. Rees	safe
						F/Sgt H.S. Webb DFM	safe
						F/Sgt T.P. Durham	safe
						F/Sgt W. Mackie	safe
						Sgt H.S. Dhu	safe
						F/O A.R. Tegart	safe
29 May	612	Whitley	BD679 'E'	Engine trouble	Lost	F/Sgt N.Earnshaw pilot	safe
						Sgt M.G. Millard	safe
						P/O J.F. Dixon nav	safe
						F/Sgt Drake	safe
						Sgt B. Dennehay	safe
						Sgt B. Langham	safe
29 May	10 OTU	Whitley	BD278 'C'	Engine trouble	Lost	Sgt K.G. Alpine pilot	safe
						P/O A.W. Appelby	safe
						Sgt G.W. Taylor	safe
						Sgt A.J. Meyers	safe
						Sgt L. Chant	safe
						Sgt D.A. Baverstock	safe
30 May	210	Catalina	FP101 'G'	U-Boat attack	Damaged*	F/L D.W. Eadie pilot	safe
						Sgt A.G. Leigh 2nd pilot	safe
						Sgt H. Roper FMA/AG	KIA
						Sgt O'Connor	safe

Date	Sqdn	Aircraft	Cause	Result	Crew	
					F/Sgt H. Sharpe eng	safe
					Sgt J A Dick WOP/AG	WIA
					Sgt S.C. Parsloe WOP/AG	safe
					Sgt L. Walker	safe
					Sgt W.L. Stubbs nav	WIA
					Sgt C. Cooper 2nd eng	safe

(* flying boat sank on landing but was recovered and repaired.)

Date	Sqdn	Aircraft	Cause	Result	Crew	
30 May	224	Liberator BZ713 'S'	Ju88s	Lost	F/Sgt H.V. Archer pilot	KIA
					Sgt J.H. Brooks	KIA
					Sgt L. Horricks	KIA
					Sgt J. Millward	KIA
					Sgt W.E. Innes	KIA
					Sgt S. Nichols	KIA
					Sgt S. Rogers	KIA
					Sgt A.S. Pudefin	KIA
30 May	10 OTU	Whitley Z9440 'N'	U-Boat attack	Lost	Sgt L.O.Slade pilot	PoW
					Sgt W.J. Wood	PoW
					Sgt W.F. Wicks	PoW
					Sgt G.F. Dimmock	PoW
					P/O R.A. Russell	PoW
					Sgt G.W. Vines	PoW
31 May	407 RCAF	Wellington MP542 'C'		Lost	F/Sgt H.C. Collins pilot	KIA
					Sgt A.C. McNab	KIA

Date	Sqdn	Aircraft		Cause	Result	Crew	
1 Jun	58	Halifax BB257 'B'		Ju88s	Lost	P/O R.G. Fowlie	KIA
						F/Sgt G.E. Greenwood	KIA
						F/Sgt J. C. Harrison	KIA
						F/Sgt B.S. Grindley	KIA
						F/L F.W. Gilmore pilot	KIA
						P/O J.R. Bickerton	KIA
						F/O J.A. Thain	KIA
						Sgt C.W. Makin	KIA
						F/Sgt S.F. Miller	KIA
						Sgt L.E. Daw	KIA
						Sgt S.D. Wyatt	KIA
2 Jun	461 RAAF	Sunderland EJ134	'N'	Ju88s	Damaged (SOC)	F/L C.B. Walker captain	safe
						P/O W J. Dowling Ist pilot	safe
						P/O J.C. Amiss 2nd pilot	safe
						P/O K.M. Simpson nav	WIA
						Sgt E.C.E. Miles eng	KIA
						Sgt P.K. Turner eng	safe
						F/Sgt E.A. Fuller WOP/AG	safe
						F/Sgt S.F. Miller WOP/AG	safe
						Sgt A. Lane WOP/AG	safe
						Sgt L.S. Watson WOP/AG	safe
						F/Sgt R.M. Goode AG	WIA

Date	Sqdn	Aircraft			Cause	Result	Crew	
3 Jun	10 OTU	Whitley	BD414	'J'		Lost	Sgt D.F. Bavin pilot	KIA
							P/O H.D. Pepper	KIA
							P/O D.T. Dorwood	KIA
							Sgt C.A. Richardson	KIA
							P/O G.A. Nicholls	KIA
							Sgt E.F. Neilson	KIA
3 Jun	236	Beaufighter JL819		'W'	Ju88s	Damaged	F/L H. Shannon pilot	safe
							P/O I.S. Walters nav	WIA
							Lt.Cdr F.J. Brookes	KIA
13 Jun	25	Mosquito	DZ685	'B'	FW190s	Lost	F/O J.E. Wootton pilot	KIA
							P/O J.M. Dymock nav	KIA
13 Jun	25	Mosquito	DZ688	'U'	FW190s	Lost	F/O J. Cheney pilot	KIA
							P/O J.K. Mycock nav	KIA
13 Jun	410 RCAF	Mosquito	DZ753	'F'	FW190s	Lost	F/O R.B. Harris pilot	KIA
							Sgt E.H. Skeel nav	KIA
13 Jun	228	Sunderland DV967		'U'	U-Boat attack	Lost	F/O L.B. Lee pilot	KIA
							F/O D.F. Hill	KIA
							P/O G. Lough	KIA
							F/O A.K. McDougal	KIA
							F/O R.J. Agur	KIA
							Sgt V. Goldstone	KIA
							Sgt R. Shaw	KIA

Date	Sqdn	Aircraft			Cause	Result	Crew	
14 Jun	415 RCAF	Hampden	X2961	'S'	Ju88s	Lost	Sgt R. Smith	KIA
							Sgt J. Fraser	KIA
							Sgt A. Carmichael	KIA
							Sgt D. Davies	KIA
							S/L J.G. Stronach pilot	KIA
							W/O W.A. Trask nav	KIA
							P/O A.B. Clegg WOP/AG	KIA
							F/O G.K. Cruming WOP/AG	KIA
14 Jun	220	Fortress	FK212	'V'	Ju88s	Lost	F/O C.F. Callender pilot	KIA
							F/O J.W. Verney	KIA
							Sgt N. Harbridge	KIA
							P/O W. Offler	KIA
							F/Sgt E. Wright	KIA
							F/Sgt W. Comba	KIA
							F/Sgt G. Dawson	KIA
							F/Sgt S Frost	KIA
14 Jun	10 OTU	Whitley	BD220	'C'	U-Boat attack	Lost	Sgt A.J. Benson pilot	PoW
							Sgt R.L. Rennick 2nd pilot	PoW
							P/O T.J.J. Lee nav	PoW
							Sgt G.T. Graves WOP/AG	PoW
							F/O A. Kingsley AG	PoW

Date	Sqdn	Aircraft		Cause	Result	Crew	
14 Jun	210	Catalina	'P'		Lost	F/O G.Silva DFC pilot	KIA
						F/O Randolph	KIA
						F/O Albon	KIA
						P/O Gardiner	KIA
						Sgt B.J. Fosh	KIA
						Sgt A.K. Hodges	KIA
						Sgt J. Reid	KIA
						F/Sgt S.C. Everitt	KIA
						Sgt Brokenshire	KIA
14 Jun	307	Mosquito	HJ648 'B'	U-Boat attack	Damaged	S/L S. Szablowski pilot	safe
						Sgt M. Gajewski nav	safe
16 Jun	59	Liberator	FL973 'C'	U-Boat attack	Damaged	F/O E.E. Allen & crew	safe
19 Jun	10 OTU	Whitley	EB344 'F'	Ju88s	Damaged	F/O C.C. Price & crew	safe
19 Jun	151	Mosquito	'S'	Ju88s/mechanical trouble, crash landed	Damaged	F/O A.D. Boyle pilot	safe
						Sgt H.M. Friesner nav	safe
20 Jun	10 OTU	Whitley	LA814 'L'	U-Boat attack	Lost	Sgt H. Martin pilot	KIA
						P/O C.M. Bingham	KIA
						Sgt W.I. Ettle	KIA
						Sgt R.W. Warhurst	KIA
						P/O A.B.C. Durnell	KIA
						P/O F.W. Tomlins	KIA

Date	Sqdn	Aircraft		Cause	Result	Crew	
22 Jun	1404 Flight	Hudson	'U'	Ju88	Damaged	Sgt Davis pilot and crew	safe
23 Jun	151	Mosquito	'X'	Collision	Lost	F/O J.D. Humphries pilot	KIA
						P/O H.J Lumb nav	KIA
29 Jun	407 RCAF	Wellington MP754	'H'		Lost	F/Sgt N.C.C. Luther pilot	KIA
						F/O E.L. Shuttleworth	KIA
						F/Sgt B.I. McLaughlin	KIA
						F/Sgt R.H. McLean	KIA
						F/O C.C. Hibden	KIA
						F/O W. Gavin	KIA
30 Jun	10 RAAF	Sunderland W3985	'T'	U-Boat attack	Damaged	F/L H.W. Skinner captain	safe
						F/O V.D. Collins 1st pilot	safe
						P/O R.R. Swinson 2nd pilot	safe
						F/O W.H. Hill nav	safe
						Sgt W. Slater eng	safe
						Sgt W.P. Greatz fitter	safe
						Sgt P. L. Johnson	safe
						F/Sgt O.A. Gibbs WOP/AG	safe
						Sgt A.R. Aldridge fitter	safe
						Sgt N.H. Orford arm	safe
						F/Sgt K.M. Meldrum WOP/AG	safe
						Sgt J.S. Burnham AG	DOW

Date	Sqdn	Aircraft			Cause	Result	Crew	
1 Jul	53	Liberator	BZ730	'O'	Ju88s	Damaged	F/O R.J. Merrifield & crew	safe
5 Jul	10 OTU	Whitley	BD359	'X'	Weather, ditched	Lost	Sgt K.R. Clarke pilot	KIA
							P/O J. Newman	KIA
							Sgt N. Allen	KIA
							Sgt H.J. Neve	KIA
							Sgt E. White	KIA
							Sgt L.G. Stewart	KIA
5 Jul	53	Liberator	BZ751	'G'	U-Boat attack	Damaged	F/Sgt W.Anderson RNZAF & crew	safe
7 Jul	248	Beaufighter		'F'	FW190s	Lost	F/O J.C. White pilot	KIA
							F/O R. C. Arthur nav	KIA
7 Jul	53	Liberator	BZ749	'E'	U-Boat attack	Damaged	F/O K.C. Boulter & crew	safe
8 Jul	53	Liberator	BZ716	'B'	Ju88s	Damaged	F/O J.F. Handasyde pilot	safe
							P/O O.G. Eaves	safe
							F/Sgt A.J. Barnes	safe
							F/O J. Witts WOP/AG	KIA
							F/Sgt A. E. Whorlow	safe
							Sgt H.D. Lindsay	safe
							F/Sgt H.A. Pomeroy WOP/AG	WIA

Date	Sqdn	Aircraft			Result	Cause	Crew	
12 Jul	228	Sunderland	DV977	'Y'	Lost	Ju88s	Sgt R. Codd pilot	KIA
							Sgt R. Martin	KIA
							Sgt J. Sowerby	KIA
							Sgt P. Harding 2nd pilot	KIA
							Sgt D. Elton	KIA
							F/Sgt R. Armstrong	KIA
							Sgt A. Sparks	KIA
							Sgt J. Graham	KIA
							Sgt E. Davidson eng	safe
							Sgt D. Waterman	KIA
							Sgt R. Whale	KIA
12 Jul	10 OTU	Whitley	BD681	'N'	Lost	Ju88s	Sgt C.T.Rudman pilot	KIA
							Sgt R.B. Turner	KIA
							Sgt W.A. Speller	KIA
							Lt J.B. Williams	KIA
							Sgt R.R. Riddle	KIA
16 Jul	304	Wellington	HE304		Lost	ran out of fuel	Sgt S. Kieltyka & crew (all parachuted to safety)	safe
16 Jul	502	Halifax	JD178	'V'	Damaged	Ju88s	F/O J.G. Grant & crew	safe
18 Jul	10 OTU	Whitley	BD276	'S'	Lost	Accident	Sgt T.E.Redway pilot	safe

(pilot overshot on landing – four of crew killed, two safe. Four groundcrew working on another Whitley injured when 'S' crashed.)

Date	Sqdn	Aircraft		Result	Cause	Crew	
18 Jul	10 OTU	Whitley	LA880 'R'	Lost		F/O G.O. Hamilton pilot	KIA
						P/O J.D. Goldring	KIA
						P/O C.W. Button	KIA
						Sgt S. Mills	KIA
						P/O S. Lees	KIA
						Sgt J.Jarman	KIA
18 Jul	224	Liberator	FL959 'N'	Damaged	Ju88s	F/O J.V. Gibson & crew	safe
18 Jul	53	Liberator	BZ731 'D'	Lost	Ju88s	F/L A.J. Dewhirst pilot	KIA
						F/O K.C. Hollison 2nd pilot	KIA
						F/O G.R. Rowland	KIA
						P/O G.W. Snelling	KIA
						Sgt J.E. Devine	KIA
						F/Sgt B.G. Kemp	KIA
						F/Sgt I. Chadwick	KIA
19 Jul	59	Liberator	FL977 'H'	Damaged	U-Boat attack	F/L E.E.Allen & crew	safe
						F/O A.W. Henry WOP/AG	WIA
19 Jul	10 OTU	Whitley	BD359 'X'	Lost	Out of fuel	Sgt R.H.Breffitt & crew	safe
20 Jul	19th US	Liberator	42-40598 'Q'	Lost	U-Boat attack	1/Lt H.E. Dyment pilot	KIA
						2/Lt C.M. Ferrini nav & crew	KIA

2/Lt M. McCormick Jr 2P KIA, 2/Lt J.A. Miller bomb KIA,
T/Sgt C.E. Owen eng KIA,T/Sgt T.L. Rose radio, KIA,S/Sgt B.B. Bromley 2/eng KIA,
Sgt D.C. Hubbard 2/radio KIA, Sgt C.H. Olsen 2/radio KIA, Cpl P.F. Kerns Jr radio KIA

Date	Sqdn	Aircraft	Cause	Result	Crew	
22 Jul	423 RCAF	Sunderland DD680 'J'	FW200	Damaged combat	F/L J. Musgrave pilot	safe
(Crew safe but three were slightly wounded)						
23 Jul	1404 Flight	Hudson 'J'	Accident	Lost	P/O Tribber & crew	killed
24 Jul	172	Wellington MP514 'Q'	U-Boat attack	Lost	F/O W.H.T.Jennings pilot	KIA
					F/O J.G. McCormack 2P	KIA
					F/Sgt J.W. Buxton nav	KIA
					F/O J. Johnson WOP/AG	KIA
					F/Sgt L. Harrop WOP/AG	KIA
					Sgt A.A. Turner WOP/AG	safe
26 Jul	304	Wellington HZ640	Ju88s	Lost	F/L S.J. Rolinski pilot	KIA
					Sgt R. Zagorowski	KIA
					F/L W. Jagiello	KIA
					Sgt S. Zawilinski	KIA
					Sgt S. Ehrlich	KIA
26 Jul	19 th US	Liberator 'L'		Damaged	F/O J. Kulicki pilot	KIA
27Jul	10 RAAF	Sunderland DV969 'E'	Ju88s	Damaged	F/O R.C.W Humble & crew	safe
					F/Sgt W. Sims 1st pilot	WIA
28 Jul	53	Liberator BZ740 'F'	Accident	Lost	F/L G.A. Davey pilot	KIA
					F/Sgt J.K.G. Freeland	KIA
					P/O N.A. Cardiner	KIA
					F/Sgt J. Marshall	KIA
					F/Sgt N.C. Taylor	KIA
					Sgt E.G. Phillips	KIA

Date	Sqdn	Aircraft	Result	Cause	Crew	
28 Jul	224	Liberator BZ781 'W'	Damaged	U-Boat attack	F/O R.V. Sweeny & crew	safe
28 Jul	4th US	Liberator 'Y'	Damaged	U-Boat attack	Maj S.D. McElroy & crew	safe
28 Jul	4th US	Liberator	Damaged	U-Boat attack	Lt A.J. Hammar & crew	safe
29 Jul	304	Wellington HE576	Lost	Accident	F/L Z.Janicki pilot	KIA
					Sgt L.J. Rodziewicz 2P	KIA
					F/Lt. Kolodziejski	safe
					Sgt M.F. Matlak	safe
					Sgt F. Zentar	safe
					Sgt K. Jozwiak	safe
29 Jul	248	Beaufighter LX819 'U'	Damaged/crash landed	Ju88	F/O J.K. Thompson pilot	inj
					Sgt G.F. Barnes nav	inj
29 Jul	224	Liberator FL965 'A'	Lost	Ju88s	F/Sgt W.E. Smith pilot	KIA
					P/O R. Ballantyne	KIA
					Sgt W. Warrington	KIA
					Sgt R. Sumner	KIA
					F/Sgt C.A. Briggs	KIA
					F/O T. Day	KIA
					F/Sgt C.T.W. Downing	KIA
					Sgt H.E. Richardson	KIA

Date	Sqdn	Aircraft	Result	Cause	Crew	
30 Jul	53	Liberator BZ730 'O'	Lost*	U-Boat attack	F/O W.J. Irving pilot	safe
					F/O R.E. Dobson 2nd pilot	safe
					F/O J. Haste nav	safe
					P/O R.G. Sharpe WOP/AG	safe
					Sgt A.J. Pudifin WOP/AG	safe
					Sgt J.G. Humphreys W/AG	safe
					Sgt J. Wildon WOP/AG	safe

(* This crew landed in Portugal but were soon released and returned to UK.)

Date	Sqdn	Aircraft	Result	Cause	Crew	
30 Jul	502	Halifax 'B'	Damaged	U-Boat attack	F/O W.S. Biggar & crew	safe
30 Jul	461 RAAF	Sunderland W6077 'U'	Damaged	U-Boat attack	F/L D.Marrows & crew	safe
31 Jul	502	Halifax 'T'	Damaged	Ju88	F/O A.J. Davey & crew	safe
1 Aug	VP63 USN	PBY-5 Catalina 08231 'J'	Lost	Ju88s	Lt W.P. Tanner pilot	WIA
					Lt B.E. Robertson nav	KIA
					Ens R.J. Bedell 2P	WIA
					ACM3c D.C. Paterson	WIA
					AP1c A.A. Rittel	KIA
					ACMM W.H. Golder	KIA
					AMM2c D.R. Carmack	KIA
					AMM3c R.B. Law	KIA
					ACRM R.C. Scott	KIA
					ARM2c W.O. Rude	KIA

Date	Sqdn	Aircraft	Cause	Result	Crew	
1 Aug	10 RAAF	Sunderland W4020 'B'	U-Boat attack	Lost	F/O K.G. Fry captain	KIA
					F/O H.R. Budd 1st pilot	KIA
					F/O J.M. Curtis 2nd pilot	KIA
					F/O J.H. Portus nav	safe
					P/O A.M. Welch	KIA
					Sgt H.B. Lydeamore	KIA
					Sgt F.O. Pettersson fitter	safe
					F/Sgt P.E. Cook WOP/AG	safe
					F/Sgt R.G. Welfare W/AG	inj
					Sgt J.E. Fryer	KIA
					Sgt J. Haslam arm	safe
					F/Sgt D.I. Conacher AG	inj
1 Aug	228	Sunderland JM678 'V'	U-Boat attack	Damaged	F/L S. White and crew	safe
2 Aug	4th US	Liberator 'T'	U-Boat attack	Damaged	Lt J.L. Hamilton & crew	safe
2 Aug	248	Beaufighter 'J'	FW200	Damaged combat	F/O J.F. Green pilot	safe
					P/O G.B. Forrest DFM nav	safe
2 Aug	415 RCAF	Hampden 'T'	Ju88s	Damaged	P/O W.R.R.Savage & crew	safe
2 Aug	307	Mosquito HJ700	Engine trouble	Lost	F/L J. Bienkowski pilot	KIA
					P/O C. Borzemski nav	PoW

Date	Sqdn	Aircraft	Cause	Result	Crew	
3 Aug	10 RAAF	Sunderland DD852 'J'	Ju88s	Damaged	F/O B.A. Williams pilot	safe
					F/O R.C. Behrndt 1st pilot	safe
					F/O A.J. Murray 2nd pilot	safe
					F/O R.W. Gross nav	WIA
					Sgt W.C. Moser	safe
					F/Sgt J.W. Guy	safe
					Sgt McVinish	safe
					Sgt R.F. Owen arm/AG	WIA
					F/Sgt H.A. Bird AG	KIA
					F/Sgt H. Pengilly WOP/AG	WIA
					F/L Dormey RAF passenger	safe
3 Aug	612	Wellington HF128 'P'		Lost	F/Sgt W.H. Smitham pilot	KIA
					Sgt J.W. Low	KIA
					F/Sgt J.W.Jones	KIA
					Sgt H. Warden	KIA
					Sgt E. Middleton	KIA
					Sgt V.F. Burnett	KIA
7 Aug	172	Wellington MB550 'Z'	Engine trouble	Lost	P/O P.W. Phillips pilot	KIA
					F/Sgt L.G. Harris 2nd pilot	safe
					F/Sgt H.A. Bate nav	KIA
					Sgt W.H.J. Ware WOP/AG	KIA
					Sgt M.H. Turner WO P/AG	safe
					Sgt G.W. Duncan WOP/AG	safe

Date	Sqdn	Aircraft		Cause	Result	Crew	
7 Aug	248	Beaufighter	'D'	FW190s	Lost	S/L R.G. Winnicott pilot	KIA
						F/O A.E. Stocker nav	KIA
8 Aug	4th US	Liberator	'Q'	Ju88s	Lost	Capt R.L. Thomas Jr pilot	KIA
	US					1Lt G.E. Good nav	KIA
						2Lt J.L. Garrick BA	KIA
						FO C.G. George 2P	KIA
						T/Sgt D.J. Gray Jr radio	KIA
						T/Sgt D.E. Bowsman rad	KIA
						S/Sgt C.J. Woodward eng	KIA
						S/Sgt J.H. Perce AG	KIA
						S/Sgt R.T.Todd radio	KIA
						S/Sgt G.E. Henriot Jr eng	KIA
8 Aug	10 RAAF	Sunderland DP177	'F'	Ju88s	Damaged	F/L N.C. Gerrard & crew	safe
11 Aug	10 RAAF	Sunderland DP177	'F'	Ju88s	Lost	F/L N.C.Gerrard pilot	KIA
						F/O K.D. Smith	KIA
						F/O I.W. Bowen	KIA
						P/O J.I. Rowland	KIA
						Sgt D.E. Bennington	KIA
						Sgt W.E. Matthews	KIA
						W/O F. Jorles	KIA
						W/O J.G.H. Webster	KIA
						Sgt J.G. Dwyer	KIA
						Sgt J.E. Challinor	KIA
						Sgt J.R. Dallas	KIA
						P/O R.J. Adams	KIA

Date	Sqdn	Aircraft	Cause	Result	Crew	
13 Aug	172	Wellington MP630	Accident	Lost	Sgt E.R.H. Widdows pilot	KIFA
					Sgt J.S. Lockwood 2P	KIFA
					F/Sgt R.G. Salter nav	KIFA
					Sgt W.F.O. Sayle WOP/AG	KIFA
					Sgt S.C. Hasler WOP/AG	KIFA
					Sgt K.H. Francis WOP/AG	KIFA
13 Aug	304	Wellington HZ638 'P'	Ju88s	Lost	P/O J.S. Kielan pilot	KIA
					Sgt W. Pastwa	KIA
					F/L S. Widanka	KIA
					Sgt J.M. Dangel	KIA
					Sgt F. Gorka	KIA
					Sgt K. Czarnecki	KIA
13 Aug	461 RAAF	Sunderland DV968 'M'	Ju88s	Lost	F/O W.J. Dowling captain	KIA
					F/O D.T. Galt DFC 1st pilot	KIA
					F/O J.C. Grainger 2nd pilot	KIA
					F/O K.M. Simpson DFC nav	KIA
					F/Sgt P.K. Turner eng	KIA
					Sgt L.S. Watson WOP/AG	KIA
					F/Sgt A.E. Fuller DFM WOP/AG	KIA
					W/O S.F. Miller WOP/AG	KIA
					F/Sgt A. Lane WOP/AG	KIA
					W/O R.M. Goode DFM AG	KIA
					F/Sgt C.D.L. Longson	KIA

Date	Sqdn	Aircraft	Cause	Result	Crew	
15 Aug	612	Wellington MP760 'Q'	Ju88s	Lost	P/O K. Harrison pilot	KIA
					P/O R.A. Wilson 2P	KIA
					P/O C.A. Phelps nav	KIA
					Sgt A.W. Monk WOP/AG	KIA
					Sgt D.B. Green AG	KIA
					Sgt J.H. Greaves WOP/AG	KIA
15 Aug	547	Wellington MP565 'T'	Ju88s	Lost	F/O J.Whyte pilot	KIA
					F/O W.J.K. Dixon	KIA
					P/O A. Fisher	KIA
					F/Sgt A.L. Bathurst	KIA
					F/Sgt L.G. Simpson	KIA
					F/Sgt H.E. Taylor	KIA
15 Aug	461 RAAF	Sunderland JM685 'X'	Ju88s	Damaged	F/L P.R. Davenport captain	safe
					F/O R.D. Lucas 1st pilot	safe
					F/O D.H. Kennedy	safe
					P/O H.H. Turnbull	safe
					F/Sgt R.A. Fowles	safe
					F/Sgt J. Russell	safe
					P/O R.G.D. Smith-Gander	safe
					P/O P.C. Bird	safe
					W/O I. Jones	WIA
					F/Sgt R.V. Woolhouse	KIA
					Sgt J.R. Edge	safe
					F/Sgt A.H. Craig	safe

Date	Sqdn	Aircraft			Cause	Result	Crew	
15 Aug	58	Halifax	HR745	'S'	Ju88s	Lost	F/Sgt I.S. Dunbar pilot	KIA
							F/Sgt J. Trotter	KIA
							F/Sgt R.J.H. Baron	KIA
							Sgt H.J. Shaw	KIA
							F/Sgt R.R.P. MacKenzie	KIA
							F/Sgt L.A. Davies	KIA
							Sgt R. Major	KIA
							Sgt S.E. Hillman	KIA
16 Aug	58	Halifax	HR746	'M'	Ju88s	Lost	F/O F.H.Jenkins pilot	KIA
							F/O H.M. Park	KIA
							P/O P.Y. Williams	KIA
							Sgt A.J. King	KIA
							Sgt G.S. Holloway	KIA
							P/O G.W. Webster	KIA
							Sgt R.S. Johnson	KIA
							Sgt W.J. Hargreaves	KIA
							Sgt A.W.S. Bundy	KIA
17 Aug	480 Gp US	Liberator			FW200	Lost combat	Capt Maxwell & crew	safe
18 Aug	10 RAAF	Sunderland	W3985	'T'	Ju88s	Lost	F/L H.W. Skinner captain	KIA
							F/O V.D.W. Collins	KIA
							F/O W.N. Hill	KIA
							F/O R.R. Swinson	KIA
							Sgt W. Slater	KIA
							Sgt W.P. Greatz	KIA

Date	Sqdn	Aircraft	Cause	Result	Crew	
					F/Sgt R.A. Gibbs	KIA
					F/Sgt K.M. Meldrum	KIA
					Sgt A.R. Aldridge	KIA
					F/Sgt H.E. Burbridge	KIA
					Sgt N.H. Orford	KIA
					F/Sgt Cosford RAF passenger	KIA
18 Aug	547	Wellington HZ407 'K'	Ju88s	Lost	F/Sgt J.Clarke pilot	KIA
					P/O N.W. Springer	KIA
					Sgt C.R. Byers	KIA
					Sgt G.B. Hasdell	KIA
					Sgt H.J. Graham	KIA
					Sgt G. Smith	KIA
18 Aug	415 RCAF	Hampden 'S'	Engine trouble	Lost	F/O R.Armstrong pilot	safe
					F/O H.R.D.S. Cudden	safe
					Sgt A.T.J.S. Mayher	safe
					Sgt T. Bileski	safe
18 Aug	19th US	Liberator	Ju88s	Lost	1Lt S.M. Grider captain	safe
					2/Lt C.H. Moore pilot	safe
					T/Sgt F.G. Antosz eng	safe
					T/Sgt G.E. Peeples radio	safe
					S/Sgt H.E. Bischoff AG	safe
					Sgt L. Rosenberg radio	safe
					2/Lt E.A.Kelton nav	KIA

Date	Sqdn	Aircraft		Cause	Result	Crew	
18 Aug	19th US	Liberator		Ju88s	Damaged	Lt A.L. Leal & crew	safe
						2/Lt P. Levine BA	KIA
						S/Sgt J.K. Daniels eng	KIA
						S/Sgt H.E. LaPlante rad	KIA
20 Aug	58	Halifax	HR774 'R'	Accident	Lost	F/O T.H. Minta pilot	injured
						P/O N.A. Lyes 2nd pilot	inj
						P/O R.W. Mee nav	inj
						Sgt L. Brewis	KIA
						W/O D.N. Lowe	KIA
						Sgt B.J. Forsyth WOP/AG	inj
						Sgt D.Jackson WOP/AG	inj
						Sgt T H. Oliver	safe
21 Aug	58	Halifax	BB279 'O'	Engine trouble	Lost	S/L H.E.Brock & crew	safe
21 Aug	311	Liberator	BZ780 'O'		Lost	W/C J.Breitcetl DFC pilot	KIA
						F/L F. Fencl 2nd pilot	KIA
						P/O E. Pavelka nav	KIA
						P/O E. Mrazek WOP/AG	KIA
						F/Sgt M. Pizur WOP/AG	KIA
						Sgt J. Felkl WOP/AG	KIA
						Sgt J. Halada AG	KIA
						W/O V. Jaks AG	KIA

Date	Sqdn	Aircraft		Cause	Result	Crew	
22 Aug	307	Mosquito	HJ655	FW190	Lost	F/Sgt T. Eckert pilot	KIA
						F/O K. Maluszek nav	KIA
22 Aug	304	Wellington	HZ576 'R'	Ju88s	Lost	F/O W.B. Porebski pilot	KIA
						Sgt K. Gawlik	KIA
						F/O B.R. Matuszewski	KIA
						Sgt W. Walkiewicz	KIA
						Sgt S. Szcepaniak	KIA
						F/Sgt T. Wojnilowicz	KIA
23 Aug	4th US	Liberator		Ju88s	Damaged	1Lt K.H. Dustin pilot	safe
						(Three crew wounded)	
24 Aug	58	Liberator	DT636	Ju88s	Lost	F/L G.A. Sawtell DFC pilot	KIA
						F/O J.M. Clarke	KIA
						F/Sgt T.R. Urquart nav	KIA
						F/Sgt A.C. Wilder eng	KIA
						F/Sgt L.C. Matthews W/AG	KIA
						Sgt J.W. Bailey WOP/AG	KIA
						Sgt B.E.Mitchell DFM WOP/AG	KIA
						Sgt W.A. Tennant WOP/AG	KIA
24 Aug	172	Wellington			Accident	W/C R.G. Musson & crew	KIFA
25 Aug	143	Beaufighter	JL886 'N'	FW190s	Lost	S/L R.A. Ullman pilot	KIA
						P/O A.G. Davies nav	KIA

Date	Sqdn	Aircraft		Cause	Result	Crew	
25 Aug	143	Beaufighter JL942	'T'	FW190s	Lost	P/O K.M. Stewart pilot	KIA
						F/Sgt W. Bunting nav	KIA
25 Aug	143	Beaufighter JM159	'P'	FW190s	Lost	F/O R.T. Chinery pilot	KIA
						W/O W.A. Jefferies nav	KIA
25 Aug	143	Beaufighter JL880	'C'	FW190s	Lost	P/O W.B.G.Bonsey pilot	KIA
						Sgt J. Bowyer nav	KIA
27 Aug	1st US	Liberator	(42-40104)	Ju88s	Lost	Lt McKinnon & crew	int/Repat.
30 Aug	311	Liberator	EV948 'M'	Ju88s	Damaged	P/O J Stach DFC pilot	safe
						F/Sgt B.Heza	safe
						F/O Dolezal	safe
						F/Sgt A. Martis	safe
						F/Sgt E. Reich	safe
						Sgt F. Benedikt	safe
						Sgt A Simek AG	KIA
30 Aug	461 RAAF	Sunderland JM707	'Z'	Ju88s	Lost	F/O C.R. Croft captain	KIA
						P/O J.A. Tamsett 1st pilot	KIA
						F/Sgt R.G. Harris 2nd pilot	KIA
						F/O G.J. Bushell nav	KIA
						Sgt H.J. Ferrett FME/AG	KIA
						F/Sgt W. Stewart FME/AG	KIA
						F/Sgt H. Smedley WOM	KIA

Date	Sqdn	Aircraft		Cause	Result	Crew	
						W/O J. Gamble WOP/AG	KIA
						F/Sgt W. Yeomans W/AG	KIA
						F/Sgt G.F. Ritchie W/AG	KIA
						F/Sgt R.J. Hunter WOP/AG	KIA
2 Sep	224	Liberator	FL938 'P'	Ju88s	Lost	F/O C.R. Wharram pilot	KIA
						Sgt R.J. Foss 2nd pilot	safe
						P/O W.R. Collins	KIA
						F/O J.C. Miller	KIA
						Sgt E.A. Maloney	KIA
						P/O J.R. Wilcox	safe
						Sgt D.H. Bareham eng	KIA
						P/O Johnstone	safe
						Sgt M.W. Dilks	safe
2 Sep	224	Liberator	FL959 'G'	Ju88s	Lost	F/O J.V. Gibson pilot	KIA
						P/O K.T. Every	KIA
						P/O V. Lower	KIA
						F/O H. R. Tierney	KIA
						Sgt A.A. Thompson W/AG	KIA
						F/O P.P.R. Mackintosh	KIA
						W/O W.J. Vocasivich WOP/AG	KIA
						Sgt K. Graves	KIA
						Sgt H.T. French eng	KIA

APPENDIX V

Since the original edition of this book was published, much more information has been received concerning the famous action of Sunderland U/461 Squadron and submarine U-461. Günther Paas had been an officer aboard U-461 on her previous patrols but was not on the fateful 30 July 1943 sortie. He has, however, managed to locate survivors among those men rescued on that day and their personal recollections have been collected. In addition he has the story from the engineer aboard U-462. He – and they – have given me permission to re-produce them here, for which I give my thanks.

The L.I. (Leitenden Ingenieurs – senior engineer officer) aboard U-462 was Hans Krüger:

'After three days [sailing] through the Bay we were positioned about 90 miles north-west of Cape Ortegal when we were located by an aircraft. All the boats were still re-charging after a long voyage underwater. A Liberator remained just outside the range of our flak and called for reinforcements. At around 1015 a Sunderland and a Catalina arrived. U-461 was the first boat to be attacked by three aircraft. In the meantime five other aircraft arrived and attacked both us and U-504. The boats all fired everything they had. At around 1100 the radio room reported surface ships moving towards us at great speed. The aircraft attacked without pause. U-461 shot at an aircraft, then a Sunderland flew in low, attacked the boat and destroyed it with depth charges. The commander and fourteen of the bridge personnel were saved, the other crew members went down with the boat.

'In the meantime we had reached mid-day; the surface ships arrived and entered the battle with their artillery. The detonations were close to us. We ran out of ammunition because of the flak barrage and in the control room we were practically up to our knees in empty cartridges. Then we were hit starboard astern and the pressure resistant hatches through to the stern were destroyed and the rudder jammed.

'The aft compartment had to be closed off and without our rudder we turned in circles. With our last bullets we gave U-504 covering fire for an emergency dive. She dived undamaged but was destroyed after eight hours of depth charging by the frigates.

'Then the order – everyone off the boat. The whole crew, including two seriously wounded men, got out of the boat before it sank and she went down flags waving. After eight hours in the water we were picked up by an English ship and went into four years of imprisonment.'

Acting Supply Petty Officer Alfred Weidemann on U-461 recalls:

'I had been relieved at 0600 and went into the interior of the boat to freshen up. Later an air-raid warning was given from the bridge. In trousers and deck shoes, and still with a piece of sea water soap in my hand, I made my way up, hand over hand, to take up my lookout position. As our fire was reliant on a 2 cm gun, I jumped into the bandstand.

'I was no expert gunner but having already had four years of warfare under battle conditions behind me I knew a bit about which way the wind blows. The aircraft grew ever more in number and audacity. We shot all that the gun held and joyfully turned it round again hoping that the aircraft would enjoy a taste of our juice, but it didn't happen that way. We played cat-and-mouse until 1100. But then it came to the kill because "Johnny" Walker was out with his destroyers on the warpath. The aircraft were closer on the ball and had the advantage.

'I believe that U-462 was the first to cop some of the damage but then the airmen had designs on us. Their on-board weapons spat out everything they had and pressed us hard. Our Vierling gun left its mounting and our crew were the worst for it.

'Bootsmannsmaat Hubert Maas had one knee shot to pieces. Obersteurman Klimaszewski was shot in the head or in the mouth and stumbled through the conning tower hatch into the boat. I dived for cover behind the bridge quarter-deck, and as I saw the machines flying towards us, I could only count the bombs as they fell; there might have been six or seven. There followed a violent explosion and I felt a burning pain as if someone had pulled a wide piece of wood from above my left buttock.

'I didn't hear the order from the "old man" – "everybody out" – because the boat had already gone under and taken me with it. I had an aviator's life jacket on with a bottle of compressed air. The going under and the tearing open of the air bottle were as one. As I saw the sun again I began to feel better. The Sunderland dropped a dinghy and when we gathered together, there were 15 of us left.'

Able Seaman Alex Franz:

'I think we still had five or seven machines around us, but when, after 2½ hours of battle the anti-submarine vessels came into view, they grew braver and began to attack us from all sides. At the end we were being attacked by four machines at once.

'The machines forward and to starboard turned. The Sunderland astern finished us off. Meantime, the pedal firing system of the Vierling was broken. I was just going to fetch the hand firing system when I noticed that my jacket was covered in blood. I said to the "old man" that I thought I'd been hit and he told me to go straight under and get myself bandaged up, but before I went I took one last look round and saw that the bows were already under water.

'The "old man" gave the order to abandon ship. I wanted to dive headfirst from the "winter garden" because I was already up to my neck in water, but we were washed overboard. The boat set itself on its head, the propellers turning high in the air. I'll never forget that scene. Those who didn't get free in time or who hung around, were taken down with her. Like Hermann Moesender, who must have hung onto the Vierling, because he came up full of panic. He hadn't inflated his life jacket and so clung to my neck and held it tight. I told him that wouldn't do and that we'd both drown; we were not going to swim to shore in any event! He quickly calmed down and let go of me.

'I didn't have an aviator's life jacket, just the old six-cell type – probably the only one on board. It was more comfortable to wear, because we also had to sleep in them, but now I had problems because I had tied it so loosely that it came up when inflated. Since I was also handicapped by my wound it was very difficult for me.

'We were scattered [in the water] over about 50 metres and someone yelled for us to get together. When we had just about managed it a machine flew over us and fired. The shots hit about 10-15 metres away so none of us were hit. Later another machine came towards us and we thought that this was it. It turned out to be a Sunderland. Four men were actually standing there next to each other, with their elbows leaning on the open door. Suddenly they threw something down – a smoke bomb – followed immediately by a dinghy. I thought it was a depth charge and wanted to dive out of the way, but of course, I couldn't with the life jacket on.

'The dinghy hadn't inflated itself so we swam around until we discovered the bottle, hanging down deep in the water. The "old man" took off his life jacket and dived, found the bottle straight away and finally the dinghy blew itself up.

'We got the seriously wounded into the boat and the others hung onto the ropes at the side and waited for rescue.'

Able Seaman Gerhard Korbjuhn, signalman on the bridge of U-461, remembered:

'When the lookout reported a single aircraft our CO looked on this machine – which was on its own, and because of our considerable armament – with negligible importance. So we continued on our way undisturbed.

'Then heavy radio activity was reported in the area by the radio room. It was already too late to dive because by now we were being circled by 6-8 aircraft, all just out of range of our weapons. When [ship] smoke eventually appeared on the horizon, the aircraft decided to attack, apparently to stop us from diving.

'They attacked simultaneously from all sides, firing with all guns and flying at such low altitude that they were barely a few metres above the water. Our Vierling gun received a hit on its mounting and would no longer swivel. I lined up the cockpit of the Halifax, as the order came to open fire, then let loose with both barrels. Then everything happened very quickly.

'I emptied my magazine, I think I hit targets too, then the low altitude flyers were only about 100 metres away. Bullets whistled past my ears with a terrible noise and I shouted over to my loader that he ought to clip on a new magazine. It was only then I noticed that he had been hit and lay senseless and bleeding on the deck. Who was he? I couldn't tell anymore.

'There were losses on the "winter garden" too but at that moment the boat was rocked by a series of enormous tremors and lifted vertically. As I now know, the pilot of the Sunderland had released his bombs and our boat had been hit more than once. The CO was asking the control room what damage had been caused, but the boat was already going under. He now ordered everybody off. I climbed onto the bench and was about to dive over the railing when the boat gave way beneath me. It was a remarkable feeling to be wrecked out in the middle of the Atlantic.

'Gradually I made out the heads that were swimming close to me. The CO urged us to stick close together because a single straggler would have little chance of rescue. It became painfully clear to me that all the rest of my comrades were dead, no one else got out from inside the boat. There was not much time to mourn them, for we were battling for our own lives. Fortunately the sea was calm and fairly warm.

'The Sunderland circled us once more. In the open hatch several airmen were standing, waving and making Victory-V signs [Oh, really! Ed.]. Then it flew quite close to us and they threw something out. When it became clear that it was an inflatable dinghy and that these airmen wanted to help rescue us, we were both relieved and thankful.

'After about three hours an English warship arrived. A large scrambling net was hung over the side so that we could clamber aboard, and be greeted by heavily armed sailors. We were taken below and provided with warm, dry clothes, chocolate and cigarettes. I got to know the "Tommies", in various situations, as fair sailors and humane people, and have regarded them highly ever since.'

Sanitätsobergefreiter (medical orderly) Wilhelm Höffken:

'[Before the attack] our doctor told me to get everything ready for an emergency, in case we have to operate. Then a message came from the control room; "Sani to the tower!" I hurried up and saw how our Obersteuermann – Helmut – had been hit. We carefully laid him down. He had been hit in the chest and throat and was bleeding heavily. Then he died. At the same moment there was an enormous crack, the boat lifted and shook itself a couple of times.

'The order came from the bridge – everyone overboard! I heaved myself upwards, I was still looking at Helmut, then water began to come through the conning tower hatch. My last thought was to open the oxygen bottle, then everything went black. As I swam upwards I came to again, and found myself directly next to Alfred Weidemann. He said to me that he had caught something in his left side. Rescue came after a while from above. An aircraft [airman] threw a dinghy down to us. We laid the wounded in the dinghy, and the rest held on tight to the outside. Suddenly my left foot began to hurt. It turned out later, when we were aboard the corvette, that the third and fourth bones in the centre of my foot were broken.

'I remained in England throughout. I went through five PoW camps and returned home on 6 October 1946.'

Leading Seaman Alois Momper:

'After we met up with the other two boats, our passage continued above water and the guns were manned. The first aircraft was soon sighted. After an hour the number of aircraft increased to, in my memory, six. They circled us at a height of 3-4,000 metres. This lasted for 2-2½ hours, while we were attacked simultaneously by three different machines. I fired at the machine attacking us from starboard. She returned fire, firing with all its guns. They must have hit one of the loaders because all of the ammunition had run out. I looked for him; he was lying close to the gun, bleeding from a dreadful chest wound. He must have been killed on the spot. At the same moment the bombs began to fall. We were engulfed by a jet of water, and I found myself eventually in the water again. I saw another man close to me. We swam towards each other and tried to stay together. We thought we were the only survivors when an aircraft, not too far away from us, dropped something down. Later we heard a whistle from this direction and swam towards it. Soon we saw the other survivors in the dinghy.

'Later the anti-submarine vessels arrived and dropped depth charges quite close to us. Eventually one of these ships returned to pick us up. We were greeted with pistols, and were led to land with our eyes bound, but treatment on board was always correct.

'After a couple of interrogation camps I arrived at Camp 15, where I met the Commander and Lieutenant. In February I was off to Canada, back to England in July 1946 and finally home in September 1947. I later got to know one of the officers from our rescue ship, in Bristol in 1947.'

The last man off the boat was Able Seaman Helmut Rochinski:

'Having surfaced at around 0600 we were still pumping out diesel when a lookout reported an aircraft at 1000. Within another half hour or so, five aircraft were in the area. My battle station was as helmsman in the tower, so I could not see what was going on on the bridge, but in one of the attacks the Vierling must have received a direct hit on its mounting and we lost it.

'We could only fire the two 2 cm gun and we had our first casualties, amongst whom was Obersteuermann Klimaszewski, who was fatally hit as he stood over the coning tower hatch. I caught him and he died in my arms. I laid my leather jacket under his head.

'Then came new orders for the helm, which I had to follow, and overhead the aircraft continued to attack. Our freedom of movement to starboard was limited as we were running in line abreast with the other submarines. U-462 was hit and then U-504 dived, leaving U-461 alone. Then the CO ordered a call to base: "Am battling five aircraft, request aerial support." I had just passed this order onto the radio room when a machine flew over us and dropped bombs. A violent tremor ran through the boat.

'The CO asked the L.I. about the condition of the boat, but in the same moment someone called out that the boat was going under and the CO ordered everyone out. That was the last order from the CO that I passed on, then I climbed the ladder, holding onto the handle of the tower as the water came over me. On the bridge I made out a couple of dead and wounded comrades, who went down with the boat. No one followed me out of the tower. I was the last man out.

'I grabbed hold of the periscope but was swept away by the waves. U-461 sank very fast and the aircraft circled over us, the Sunderland dropping a dinghy. We put some wounded men into it while the rest of us clung to ropes.

'After some hours the corvette HMS *Woodpecker* picked us up and after a few days we arrived in a British port and were then sent off to a PoW camp.'

AVISO

EL dia 20 de abril el Almirantazgo británico avisó oficialmente por radio que las embarcaciones pesqueras que penetrasen en las zonas declaradas peligrosas para la navegación comercial, lo harian por su propia cuenta y riesgo.

Aunque los pesqueros españoles han hecho caso omiso deeste aviso, los aviadores ingleses, por consideración hacialos subditos de un país neutral, no atacaron esos barcos españoles aunque la ley de guerra les autoriza plenamente para hacerlo.

Las fuerzas aéreas de las Naciones Unidas no pueden mantener más tiempo su actitud pasiva, ni permitir nuevas infracciones.

Hoy os damos un último aviso. A partir del dia 1 de junio toda embarcación española hallada en zona prohibida será tratada como enemiga y atacada al momento sin previo aviso.

WARNING

The day of the 20th April, the British Admiralty officially advised over the radio that the fishing boats that penetrated into the declared dangerous zones for commercial navigation would do so at their own cost and risk.

Although the Spanish fishermen had ignored this advice, the English airmen out of consideration for the subjects of a neutral country did not attack these Spanish ships, although the law of war fully authorized them to do so.

The airforce of the United Nations cannot sustain thelr passive attitude for much longer nor allow new infringements. Today we give you a final warning. After 1 June all Spanish boats found in a prohibited zone will be treated as an enemy and attacked without prior warning.

AUX MARINS PÊCHEURS FRANÇAIS

IL faut que les sous-marins allemands soient coulés. L'issue de la Bataille de l'Atlantique en dépend.

Ces sous-marins se servent de plus en plus de vos ports occidentaux. Ils traversent vos lieux de pêche et se servent même de certains de vos bateaux à des fins militaires.

Nous vous avons déjà avertis que votre présence au large gêne nos opérations navales et aériennes contre l'ennemi. A plusieurs reprises nous vous avons avertis que tout bateau sortant des eaux côtières le ferait à ses risques et périls.

Nous vous disons de nouveau qu'à partir du 1er septembre tout bateau sortant des limites déjà annoncées court le risque positif d'être attaqué.

Nous savons combien il vous est difficile de vous conformer à ces prescriptions, mais nous sommes fermement résolus à poursuivre et à intensifier nos attaques contre les sous-marins et à hâter ainsi le jour de notre victoire commune.

Nous sommes par conséquent obligés de faire interrompre la pêche dans vos lieux de pêche habituels.

Nous savons de manière certaine que les Allemands, de leur côté, essayeront de vous forcer à partir au large, lorsqu'ils le jugeront utile, afin de compliquer par votre présence notre chasse incessante aux sous-marins ennemis.

Ils n'hésiteront pas à vous sacrifier — vous et vos bateaux — à partir du moment où ils ne seront plus en état de se servir de vous pour leurs propres fins.

N'attendez pas ce moment !

Nous vous offrons une alternative vous permettant de vivre et de pêcher en toute sécurité.

Venez rejoindre dans nos ports de pêche vos camarades bretons qui s'y trouvent déjà.

Vous trouverez chez nous ce qui actuellement vous manque le plus en France . . . des conditions de pêche très avantageuses, bons vivres, bons vêtements, des engins de pêche de premier ordre et . . . . la liberté.

Si vous venez les rejoindre, nous disposons de moyens sûrs nous permettant de donner de vos nouvelles aux vôtres restés en France sans risque de les compromettre.

CAP SUR L'ANGLETERRE !

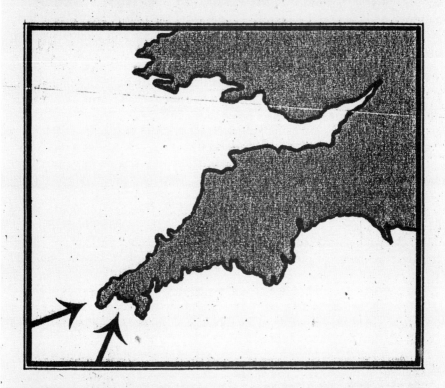

Ceux qui partiront seront protégés au cours du trajet par la R.A.F. !

Passez le mot aux autres—à tous vos camarades en mer !

Les pêcheurs bretons en Angleterre vous attendent avec impatience. En attendant, vos amis de la Royal Navy et de la R.A.F. vous saluent.

PROPAGANDA LEAFLET – TRANSLATION

This was a propaganda leaflet dropped by the RAF over Brittany in 1943, warning Breton fishermen of the dangers of fishing in areas in the Biscay and Western Channel, while also encouraging them to defect to Britain to join either the Royal Navy, Royal Air Force, or to join other fishermen operating from the Cornish peninsular.

TO THE FRENCH FISHERMEN

It is necessary for German submarines to be sunk. The outcome of the Battle of the Atlantic depends on this.

These submarines are using your western ports increasingly. They cross your fishing grounds and they also take certain of your boats for military use.

We have already warned you of the difficulty of your presence during our naval and air operations against the enemy. Several times we have warned you that all boats leaving coastal waters are at great risk.

We will say to you again that from 1ˢᵗ September all boats going beyond the limits imposed, court the risk and the possibility of attack.

We know it is difficult for you to conform to this but we are firmly resolved to intensify our attacks against submarines to hasten our joint victory.

We are consequently obliged to interrupt your daily fishing expeditions.

We know for sure that the Germans are trying to force you to sail for the open sea since they consider your presence useful as it complicates our ceaseless hunt for enemy submarines.

They will not hesitate to sacrifice you—you and your boats—if it will help them.

Do not wait for this moment!

We will offer you an alternative to live and fish in total safety.

Come and join us in our ports with your Breton friends who you will find there already. You will find we have got what you need most in France ... advantageous fishing conditions, good life, good clothes, good fishing boats ... and your freedom.

If you join us we can all pull together to rid France of danger, so you can regain your rightful position.

HEADLAND OF ENGLAND

Those who will leave will be protected in the course of the journey by the RAF!

Spread the word to others—all your friends at sea!

The fishermen of Brittany and England are waiting for you anxiously. Meantime your friends of the Royal Navy and Royal Air Force salute you.

BIBLIOGRAPHY

Aircraft versus Submarine, Alfred Price, Wm Kimber, 1973.

Coastal Command Leads the Invasion, S/Ldr M. Wilson & F/L A.S.L. Robinson, Jarrolds Ltd,1945.

They Shall not Pass Unseen. Ivan Southall, Angus & Robertson, 1956.

Air War Against Germany & Italy 1939-1943, John Herington, Australian War Memorial, 1954.

Men of Coastal Command 1939-1945, Chaz Bowyer, Wm Kimber, 1985.

The Strike Wings, Roy Conyers Nesbit, Wm Kimber, 1984.

The Hunters and the Hunted, Jochen Brennecke, Burke Publishing Co., 1958.

Iron Coffins. Herbert A. Werner, Arthur Barker Ltd, 1970.

Aircraft Illustrated Extra, No. 14, Ian Allan Ltd.
  And since the original edition:

Bloody Biscay, Chris Goss, Crécy, 1997.

U-Boat Operations of the Second World War, by Ken Wynn, (Vol.1 & 2), Chatham, 1998.

Search, Find & Kill, Norman Franks, Grub Street, 1995.

Dark Sky, Deep Water, Norman Franks, Grub Street, 1997.

U-Boat versus Aircraft, Norman Franks & Eric Zimmerman, Grub Street, 1998.

234

INDEX